A LITTLE HISTORY OF POETRY

'Books about poetry are rarely page-turners, but Carey's
little history is gripping, is unputdownable! Reading this book
and its galaxy of poets is like looking up at the sky and seeing the
whole wheeling and constellated universe.'
Daljit Nagra, author of *Look We Have Coming to Dover!*

'I have been dipping into John Carey's masterly *A Little History
of Poetry*, where old and new wines are mixed to great effect.'
Edna O'Brien, *Guardian*

'If this dazzling book, as packed with gems as a billionaire's birthday
bash, doesn't make you want to rush to your local bookshop to buy
some poetry for the long summer, then check your pulse.'
Roger Alton, *Daily Mail*

'It's populist, no-nonsense and anti-elite in its sympathies.
Many people may find new favourites here.'
Stephanie Burt, Professor of English, Harvard University

'*A Little History of Poetry* succeeds because it communicates
Carey's love for a poet clearly and infectiously.'
Harry Cochrane, *TLS*

'This characterfully compered mini-anthology would
make a great guide for anyone just beginning to
explore poetry, at any age.'
David Sexton, *Evening Standard*

'*A Little History of Poetry* is delightful and succinct: 40 perceptive
chapters in 295 pages, covering nearly 200 poets.'
Brian B. McClorry SJ, *Thinking Faith*

JOHN CAREY

A LITTLE
HISTORY
of
POETRY

YALE UNIVERSITY PRESS
NEW HAVEN AND LONDON

For information about this and other Yale University Press publications, please contact:
U.S. Office: sales.press@yale.edu   yalebooks.com
Europe Office: sales@yaleup.co.uk   yalebooks.co.uk

Set in Minion Pro by IDSUK (DataConnection) Ltd
Printed in Denmark by Nørhaven, Viborg

Library of Congress Control Number: 2019956794

ISBN 978-0-300-23222-6 (hbk)
ISBN 978-0-300-25503-4 (pbk)

A catalogue record for this book is available from the British Library.

10 9 8 7 6 5 4 3 2 1

Contents

CHAPTER 1

Gods, Heroes and Monsters
THE EPIC OF GILGAMESH

What is poetry? Poetry relates to language as music relates to noise. It is language made special, so that it will be remembered and valued. It does not always work, of course. Over the centuries countless thousands of poems have been forgotten. This is a book about some that have not.

The oldest surviving literary work is *The Epic of Gilgamesh*. It was composed nearly 4,000 years ago in ancient Mesopotamia (roughly equivalent to where Iraq and eastern Syria are now). No one knows who wrote it, or why, or what readership or audience it was intended for. It is preserved on clay tablets in the earliest known alphabet, which is called cuneiform script because the scribes who wrote it formed the letters by making wedge-shaped (cuneiform) dents in wet clay with bits of reed.

For centuries the secret of how to read cuneiform script was lost. Then, in the 1870s, a self-taught, working-class Londoner called George Smith, studying clay tablets in the British Museum, cracked the code and brought *The Epic of Gilgamesh* to light.

The epic tells the story of a king, Gilgamesh, whose mother is a goddess. He rules the city of Uruk (now Warka in southern Iraq). He is a great warrior and builds a magnificent city using glazed bricks, a new technique. But he is lustful and tyrannical, seizing and violating brides on their wedding day. So the gods create a wild man called Enkidu to stop Gilgamesh oppressing his people.

Enkidu is made from the clay the mother goddess washes from her hands, and he is an animal rather than a human. He is covered in hair and lives with the gazelles, eating grass as they do. However, a votaress of the temple in Uruk seduces him and after seven days and nights of fervent love-making he becomes human. She teaches him to wear clothes and eat human food.

Gilgamesh falls in love with Enkidu, caressing him like a woman. But when Enkidu tries to stop him violating brides, they fight. They turn out to be equally matched, so they kiss and make friends and embark on heroic adventures. Together they go on a quest to the Cedar Forest and kill the monster Humbaba who lives there. This angers the gods, since Humbaba was their monster. While Gilgamesh is washing after the fight the goddess Ishtar sees him, falls in love, and proposes marriage. But she is the goddess of sex and violence and all her lovers come to a bad end, so Gilgamesh rejects her. She is angry, and calls on her father, the sky god, to send another monster, the Bull of Heaven, to kill Gilgamesh. Instead Gilgamesh and Enkidu kill the Bull, which angers the gods still more, and they sentence Enkidu to death.

Gilgamesh mourns him bitterly and sets off to discover the secret of eternal life. He is ferried across the waters of death and finds the immortal man Utnapishtim, who survived the great flood, in which all other humans died, by following the gods' instructions and building a boat. Gilgamesh dives into the ocean to find a plant that is said to make whoever possesses it young again. Though he finds it, and brings it to the surface, it is stolen by a snake, and Utnapishtim tells him that no one can defeat death. So Gilgamesh returns to Uruk, having learned that, though he is mighty and famous, he will be equal in death with all other human beings.

There are clear parallels between *The Epic of Gilgamesh* and Homer's *Odyssey*. This may be the result of direct influence, or because some elements in the Gilgamesh story are common in myth and folklore worldwide. In many mythologies and religions gods favour or victimise human heroes, and human heroes fight with monsters and descend into the underworld, the realm of death, and then return to the living world. Through Homer, these motifs have become part of Western poetry's imaginative universe.

It is not clear that *The Epic of Gilgamesh* was thought of as poetry in our sense of the word. It may have been thought a true account of the gods and their relation to humans. In *Gilgamesh* there is a chief god called Marduk, but there are many other gods and they quarrel, get drunk and make mistakes. They originally made humans immortal, but then they invented death, sending the flood to destroy the human race (except Utnapishtim), because they were noisy and kept the gods awake.

Did this strange story have any effect on the development of modern beliefs and traditions? Possibly. In 597 BC Judah was conquered by Nebuchadnezzar, king of Babylon, and its people were taken into captivity. Their exile is recalled in Psalm 137, 'By the waters of Babylon we sat down and wept, when we remembered Sion.' For more than fifty years the people of Judah had to live in subservience to the triumphant Babylonians, and hear about their strange gods. But in 539 BC the Persians conquered Babylon, and the freed Jewish captives returned to Judah. It seems they then set about amalgamating their legends into a sacred book, the Torah, consisting of the first five books of what is now called the Old Testament. They tried, it seems, to keep their legends untainted by the Babylonian beliefs they had lived among. But the flood that destroys mankind in the Book of Genesis and the snake that tricks Eve in Eden may derive from the flood and snake in *Gilgamesh*.

Most importantly, the Torah asserts that Yahweh, all-powerful and all-knowing, is the only true God, and all other gods, like those of Babylon, are false. This major change brought problems. For if God is all-powerful and all-knowing, why is the world full of misery and suffering? Why didn't God make things better? This problem has been exercising the minds of theologians for centuries, and different religions have different answers.

In the Torah, man is to blame for the state of the fallen world with its misery and suffering, because Adam ate the apple, although God had warned him that if he ate it he would die. In Christianity this explanation is accepted, though usually with modifications that make the Adam and Eve episode a story, or 'allegory', rather than literal truth. But Christianity adds an extension to the story, which is that God sent his son, Jesus Christ, to redeem humankind by dying on the cross, so that all who believe in him will have immortal life.

A different answer to the problem of human suffering is found in some Eastern religions and relates to the idea of *karma*, according to which an individual's good deeds and intentions lead to happiness, evil deeds and intentions to suffering. In many Indian religions, including Hinduism, Buddhism, Jainism and Sikhism, *karma* is linked to a belief in rebirth, and one's deeds and intentions in this life affect the nature and quality of one's future lives. Being born blind, for example, may be the result of sins in a previous life. The Abrahamic religions (Judaism, Christianity and Islam) do not have the concept of rebirth, so this solution to the problem of divine justice is not open to them. But in the Hindu scripture, the Bhagavad Gita, Lord Krishna teaches that every creature in the universe is subject to rebirth.

As we shall see, some Western poets have been drawn to the idea of rebirth. But it is not present in *The Epic of Gilgamesh*. Gilgamesh thinks he can conquer death, but is mistaken. When Utnapishtim tells him that no one can escape death it is the earliest known literary statement of what will become one of poetry's major concerns down the centuries – how to confront death, one's own or other people's, yet make something valued and beautiful out of it. Shakespeare does this in, for example, the song from *Cymbeline*:

> Fear no more the heat o' the sun,
> Nor the furious winter's rages,
> Thou thy worldly task hast done,

Home art gone, and ta'en thy wages:
Golden lads and girls all must,
As chimney-sweepers, come to dust.

Fear no more the frown o' the great;
Thou art past the tyrant's stroke;
Care no more to clothe and eat;
To thee the reed is as the oak:
The sceptre, learning, physic, must
All follow this, and come to dust.

There are, of course, religious poems that hold out hopes of an afterlife. But Shakespeare's poem does not. It presents death as an escape and a release.

Like death, love is one of poetry's perennial subjects, and it is already central to *Gilgamesh*, where love is presented as a civilising force, something that is needed to make you fully human. A week of love-making turns Enkidu from a beast into a man. Unlike the Adam and Eve story in Genesis, *The Epic of Gilgamesh* also celebrates deep, same-sex love between two males, and some of the greatest love poems we shall come across in this book are addressed by men to men and women to women.

There are other aspects of *Gilgamesh* that resonate in later poetry. Gilgamesh is a tyrant, and he is guilty, like Homer's Odysseus, of what was called in Greek 'hubris', meaning arrogance. The gods disapprove of this, and of his tyranny, which is why they send Enkidu to correct him. *The Epic of Gilgamesh* is in this respect a political poem, carrying a reproof and a warning for tyrants. Generalisations about poetry are rash, but in the main poetry, especially modern poetry, is sceptical of power, wealth, luxury and celebrity, and sceptical, too, of people who admire them.

The Epic of Gilgamesh tells us nothing about what it sounded like when it was read or sung. So it lacks, for us, the vital dimension of poetry that relates to rhythm, metre and rhyme. As we shall see, poets differ about what poetry should sound like, and how much this matters. Some argue that sound is all-important, and meaning negligible. Others consider meaningless poetry futile. Some believe that the sound of poetry, its beat and rhythm, relate to our earliest experience in the echo-chamber of the womb.

As we have seen, part of the wisdom of poetry is that it reminds us we must die. But poems, or some poems, do not die, but survive far beyond the span of human life. Why this should happen is mysterious. How can it be that a poet can take a few words from the vast avalanche of language that hurtles past us every day, arrange them in a certain order, and make a deathless work of art? No one has ever been able to explain it. But that, it seems probable, is every poet's aim. Why else go to the trouble of creating a poem and labouring to perfect it, if it is to be instantly forgotten? Even when the poet tells us everything turns to dust, the poem is meant not to. Some poets, Shakespeare for example, in Sonnet 55, are outspoken about it:

Not marble, nor the gilded monuments
Of princes shall outlive this powerful rhyme . . .

Because no one knows what makes a poem immortal, it follows that the standards for judging poetry are subjective, not scientific facts. My preferences will not be yours, for we bring different minds and different pasts to what looks superficially like the same poem. There are no rights or wrongs in aesthetic judgement, only opinions. I hope you will find poems in this book that you did not know before, that they become part of your daily thoughts, and that you will trust your own judgement of them.

CHAPTER 2

War, Adventure, Love
HOMER, SAPPHO

Who Homer was, and whether the Homeric epics were the work of one poet, is not known. They probably date from about 700 BC. The *Iliad* is the first surviving war poem. It tells of the battles fought between Greeks and Trojans in the last few weeks of the ten-year siege of Troy, ending in the killing of Hector, leader of the Trojans, by the Greek warrior Achilles.

In its attitude to war the poem is contradictory. It presents war as both glorious and horrible. Cowardice is despised. Yet the brutality and futility of war are exposed. This contradiction is reflected in two contrasting styles that run through the battle scenes. The warriors address each other in formal, rhetorical terms, like orators. But they die like slaughtered beasts. A spear crashes into a mouth, shattering teeth and bones; a youth is plucked from his chariot on a spear's point, writhing like a hooked fish.

The divided feelings about war that the *Iliad* registers seem to be deeply embedded in human nature. Even today, celebrating the glory and lamenting the waste of war go together, as any Remembrance

Day ceremony shows. Exposing this rift within us is one thing that gives the *Iliad* its universality and depth.

Another thing is its portrayal of human feeling. The gods and goddesses who intervene in the action of the epic – Zeus, Apollo, Athena, Aphrodite and the rest – are presented as frivolous, malevolent, petty and quarrelsome. The effect is to make the human beings, by contrast, dignified and elevated. They feel real pain and grief, and are capable of heroism, as the gods, being immortal, are not.

One of the most famous scenes in the poem comes in Book 6, where Hector's wife, Andromache, is weeping as she tries to persuade him not to go out to battle. But Hector replies that he would feel 'deep shame' before the Trojan men and women:

if like a coward I were to shrink aside from the fighting.

He refuses to yield to his wife's pleas, though he knows that he is fated to die in battle and foresees that Troy will be destroyed along with his father, King Priam, and all his people.

A nurse is in attendance, holding their little son Astyanax, 'beautiful as a star'. The child screams with terror at the sight of his father's armour and the horse-hair plume nodding fiercely on his helmet, and nestles up against his nurse as if to get away. Hector and Andromache laugh at the sight of the boy's fear, but Hector takes his gleaming helmet off and places it on the ground. Then he takes the child, kisses him, and dandles him in his arms, praying as he does so:

Zeus, and you other immortals, grant that this boy, who is my son, may be, as I am, pre-eminent among the Trojans,
great in strength, as I am, and rule strongly over Ilion;
and some day let them say of him: 'He is better by far than his father',
as he comes in from the fighting, and let him kill his enemy
and bring home the blooded spoils, and delight the heart of his
    mother.

With that he gives the child to Andromache, who takes him 'to her fragrant bosom, smiling in her tears'. Hector pities her, strokes her and speaks comfortingly, telling her that no one can send him down to Hades before his time comes.

Many thousands of words have been written about this short scene. It transfers to a family setting the divided reactions to warfare we noticed in the battle scenes. To us it seems horrible that Hector should want his little son to grow into a killer and come back from battle covered in someone else's blood. To pray for this to happen seems like the action of a brute. But we are made to see that Hector is not a brute. He loves his child tenderly, and tries to comfort his wife in her distress. He also foresees that fighting will not achieve anything. He knows that he and his father and Troy are doomed. So going back to re-join the battle does not make sense even on a practical level. It will do no good. Yet we can see why Hector feels he must do it.

So the *Iliad* is a tragedy. But the *Odyssey*, though it is a sort of sequel to the *Iliad*, telling of Odysseus' ten-year voyage to reach his home on the island of Ithaca after the Trojan War, is a totally different kind of poem. It is an adventure story, and it introduces a type of fictional character that will appear in countless adventure stories down the ages. You could call this type the indestructible hero. Like James Bond or Tolkien's Hobbit – or Alice in *Alice in Wonderland*, who is an indestructible heroine – Odysseus survives every danger, however improbably. So compared to the grim realism of the *Iliad*, the *Odyssey* could be classified as a fantasy.

In the first part of the poem we learn what has happened in Ithaca while Odysseus has been away. His wife, Penelope, is being harassed by scores of unruly young men who, believing Odysseus dead, want to marry her. Odysseus' and Penelope's young son, Telemachus, cannot control these intrusive suitors and, helped by the goddess Athena, he sails to the Greek mainland where he learns that his father is being held captive by a nymph called Calypso who is in love with him.

The second part of the poem starts with Odysseus still on Calypso's island. But she finally agrees to let him go, so he builds a raft and sets off, only to be wrecked by the sea-god Poseidon, who has a grudge against him.

He swims to the nearest land, crawls ashore caked with salt, and falls asleep. The sound of girls laughing wakes him, and he emerges, naked, to find a princess, Nausicaa, and her maids, who have been washing clothes and are now playing ball. Because of its erotic charge, this is one of the poem's most famous scenes.

Nausicaa takes him to her parents' palace, where he is welcomed, and they ask him how he came to be cast up on their island. At this point Odysseus becomes the narrator, and the story he tells is weird and wonderful. It reads like a pack of lies dreamed up by a wily old wanderer who has to find some excuse for taking ten years to sail home, a distance of some 500 miles.

He left Troy, he says, with twelve ships, and landed on the island of the Lotus Eaters, who gave his men a kind of super-sedative fruit that made those who ate it forget their homes and families. Next, he and his men were captured by a one-eyed, man-eating giant called Polyphemus, but escaped by blinding him with a sharpened stake. Next Aeolus, god of the winds, gave Odysseus a leather bag containing all the winds. But his men foolishly opened it, letting the winds out, so that their ships were driven back even though they had already sailed within sight of Ithaca.

After that they sailed into a bay where giant cannibals sank eleven of their twelve ships by hurling rocks from the cliffs. Only Odysseus' ship escaped, and reached the island of the goddess Circe, daughter of the sun god, who turned half his men into swine. However, the god Hermes gave him a drug that made him immune to Circe's magic, and she told him how to reach the world of the dead on the western edge of the world. There he communed with various ghosts, including Achilles and Agamemnon, his comrades in the Trojan War, and his own mother.

Sailing back to Circe's island he passed the land of the Sirens, who lure sailors to their destruction on the rocks with their enchanting music. But he plugged his men's ears with bees' wax, and ordered them to tie him to the mast so that he heard the Sirens' sing, and survived. Nearby were a lethal sea-monster-cum-whirlpool called Charybdis, and another sea-monster with six heads, called Scylla. Successfully navigating the strait between them, Odysseus reached an island where, while he was asleep, his men made the bad mistake of killing and eating some cattle sacred to the sun god Helios. As punishment, Zeus sent a storm that wrecked their ship, drowning everyone except Odysseus. He survived by clinging to some driftwood, and then was almost sucked down into Charybdis, but was washed up on Calypso's island, where the narrative of his adventures began.

Nausicaa's parents, having heard his story, help him to get back to Ithaca. He disguises himself as a beggar, and no one knows him except his old dog, which dies of joy on seeing him, and his old housekeeper who recognises a scar on his leg while she is washing his feet, but does not give him away. Choosing his moment, he reveals himself to his son Telemachus and to two of his former slaves, a swineherd and a cowherd, and together they take a terrible revenge, slaughtering the suitors and strangling twelve maidservants who had betrayed Penelope.

How far we are meant to assume that Odysseus' story is a pack of lies is impossible to say, and pointless to ask. For what the *Odyssey* does, far more than the *Iliad*, is open the door to the monsters, phantasms and nameless horrors that live on the far side of logic and reason. Entering this imaginary realm is something poetry has always done, and some of the *Odyssey*'s creatures, such as Scylla and Charybdis and the Sirens, have become almost proverbial, referred to in later poems worldwide. That may mean that Homer was uncannily attuned to humanity's collective unconscious. But it may also be because his writing is so graphic that it stamps itself on the memory. He works through vivid, direct language – Odysseus grinding out Polyphemus' eye with an olive-wood stake, for example, or Scylla grabbing six men from his ship and whirling them in the air, shrieking, or the maidservants strung up by their necks and slowly choking (the first depiction of a hanging in world literature). Scenes like these are difficult to forget, even when you want to.

Unlike a lot of poetry, Homer's can survive translation into other languages, partly because of the simplicity, speed and directness of his narrative technique. There have been many English translations, but the earliest was by George Chapman in 1614. Its most famous reader was the English poet John Keats, who knew no Greek, and whose sonnet – 'Much have I travelled in the realms of gold' – written in 1816, records his wonder on reading Homer in Chapman's translation.

Sappho (*c.* 630–*c.* 570 BC) is the only Greek poet apart from Homer that most people have heard of today. In antiquity critics referred to her as 'The Poetess' as Homer was 'The Poet'. She was born on the island of Lesbos (from which we get the word 'Lesbian'). Most of her poetry is lost. Apart from one poem – an 'Ode to Aphrodite', in which she asks for the love goddess's help – only fragments remain.

But enough survives to show why critics were so wild about her. Her poetry is clear, sensuous and passionate. The loved one is a ripe, red apple, high on a tree, out of reach. Or she is a mountain hyacinth, which the shepherds trample on with their clumsy feet, leaving a purple stain on the earth. In another poem she derides the Homeric gods for their callousness, and mocks those who worship them.

In a poem identified as 'Fragment 31', Sappho watches the woman she loves talking and laughing with a man, and she goes into shock. Her heart thumps, her skin seems on fire, she can't speak, her eyes dim, her ears ring. Trembling, she breaks out in a cold sweat. It is the first description of the symptoms of passionate love by a woman in Western literature.

CHAPTER 3

Latin Classics
Virgil, Horace, Ovid, Catullus, Juvenal

Just before the beginning of the Christian era three poets were born whose writings were to become cornerstones of Western civilisation.

Not much is known about the origins of the oldest, Virgil (70 to 19 BC), but he probably came from a land-owning family near Mantua. According to legend he was shy and modest, and his schoolmates nicknamed him 'the maiden'.

He grew up in turbulent times. Julius Caesar had put an end to the old Roman republic by seizing dictatorial power, and civil war raged both before and after his murder in 44 BC. Not until 27 BC did his adopted son emerge victorious, and establish himself as Caesar Augustus, the first Roman emperor. Virgil's early poetry caught the attention of Augustus' cultural adviser, Maecenas, and he recruited the young poet to what became, in effect, the emperor's propaganda ministry.

Virgil's masterpiece was his twelve-book epic poem, the *Aeneid*. He started it around 29 BC, and its political aim was to glorify

Augustus and legitimise the dynasty he founded. Its hero is a Trojan, Aeneas, briefly mentioned in the *Iliad*, who, in Virgil's reconstruction of history, is destined to become the ancestor of the Romans. Aeneas's mother is the goddess Venus, but his enemy among the immortals is Juno, who plagues him with disasters. He escapes with his band of followers from the sack of Troy, carrying his father Anchises, and accompanied by his little son, but his wife dies in the general carnage.

The first six books of the epic recount the adventures Aeneas and his men undergo prior to making landfall in Italy. The last six books tell of their wars against the native Italian tribes, culminating in Aeneas's defeat of Turnus, leader of the Rutuli. By writing about both adventure and warfare, Virgil intentionally challenges comparison with the Homer of the *Odyssey* and the *Iliad*. His poem, like the empire it glorifies, aims to be a world-beater.

Aeneas is depicted as an ideal leader, and characterised as *pius*. This is not quite the same as the English word 'pious'. It includes duty to family and nation, as well as obedience to the gods. His test comes when he and his men are cast up on the African coast near Carthage, and Dido, the queen of Carthage, offers them hospitality. It is to her that Aeneas recounts the destruction of Troy and the perils he and his men have been through. She falls in love with him, and he is touched by her sympathy. While sheltering in a cave during a hunting trip, they make love. But Jupiter sends Mercury to remind Aeneas of his destiny and, though torn, he forsakes Dido and sails away. Furious, she builds a funeral pyre and stabs herself, vowing eternal enmity between Carthage and Aeneas's descendants. Out at sea Aeneas and his men see the blaze of the pyre that consumes her.

The Dido episode had a political purpose. The great maritime empire of Carthage had been the rival of the Roman republic in its early days, and there had been three horrendously costly wars between the two powers. At the end of the third, Carthage was burnt to the ground. The Dido episode puts these tragedies into the context of divine destiny.

The most politically significant part of the poem, from the viewpoint of Augustan propaganda, comes in Book 6 where Aeneas, with Venus's help, finds the magic golden bough that admits him to the underworld. There, among the souls of the dead, he encounters his father Anchises, who foretells the future of Rome, including the advent of the divine Augustus and the emperors that will follow him.

For posterity, however, the epic's vividness and emotional depth mattered far more than its politics. Its incidents etched themselves on the European imagination – not just the sensational highlights, such as Aeneas's flight from Troy and Dido's operatic death, but relatively minor episodes like the crushing of Laocoon and his sons by sea-serpents during the siege of Troy as described by Aeneas. The poem has, too, been quarried for wise sayings, for example Aeneas's words to his men in the midst of their afflictions (*Aeneid*, 1.203), which translate roughly, 'Perhaps one day it will give us pleasure to remember even these things.'

The second of the three great poets, Horace (65 to 8 BC), was the son of a freed slave, but had an expensive education, partly in Athens. He served as an officer in the republican army that Augustus defeated at the Battle of Philippi in 42 BC. After that he decided to throw in his lot with the winning side. Maecenas rewarded him with a farm in the Sabine hills, and wangled him a civil service job. In return, Horace's poetry lavishes praise on Augustus as a divine ruler.

He has been criticised as a time-server. But his easy-going nature is one factor that gives his poems their charm. There is no point, he advises, in fighting against the inevitable. He preens himself on his prowess as a lover, while admitting that age has blunted his ardour. He seems to have kept going as long as he could, though. The Roman historian Suetonius alleges that he had his bedroom walls covered in obscene pictures, with mirrors positioned so that pornography met him wherever he looked.

Like Virgil and Ovid, Horace wrote poetry in several forms. But he is chiefly remembered for a single masterpiece, the *Odes*, consisting of just over a hundred shortish, personal poems. Their subjects are various, and they obey no particular order. Some congratulate Augustus on his victories, some hymn the coming of springtime or celebrate the delights of country life on his Sabine farm, with its lovely fountain, deliciously cool even on torrid days. Some sing the virtues of wine, and invite friends to come and share it. He condemns avarice and luxury, in line with Augustus' plans to reform public morality, and recommends a return to the pure, simple ideals of ancient times, His poems to women are frank, teasing them or telling them off as he thinks fit. He pays due reverence to the Roman gods – Apollo, Venus, and the rest – and honours them with simple sacrifices. Be content with your lot is his advice.

All this may sound rather humdrum. But it is the brilliance of his writing that has secured his immortality – as he knew it would. 'I have built a monument more permanent than bronze,' he boasted (*Odes*, 3.30). The effect is one of brevity, elegance and extreme cleverness. This is poetry for the educated, not the mob. 'I hate the unholy rabble,' he admitted (*Odes*, 3.1). Yet several of his taut, pregnant phrases have passed into common English usage, most famously *carpe diem*, meaning 'seize the day' (*Odes*, 1.11).

Ovid (48 BC to AD 17), the youngest member of the great trio, belonged, like Virgil and Horace, to Augustus' circle of poets. He enjoyed a scandalous reputation, writing impudently immoral poems describing his love affairs (called the *Amores*) and an instruction manual on seduction (the *Ars Amatoria*). He married three times and divorced twice before he was thirty. Nine years before his death Augustus exiled him (no one knows why) to Tomis on the Black Sea, and he wrote poems about that.

But his masterpiece was the *Metamorphoses* (meaning 'Transformations'). It is a fifteen-book epic covering the history of the world from the creation to the deification of Julius Caesar (which happened the year before Ovid's birth). But this historical framework is no more than a carrier-bag. The *Metamorphoses* is really a glorious medley of myths, over two hundred and fifty of them, some tragic, some comic, some grotesque. Ovid jumps from story to story with scarcely any attempt at connection, but all the myths are about love, and they all involve someone being magically turned into someone or something else. Humans are turned into animals or birds or plants or stars; gods take on ungodly shapes to seduce nymphs or maidens. Jupiter becomes a swan to woo Leda and, disguised as a white bull, swims out to sea with the beauteous Europa on his back; Pluto, god of the underworld, drags Proserpina down to his dark realm. Sometimes their prey changes shape to save herself. Chased by Apollo, Daphne becomes a laurel bush.

Gods and goddesses are shown as not just lustful but horribly vindictive and vain. A flute-player, Marsyas, dares to challenge Apollo to a musical contest and is flayed alive by the god for his effrontery. A shepherd's daughter, Arachne, competes at weaving with the goddess Athena, and wins. But Athena, in jealous rage, rips her work to pieces and turns her into a spider. Offending the immortals, even by mistake, earns fearful punishment. The huntsman Actaeon comes upon Diana bathing, and, turned into a stag, is torn to pieces by his own hounds.

Some stories have moral meanings. Greedy Midas turns all he touches to gold, and starves to death. Vain Narcissus pines for his reflection in a pool. Overweening Phaeton tries to drive the chariot of the sun and plunges to destruction. But the myths feed a hunger for the marvellous that is deeper than morality. There are monsters – the bull-man Minotaur lurking in his labyrinth; the Gorgon, Medusa, slain by Perseus to save Andromeda. There are sex-changes. A beautiful boy and a nymph unite to form the bisexual Hermaphroditus. The prophet Tiresias lives for seven years as a woman, marries, has children, then becomes a man again. (Asked whether men or women got more pleasure from love-making, Tiresias replied that women did – ten times more. Juno blinded him as punishment.)

The influence of the *Metamorphoses* spread much wider than literature. Countless paintings and sculptures in the Renaissance took their inspiration from the stories Ovid tells – Cellini's *Perseus with the Head of Medusa*, Bernini's *Rape of Proserpina*, Titian's *Actaeon Surprising Diana* and *Rape of Europa*, Veronese's *Venus and Adonis*, and many more. To say that the Renaissance would not have happened without the *Metamorphoses* would be going too far. But not much.

Two other great Latin poets have left their mark on world litera-ture. Catullus (84 to 54 BC) lived in the last days of the Roman

Republic, before Augustus came to power. His poetry influenced Virgil, Horace and Ovid, and was influenced by Sappho. His *Carmina* consist of 116 mostly short poems, some homosexual, some obscenely vituperative, some explicit enough to shock the faint-hearted. Many are about a real-life love affair and reflect its ups and downs, from tenderness to jealous fury. He calls the loved woman 'Lesbia', but her real name was Clodia. She was married, promiscuous, and came, like Catullus, from a high-ranking family. Two of his poems that have proved popular with later poets are about her pet sparrow (a bird that, some think, has an improper double meaning).

Almost nothing is known about the life of Juvenal (*c.* AD 55 to *c.* 138), but he wrote sixteen *Satires*, and said that their subject was 'whatever men do – prayer, fear, rage, pleasure, joy, running about'. They are sometimes scathingly comic and, taken together, amount to a blistering denunciation of the public and private life of first-century Rome. They have been eagerly translated, adapted and imitated down the ages, which suggests that human vices have not altered much over time, nor our pleasure in reading about them. The *Satires* are the source of several common sayings, for example, 'bread and circuses' (meaning the kind of pleasures the mob chases after), 'a sound mind in a sound body', and 'who will guard the guards?' (meaning who will keep an eye on those who are supposed to keep an eye on us?). That said, the *Satires'* treatment of women, gays, Jews, foreigners, and other people the author regards as social deviants is deeply repellent to us nowadays. Some prefer to read them as ironic, meaning the opposite of what they say.

CHAPTER 4

Anglo-Saxon Poetry
BEOWULF, LAMENTS AND RIDDLES

The empire foreseen by Virgil and the Roman poets did not prove eternal after all, and the last Romans left Britain around AD 410. In the 150 years that followed, immigrants – perhaps as many as 100,000 – arrived from the continent. Now known as the Anglo-Saxons, they were mainly from Germanic tribes, and they brought with them their own language and a heroic code of honour, which included loyalty to one's lord and kinsfolk, and a warrior's duty to avenge wrongs through the blood feud.

Christianity, with its doctrine of forgiveness, reached Britain towards the end of this immigration, and declarations of Christian belief are found in Anglo-Saxon poetry side by side with adherence to the pagan heroic code. Some consider this a flaw. But it may also be the reason any Anglo-Saxon poems have survived at all. Anglo-Saxon poetry was, it seems, mostly composed and transmitted orally, not written down, whereas reading and writing were virtually confined to the monasteries. Monastic scribes would naturally choose to preserve poems that had some Christian content. They may even have inserted Christian references while copying.

Beowulf, the great treasure of Anglo-Saxon poetry, is an epic of just over 3,000 lines, and was probably composed around AD 700. Its poet is unknown, and it survives, untitled, in a single manuscript written some 200 years later. Together with expressions of the heroic code it contains quite frequent biblical references, though only to the Old Testament; Christ is not mentioned. Set in Scandinavia, it tells the story of Beowulf, a legendary hero of the Geats, a people who inhabited what is now southern Sweden. Beowulf sails to the aid of Hrothgar, king of the Danes, whose 'mead-hall', or royal residence, called Heorot, has been ravaged by a man-eating monster, Grendel. Beowulf lies in wait for Grendel, grapples with him single-handed, and tears off his arm. The monster flees, fatally hurt, and his arm is hung in Heorot as a trophy.

But Grendel's equally fearsome mother attacks Heorot to avenge her son, slays one of Hrothgar's warriors, and makes off with his corpse. Following her blood-soaked trail, Beowulf comes to a hellish lake, swarming with vile life-forms. Diving in, fully armed, he swims down to her underwater hall, where she lies in wait mourning over her son's dead body. After a furious fight Beowulf beheads her and her son and returns to dry land triumphant, to be rewarded with treasure, and with a Christian sermon on the dangers of pride, by a grateful Hrothgar.

Fifty years pass. Beowulf is now king of the Geats, and his realm is being ravaged by a fire-breathing dragon, the guardian of a treasure-hoard. With eleven chosen comrades Beowulf confronts the monster. But fate (*wyrd* in Anglo-Saxon) is against him. His sword snaps, and the dragon sinks its poison fangs into his neck. His comrades flee in terror, all except one, Wiglaf, who stands firm with his doomed king. Together they kill the dragon, and Beowulf feasts his eyes on its treasure as he dies. Afterwards the Geats build a pyre for Beowulf, heaping the dragon's treasure on it, and when it has burnt they place all that remains in a burial mound on a headland, as a lasting memorial.

But a plot summary can give no idea of *Beowulf*'s magnificence. The poem grips and thrills because of its power to convince the reader of the reality of its impossible events. It does this by both stimulating and thwarting our imagination. We have no distinct idea, for example, what Grendel or his mother look like. When Grendel attacks Heorot he is said to grab thirty warriors at one go and carry them off to his lair, and after Beowulf has cut his head off it takes four warriors to carry it (lines 123, 1637). How a mere human could grapple with a creature this size is not explained. The directness and conviction of the style simply sweep away such cavils.

The poem's verse-form drives it with insistent momentum. Anglo-Saxon metre is as relentless as a drum-beat. The lines of verse have no fixed number of syllables, and they do not use rhyme. But each line is divided into two parts, with a breathing space between, each part has two stressed syllables, and the stressed syllables in one half-line must start with the same consonant as either one or both of the stressed syllables in the other half-line. The result is called 'alliterative' verse. Here is an example (*Beowulf*, line 102). It means, 'That grim demon was called Grendel'.

Waes se grimma gaest Grendel haten

The three thumping 'g' sounds bind the line together, but the other syllables are arranged as the poet pleases.

A disadvantage of alliterative verse was that the poet had to find a lot of words starting with the same consonant. It was a particular problem with things he had to refer to frequently, such as swords, warriors or the sea. One solution was to use a kind of metaphor, known as a kenning. For example, the sea can be called 'the whale's road' or 'the swan's way' or 'the gannet's bath' and so on.

From the viewpoint of the Anglo-Saxon audience, the poet's quest for alliterating synonyms must have made poetry very strange. *Beowulf* contains about 3,100 distinct words, and almost one third of them occur only in *Beowulf* or other poems, never in Anglo-Saxon prose. Perhaps for the poem's original listeners this vocabulary, remote from ordinary usage, would help to create a sense of wonder to match the poem's heroic other-world.

Beowulf ends in sorrow. Now that their king is slain, the poem foretells, disaster will overtake the Geats. They will tread the path of exile, bowed under woe. Harps will no longer awaken the warriors, but ravens will circle over them, scenting carnage. This is typical Anglo-Saxon gloom. Almost all the poems that survive (apart from biblical paraphrases) are laments for lost happiness.

Among the most famous is the poem now known as *The Wanderer*. It is spoken by an exile, friendless, surrounded by strangers. Sadly he remembers his lost lord, his 'gold-friend', and the feasting and treasure-giving that made the mead-hall joyous. He drifts into a dream, imagining the kisses and embraces of his dear lord. But then he wakes up to reality: frost, snow, hail, the screaming seabirds, the ice-cold sea, and the memory of his slaughtered kinsfolk. At the end he turns to God, telling us that it is best to seek mercy from the Father in heaven, the source of all certainty.

The Seafarer is in some ways similar. The speaker recalls past delights – cities, with their gardens and blossoming groves, 'joy in women' and the cuckoo's song – and contrasts them with his present miseries – storms, cold, hunger, the bleak sea and the eagle's screech. But he blames himself. He chose the seafaring life because it offered adventure. As he reflects on his choice, the poem juggles Christian and pagan values. Life on land is 'dead', says the speaker. But the seafaring life may earn the praise of posterity, which is 'the best thing'. By pursuing 'brave deeds, opposed to the devil', he will 'live for ever among the angels'. It is a poem that struggles with irreconcilable ideals.

The Dream of the Rood, the most famous Anglo-Saxon religious poem, finds a simpler solution to the conflict between Christianity and the warrior-code. It is spoken in part by the cross (rood) on which Christ hung, and it presents him as a 'young warrior' who strips himself as if for an athletic contest. The cross which he embraces becomes a 'tree of victory', adorned with gold and gems, like a warrior's trophy. The shortcomings of this as a version of Christianity are clear. But the cultural rift that the advent of

Christianity brought must have been colossal, unlike anything before or since, and the poem strives to bridge it.

The sense of loss that haunts Anglo-Saxon poetry may reflect folk-memories of the Roman occupation. In a poem usually called *The Ruin* (now thought to describe the city of Bath), the poet tells us of great buildings, 'the work of giants', that are empty and devastated. Once they were full of gold-bright, wine-flushed men, treasure and precious stones. There were troop-roads and baths heated by hot springs. Now the red-tiled roofs have collapsed and the 'master-craftsmen' have departed. This and the exile poems should perhaps alert us to a further depth in *Beowulf*. For Grendel and his mother are exiles, wandering the moors and waste places, and envying the gold-bright, wine-flushed men in Heorot. To an Anglo-Saxon listener they may have seemed pitiable as well as hateful.

Two further exile poems, now called *The Wife's Lament* and *The Husband's Message*, carry the usual exile motifs but also seem to be riddle poems. Anglo-Saxon poetry is not rich in humour, and its never-never land of lords doling out treasure to carousing warriors was far removed from the lives most Anglo-Saxons lived. The riddle poems, of which about ninety survive, all in a single manuscript, fill these gaps.

The point of a riddle poem is that you have to try to guess who or what the speaker is. They are tricky. Some remain unsolved after a thousand years. To write a riddle the poet had to imagine how another being might feel or think. Some of the speakers are animate – an ox, an oyster, a swan, a nightingale. A badger tells us what it was like to escape with his family from a dog crawling into his sett. Other speakers are tools or household objects – a plough, a rake, a key, a weathercock, a weaver's loom. This closeness to real life and the playful imagining are unlike anything else in Anglo-Saxon poetry. Some of the riddles are dirty jokes. An onion (or a penis, depending on how you read it) speaks of his usefulness to housewives. No one thinks like that in *Beowulf*. We seem to have hopped forward four centuries to the age of Chaucer.

Do the British inherit any national traits from the Anglo-Saxons? The question is much disputed. Anglo-Saxon poets enjoyed complaining about the weather, so that may indicate some kinship. They had a liking for ironical understatement (called 'litotes'). Hrothgar, for example, having described the hellish lake where Grendel's mother lurks, adds, 'That is not a good place' (*Beowulf*, 1372). Maybe this relates to the stiff upper lip that is supposed to characterise Britons in adversity.

More persuasive is an incident in the poem *The Battle of Maldon*, which could be seen as the first recorded British sporting gesture. The battle was fought in AD 891 beside the river Blackwater in Essex. Some shiploads of Vikings had landed on the river's far bank, while on its near bank a collection of local farmers and villagers were drawn up under the command of an alderman, Byrhtnoth. The Vikings could not cross the river because two of Byrhtnoth's men held the only bridge. The Viking chief asked Byrhtnoth to allow his warriors across so that they could fight on equal terms. Byrhtnoth agreed, and disaster ensued. Some of the Anglo-Saxons fled, the rest, including Byrhtnoth, were killed.

Commemorating a military disaster as heroic prompts comparison with 'The Charge of the Light Brigade' or the Dunkirk spirit. But it seems the poet took a more critical view. The word he uses to describe Byrhtnoth's rash gesture is *ofermod*, which means something like 'excess of courage', and in every other place where it occurs in Anglo-Saxon it refers to Satan.

All the same, the defiant words that Brytwold, one of the last to be cut down, speaks to his doomed comrades are an irresistible expression of the Anglo-Saxon heroic spirit. They are best in Anglo-Saxon, but this is a rough translation.

Resolve shall be the firmer, heart the harder,
Courage the keener, as our strength lessens.

Not many poems give you a code to live – and die – by. This one does.

CHAPTER 5

Continental Masters of the Middle Ages
DANTE, DANIEL, PETRARCH, VILLON

Of all world-famous poets none is less likely to appeal to the modern reader than Dante Alighieri (*c.* 1265–1321). This is not just because his poetry is soaked in medieval theology. It is also because his beliefs are, for us, often repellent. He does not seem to have been attractive as a man, either. He comes across as vengeful and unforgiving.

The *Divine Comedy* (1320), usually accounted his greatest work, recounts his imaginary visit to Hell, Purgatory and Paradise. At first he is guided by the Roman poet Virgil, and then by the sanctified spirit of a dead woman, Beatrice Portinari, a Florentine banker's daughter whom, according to Dante's own account, he had glimpsed and fallen in love with when they were both children. Though he saw her later only rarely, she became his model of female perfection. His wife Gemma Donati, on the other hand, who bore him several children, is never mentioned in his poetry.

The punishments Dante invents for the damned suggest an ingenious interest in cruelty. His depiction, at the start of the *Divine*

Comedy, of the recently dead who are bound for perdition is horrifying. Men, women and children, naked, and goaded by hornets and wasps, scream, blaspheme, and curse their parents, themselves, and the human race, as they await allocation to their places in Hell. The torments they are doomed to suffer are revealed to Dante and Virgil as they descend through Hell's circles and view the damned. Some are hanged on thorn trees and whipped by horned demons. Others are entombed in red-hot sepulchres, or plunged head-first in boiling oil or pitch or steeped in human excrement. The punishments in Purgatory can be almost as hideous. There the envious have their eyelids stitched together with iron wire, while their tears seep through the stitches.

The punishments of the damned are eternal. There is no escape into merciful death. Thieves, for example, run naked among venomous snakes and, when bitten, crumble to ash, but are reconstituted to suffer again. Heretics, that is, those whose beliefs differ from current Christian orthodoxy, suffer as cruelly as criminals. Muhammad, the founder of Islam, is damned for causing the rift between Islam and Christianity. So he is cleft in two from the chin to the midriff, with his entrails dangling between his legs, smelling horribly, and remains like that eternally.

When Dante recognises his former enemies among the dead, he is not above intervening to intensify their suffering. In Hell's fifth circle, among the dead condemned to wallow in mud and slime, he sees Filippo Argenti, a Florentine knight from an opposing faction, and asks Virgil to have him doused in filth more thoroughly. Virgil obliges. In the frozen lake that is Hell's ninth circle, Dante tugs handfuls of hair out of the scalp of one of the damned to make him identify himself. He turns out to be Bocca degli Abati, a traitor to Dante's cause. The contemporary Dante hated most bitterly, Pope Boniface VIII, is allocated a special place of torment, reserved for ex-popes, in hell's eighth circle.

All these punishments are presented as exhibiting God's wisdom and justice, even when the victims are innocent. Virgil explains that he, and virtuous heathens who lived and died before Christ's birth, are condemned to Hell's first circle, where, though there is no actual torment, there is perpetual darkness and continual sighing. Innocent children, who die unbaptised, remain there forever.

In Paradise, Beatrice is Dante's guide until almost the end, when she leaves him and he glimpses her, enthroned in eternal light. Her purity and saintliness are key elements in the *Divine Comedy*, and also in Dante's *Vita Nuova* (1295), a series of short adulatory poems with prose commentaries, written after Beatrice's death. This sanctification might appear to be a way of honouring women. But it is also a means of depriving them of full womanhood. In particular, it deprives them of their sexual nature, and in this respect it is merely the obverse of the revulsion from the female body found in some medieval theologians. This is illustrated in *Purgatory*, Canto 19, where Dante is lulled to sleep by the bewitching song of a Siren until Virgil rips open her clothing to reveal her belly, which releases so foul a stench that it wakes Dante up.

Dante's unsexing of woman was deliberate, and was meant to distinguish him from previous poets, especially troubadours such as Arnaut Daniel (fl. 1180–1200). Daniel's poetry, written in his native Provençal dialect, is joyously erotic, celebrating human love as a part of nature, along with trees, flowers and birdsong. He remembers his love's blonde hair and her lithe body, and the joy of undressing her, kissing and laughing, and watching her flesh in the lamplight. He is sure no hermit, monk or priest was ever as devoted to God as he is to her.

By contrast Dante's love poetry in the *Vita Nuova* is vapid and abstract, as he perhaps realised. In *Purgatory* (Canto 26) the poet Guido Guinicelli points out Arnaut Daniel to Dante, and praises him as '*il miglior fabbro*' (the better craftsman) – better, that is, than other poets who write in their native language rather than in Latin. However Daniel, when Dante finds him, has risen above human love. He suffers among the lustful, burning in the refining fire of Purgatory. Ignoring Guinicelli's compliment, he regrets his past folly and begs Dante to pray for him.

Though the *Divine Comedy* was hailed as a masterpiece during the later Middle Ages, its reputation dwindled during the Enlightenment. It revived among the Romantics and the Pre-Raphaelites, and

William Blake illustrated it in a series of drawings and watercolours. In the early twentieth century T.S. Eliot and Ezra Pound gave it cultural currency, using it as a source for esoteric references. Eliot dedicated *The Waste Land* to 'Ezra Pound, *il miglior fabbro*'.

Petrarch (1304–1374) seems to have been more likeable than Dante (whose *Divine Comedy* he confessed he had not read). He did not meddle in politics, recommending instead a solitary, contemplative life. A classicist (though he knew no Greek), he rediscovered lost Latin texts, and so was a motive force behind the Renaissance. As a minor church official he could not marry, but an unknown woman or women bore him two children and he adopted them as his own. He enjoyed travel, and is known as the first mountaineer, climbing Mt Ventoux in Provence (6,273 feet) in April 1336, just for fun. His collection of 366 love poems, mainly sonnets, recording his love for a woman he calls 'Laura', came to be known as *Il Canzoniere* ('The Songbook') and was admired and imitated throughout Europe.

It would be good to be able to report that it still repays reading. But to the modern reader it is numbingly tedious and repetitive. Petrarch's love is chaste and continues for twenty-one years. In that time he does a lot of weeping, but little else. He longs to spend a night with her, but knows he never will. In Poem 111, after he has adored her for fifteen years, she deigns to look at him. Two years later, in Poem 155, she weeps and speaks 'gentle words'. In Poem 201 he finds a glove she has lost and gives it back. That is virtually the sum total of the action.

On 6 April 1348 she dies (possibly of the Black Death), but that changes things less than might be expected. Petrarch still spends a lot of time in tears, and writes poems about her for another decade. His thoughts are turned to heaven, where she is now, but his love for her had always been religious. Her eyes had shown him 'the way that leads to heaven' (Poem 72). In some respects things get better after her death. She comes to him in dreams and sits on the edge of his bed (Poem 359). She says she is waiting for him in heaven, and tells him that she was harsh only to save their souls (Poem 341). He comes to believe she resisted his desires for his sake, 'my pain was my salvation' (Poem 290).

Throughout, Laura is deprived of a body almost as thoroughly as Dante's Beatrice is. References to her person are chastely unspecific. She has golden hair, slender white hands, and a milk white neck. All other body parts are missing. Physical reality intrudes only after her death, with the realisation that she is 'now a little dust that feels nothing' (Poem 292).

On the plus side, you can see how the *Canzoniere* must have seemed like a breakthrough to contemporary poets. They validate human love as a subject for serious poetry, and they claim implicitly that the inner conflicts of a single human being are worthy of a lifetime's poetic dedication. They also configure the poet as separate from the rest of humanity. Petrarch flees the 'hostile, odious crowd' (Poem 234), and after Laura's death the world is 'a waste land to me of bitter and savage creatures' (Poem 310). Solitariness has been popular with Western poets ever since. In addition, though the dead hand of medieval theology lies on Petrarch's poetry, as on Dante's, he sometimes escapes it, thanks to his classicism. He gives Laura power over nature, like the mythical poet Orpheus. Her words made mountains move and halted rivers (Poem 156). The countryside was happy for her, and there cannot have been a stone, he declares, 'unused to burning as my flame burns' (Poem 162). Four centuries later the same idea, expressed by Alexander Pope and set to music by Handel in his opera *Semele*, became world-famous:

Where'er you walk, cool gales shall fan the glade,
Trees where you sit shall crowd into a shade,
Where'er you tread, the blushing flowers shall rise,
And all things flourish where you turn your eyes.

The term *poète maudit*, meaning 'accursed poet', and applied to poets who rebel against society's norms, was not invented until the nineteenth century. However, it was with François Villon (c. 1430–c. 1462) that Europe acquired its first *poète maudit*. Born in Paris to unknown parents, he adopted the name Villon from his foster-father, a law professor. He took his BA in 1449 and his MA in 1452. In 1455 he fatally stabbed a priest in a street brawl, but petitioned the king and was pardoned. Later the same year he was with a gang who burgled the Collège de Navarre. After that he fled Paris and temporarily vanishes from the record, though he claims that in 1461 the Bishop of Orleans locked him in a dungeon and tortured him. Back in Paris in 1462 he was in a scuffle that left a Papal notary dead, and was sentenced to hang. On appeal this was commuted to banishment, but no more is known of him.

He wrote twenty shorter poems and two mock last-will-and-testaments, totalling 2,300 lines, in which he leaves a miscellany of junk, plus various items not his to bequeath, to a broad swathe of beneficiaries, some with names twisted into obscene puns. His tone is by turns scathing, sardonic, pious, vituperative, comic, arrogant and trenchantly self-critical – but it is always unmistakable, and he treats subjects other poets had ignored – sex, crime, money troubles, drinking, poverty, pain, hunger. His cast of characters runs from hawkers, criminals, fishwives, lamplighters and down-and-outs who sleep under market stalls, chilled and filthy, to bankers and lawyers. His speakers include a hanged corpse, complaining that crows have stolen his eyebrows and beard for their nests, and an old woman lamenting what time has done to the 'little garden' (*jardinet*) between her legs.

Among moderns, Villon was admired by Arthur Rimbaud, Paul Verlaine, Bertolt Brecht and Ezra Pound, who recommended him as a model. His persistent theme is time's transience, expressed in his most famous line, '*mais où sont les neiges d'antan?*' which Dante Gabriel Rossetti (1828–1882) rendered as, 'But where are the snows of yesteryear?'

CHAPTER 6

A European Poet
CHAUCER

Geoffrey Chaucer (1343–1400) was not only the greatest medieval English poet, he was also a European, weaving other literatures into his poetry – French and Italian, and what had come down to him from the Greeks and Romans. The son of a London vintner, he served Edward III as courtier, soldier, diplomat and civil servant. He travelled widely in France, Spain and Italy, and may have met Petrarch, and possibly Giovanni Boccaccio, whose *Decameron* became a model for his *Canterbury Tales*. A perk of his civil service job (which he seems to have shamefully neglected) was a free flat over London's Aldgate, and he writes jokily about how, when he has finished his daily 'reckonings', he hurries home and buries himself in books till he is 'dazed' with reading. He seems to have preferred scholarly seclusion to family life. At twenty-two he married a court lady, Philippa de Rouet, who bore him three children, but they mostly lived apart.

A good starting point for newcomers to Chaucer is his early poem *The Parlement of Foules* ('The Parliament of Birds'), where a broad cross-section of English birds gather on St Valentine's Day to choose their mates. They are naturally eager to get on with it, but proceedings are held up by the eagles, the most noble birds present. Three male eagles, it turns out, are in love with the same female eagle, who seems reluctant to be chosen as a mate at all. Her wooers compete in courtly protestations, vowing to serve her till death. The other birds, led by the goose, cuckoo and duck, urge them to quit their 'cursed pleading', and the goose squawks coarsely, 'If she won't love him let him love another.' The sparrow-hawk remarks tartly that that's just how you'd expect a goose to talk. However the other birds agree with the goose, and eventually Lady Nature rules that the eagle can wait another year before she's married. The poem closes with all the birds singing a hymn to St Valentine.

There are four very Chaucerian things about this poem. First, it's funny, which Dante and Petrarch never are. Second, like the *Canterbury Tales* it's about the different levels of society and how they interact. Third, Chaucer sees both sides. He is genial and tolerant. The goose is as much in the right, and in the wrong, as the eagles. Fourth, by making his birds talk like people he suggests that all life – humans, birds, animals, the green world – is bonded together by Nature.

Not that Chaucer was a nature-worshipper. He was a Christian. But he was intrigued by the problem of how God governed the world, and he saw what we call 'nature' as part of this. He also wondered whether humans can have free will if (as Christians believe) God knows what will happen in the future. The most famous philosopher who considered these questions was Boethius, whose *Consolation of Philosophy* (523 CE) Chaucer translated into English and often quotes in his poems. The same questions gave him an interest in astrology, which is the theory that the stars and planets determine people's characters and actions. A scientific instrument used in making astrological calculations was the astrolabe, and Chaucer wrote a prose *Treatise* about it for his little son Lewis.

Chaucer's greatest completed poem (the *Canterbury Tales* were never completed) is *Troilus and Criseyde*, which is a version, short-ened and altered, of Boccaccio's poem *Il Filostrato*. Set during the

Trojan War, it tells how Troilus, a son of King Priam of Troy, falls in love with the beautiful Criseyde, whose father has left Troy and joined the Greeks. When she hears of Troilus's love, Criseyde is terrified. But her wily uncle Pandarus, Troilus's friend, talks her round, brings them together, and they become lovers. Then tragedy strikes. The Trojans, knowing nothing of their secret love, agree that Criseyde should be sent to the Greek camp in exchange for a captured Trojan warrior. She promises Troilus she will soon return to Troy, but she never comes and, learning that a Greek warrior, Diomed, is now her protector and lover, Troilus despairs. He seeks death in battle, and is killed by Achilles.

One of the triumphs of Chaucer's art is the first night the lovers spend together. It shines with images, both cruel and tender, from the natural world. Criseyde, helpless in Troilus's arms, is like a lark caught by a sparrow-hawk. But as her fear melts away she 'opens her heart' to him, and it is like a nightingale that had been scared by something in the hedgerow, but then sings out when the danger is past. Amazingly, at this moment of bliss, Chaucer quotes from Dante's *Paradiso* ('Benign love, thou holy bond of things'). Dante, of course, was referring to a quite different kind of love from two lovers naked in bed. But Chaucer dares to challenge Dante's priorities. If love-making is natural, and nature is God's creation, why should lovers not be seen as holy?

The Dante quotation is just one of multiple borrowings that make this a European poem. Virgil, Ovid and Horace are repeatedly quoted too, and Boethius and Boccaccio and the French *Roman de la Rose*, which Chaucer translated. The love song Troilus sings when first smitten is a Petrarch sonnet. The borrowings are not alien but assimilated into Chaucer's voice. One of his most beautiful stanzas is spoken by Criseyde when she hears she must leave Troilus. She vows that, though they may be parted on earth, yet in the afterlife, 'in the field of pity, out of pain', they will be together. The sources for what she says are Virgil and Ovid, but her words are pure Chaucer.

Astrology is a persistent backdrop to the poem. Chaucer fills us in on what conjunction of stars and planets affects the action at crucial moments. The 'smoky rain', for instance, that traps Criseyde in Pandarus's house, results, we're told, from the moon, Saturn and Jupiter being in the constellation of the Crab. Astrology lifts blame from humans, at least partly, and so does Chaucer. He is unwilling to blame Criseyde for being unfaithful. If he could excuse her in any way, he says, he would, 'For she so sorry was for her untruth.' Not that he downplays Troilus's suffering. That is achingly conveyed as he waits and waits in vain.

As you might expect with Chaucer, the poem ends in laughter. When Troilus is killed his soul flies up through the spheres of the universe, and, looking back at 'this little spot of earth', he laughs at how trivial human life is compared to heavenly truth. This world-scorning laughter is firmly Christian. But even here Chaucer sees both sides. For at the poem's end he worries about how the English language is changing, and whether future readers will be able to understand his poem, and get the metre right. He prays they will, and sends his poem out into the world – 'Go, little book' – to take its chance. It is an astonishing moment. For he seems to foresee, half a century before the invention of the printing press, that his readership will extend far beyond his own place and time. He was right, of course, and these concerns are natural in a poet. But they hardly fit in with Christian scorn for the world.

The *Canterbury Tales* is the work of Chaucer everyone has heard of, and its *Prologue* is so familiar it's easy to forget how epoch-making it is. It tells us, as nothing else does, how the different levels of medieval society dressed, talked, joked, swore and viewed one another. It is revolutionary. No one before had created a character like the Wife of Bath, with her frank treatment of female sexuality. The poem's exposure of the profiteering in the Catholic Church, represented by the venal Pardoner and the lecherous, drunken Summoner, is an early warning of the outrage that was to lead, a century later, to the Protestant Reformation.

Finding a tale that matches the brilliance of the *Prologue* is quite difficult. A general favourite is the *Nuns' Priest's Tale*, which is an animal fable like *The Parlement of Foules*, only better. The hero, Chauntecleer the cockerel, is a gorgeous creation, a symphony of coral, jet, azure and gold with nails 'whiter than the lily flower', and he is deliciously vain and pompous. A practised ladies' man, he assures his hen, Madame Pertelote, that *mulier est hominis confusio* is Latin for 'Woman is man's joy and all his bliss', when it means just the opposite. It is the happiest of the tales, and seems to radiate an artist's sheer enjoyment of his art. Even the old widow's meagre diet – milk, brown bread, boiled bacon, and sometimes an egg or two – sounds quite appetising.

But whichever tale is your personal favourite, two undoubted masterpieces are the *Knight's Tale* and the *Miller's*. The knight outranks all the other pilgrims so it is his privilege to start, and he chooses, of course, the subject of chivalry. His tale is a cut-down version of a full-scale epic by Boccaccio, the *Teseida*. But the wonder, given this patchwork origin, is the perfection of its structure. From the first moment, when the two knights, Palamon and Arcite, glimpse through their narrow prison window the beautiful Emily gathering flowers, the tension mounts, the vistas widen and the splendours multiply, as Theseus arranges the great tournament. The arena arises, with its temples and treasures, and the warriors arrive – knights ablaze with gold and rubies; tame lions and leopards romping around them. Then with the tragedy of Arcite's fatal injury the panoply suddenly collapses. It is replaced by raw, clinical details, sick-room words like 'vomit' and 'laxative', and a stark assessment of man's lot:

Now with his love, now in his colde grave
Allone, with-outen any companye.

But the poem has one more wonder for us. A wood is felled to build Arcite's funeral pyre. The knight lists the trees as they come crashing down – oak, fir, birch, a whole forest-catalogue. He tells how the woodland creatures, birds and animals fly out in alarm from the ruin, and how the woodland gods, nymphs, fauns and dryads flee in terror too, and how, he adds, 'the ground aghast was at the light', because it was not used to seeing the sun. The shocked, pale face of the earth is a graphic take on Chaucer's seeing humans and nature as one.

The *Miller's Tale* is deliberately designed to annoy the knight, as well, of course, as the reeve (or 'magistrate'), and it mockingly repeats the knight's 'Allone, with-outen any companye' in its opening lines. It is ribald and obscene, but a marvel. Essentially it is a dirty joke turned into a great work of art, and in that respect it seems unique in literature. Its farcical structure is masterly. The moment that knots the plot's strands together is when Nicholas, fearfully burnt in the buttocks by vengeful Absolon, yells 'Water', and poor deluded John, hanging in his tub up in the rafters (whom readers have quite likely forgotten all about, by this time), thinks Noah's flood has arrived, cuts his rope and crashes to the floor, breaking his arm.

The characterisation, touched on in swift detail, is completely convincing. We believe that clever, handsome Nicholas's idea of wooing would indeed be to catch a woman by the 'queynte'. We understand why fastidious Absolon, in a frenzy of disgust, scrubs his lips with every abrasive that comes to hand when he realises that what he has kissed in the dark was not Alison's mouth. And eighteen-year-old Alison, soft, straight and weasel-slim, is Chaucer's most enticing woman. We know everything about her, from her clothes and plucked eyebrows and fancy handbag to what her breath smells like (mead made with honey, and apples stored in hay). Whatever else of Chaucer's you read, you should not miss the *Miller's Tale*, and if you have read it, treat yourself and read it again.

CHAPTER 7

Poets of the Seen World and the Unseen
THE GAWAIN POET, HAFEZ, LANGLAND

No one knows who the Gawain poet was. Besides writing *Sir Gawain and the Green Knight* he probably wrote three other poems found in the same manuscript, *Pearl*, *Purity* (or *Cleanness*) and *Patience*. He lived around the same time as Chaucer, but wrote in a different dialect, reflecting the speech of Cheshire or Derbyshire. To Chaucer he would have seemed a northerner. He also used alliterative verse, as in *Beowulf*, which Chaucer would have thought old-fashioned. But the Gawain poet combines it with rhyme, sometimes intricately patterned.

He creates a world of brilliant surfaces, and maybe the Gawain story attracted him because of its opportunities for spectacular special effects. During King Arthur and Queen Guinevere's Christmas revels at Camelot a gigantic knight, green in colour from head to foot, and mounted on a green horse, bursts into the hall. He carries a holly bough and a massive axe, and issues a strange challenge, daring any knight present to take the axe and strike him with it, on condition that, in a year's time, the same knight will seek him out and take a blow from the axe in return.

The scene is resplendently detailed – the knight's red eyes rolling in his green face; his enormous axe, green and gold and razor sharp; his green charger with its green tail bound up in an intricate knot on which gold bells ring. Amazed, Arthur's knights are struck dumb. But Gawain begs the king to be allowed to accept the challenge and, grasping the axe, strikes off the Green Knight's head. Blood spurts from the severed neck, yet the knight remains firmly on his feet, grabs his head, turns it so that its eyes are fixed on Guinevere, and its lips move, repeating the terms of the challenge. Then he dashes off, flashing fire from the flints struck by his horse's hooves.

The elaborate detailing continues as the poem moves towards its climax. Gawain dons his armour before leaving Camelot and each item is lovingly described – the brightly polished knee pieces, fastened with gold knots, the 'aventayle' (chain mail protecting the neck), the 'vryson' (silk, embroidered with parrots and periwinkles, attaching the aventayle to the helmet). After riding many days through wild country, he comes upon a wondrous, white castle, huge, but so light against the sky 'That pared out of paper purely it seemed'.

The knight who owns it tells Gawain that the Green Chapel, where he is to meet the Green Knight, is close by. He invites him to stay in the interim, and proposes a wager. Each day he will go hunting, while Gawain remains behind, and at the day's end each of them will give the other whatever he has gained during the day. The knight goes hunting on three days, killing, successively, many deer, a wild boar and a fox, and the hunts are glorious, cruel, bloody set pieces. Meanwhile Gawain, in bed, is visited and tempted by the lady of the castle. Politely but firmly he rejects her advances, accepting each time only a chaste kiss, which he duly pays to the knight when he returns from hunting (without saying who gave him the kiss, since that was no part of the wager). But on the third day the lady offers, besides kisses, a green and gold girdle, which she says will save his life. What happens after that you must read the poem to find out. It is supposed to be a thriller, and it would be a pity to spoil it.

Spectacular visual effects combine with moral and religious lessons in the other three 'Gawain' poems too. In *Pearl* a father whose baby daughter has died dreams that he sees her as a holy lady in a wondrous landscape on the far side of a stream in which emeralds and sapphires gleam like wintry stars. *Purity* climaxes with a retelling of the biblical story of Belshazzar's feast (Daniel 5), where the phrase 'pared out of paper' reappears. As the dishes are carried in by servitors ablaze with azure and indigo, canopies flutter over them, 'pared out of paper' and tipped with gold. *Patience* is a retelling of the biblical Book of Jonah – as full of wonders as anything in *Gawain*. Thrown overboard in a tempest, Jonah is swallowed by a gigantic whale, compared to which he is like a mote of dust blown through a cathedral door.

Gawain and the Green Knight sharply divides sexuality from religion, making sex a temptation to be resisted. That is usual in medieval Christianity, though it contrasts with Chaucer's integration of human love with the innocent, procreating natural world. A more extreme contrast is with the great Persian poet, Hafez (1315–1390), who was writing at the same time as Chaucer and the Gawain poet. He was born in Shiraz, Iran, but not much is known of his life. He is said to have learned the Quran by heart as a child, and worked as a baker, before becoming a court poet. He studied Sufism, an Islamic form of mysticism, under a Sufi master. His lyrical poems, called *ghazals,* use love, wine and women to express the ecstasy of divine inspiration. This treatment of bodily joy, not as a temptation but as a mystical equivalent of the divine, is an achievement that would be inconceivable in Western poetry of the Middle Ages (though it can be matched in the Old Testament Song of Songs). Even today, Western readers of Hafez's poems (which are available in translation) still find it difficult to relate them to religious experience. In Iran, however, they are prized as the greatest achievement of Persian literature, and have passed into common currency, being drawn on for proverbs and sayings. Hafez is still Iran's favourite poet, and it is said his works can be found in almost every Iranian home.

Unlike Chaucer, the poet who wrote *Gawain and the Green Knight* seems entirely satisfied with the society he lives in. He is not critical of either courtly life or the Church. He evidently admires the refined manners ('frenkysch fare') at Camelot, and Gawain is a devout Christian, going to mass and confession before his ordeal. You would not guess that this was the age of the Black Death (1348), the Peasants' Revolt (1381), or John Wycliffe and the Lollards, forerunners of the Reformation.

In William Langland's great poem *Piers Plowman* these political and social issues are paramount. Though he was not a revolutionary himself, his ideas were, and were taken up by the Lollards and the leaders of the Peasants' Revolt. His life is largely unknown. He was obviously learned and a thinker. He refers to his wife, 'Kitte', and a daughter, 'Kalote', and says he gave up intellectual struggle and 'followed the flesh' for forty-five years, then lived 'In manner of a mendicant [a beggar] many years after'. But now, old and poor, he is prompted to begin his poem. Written probably in the late 1370s and early 1380s, it exists in three widely different versions (the A, B and C texts). It was unfinished, and perhaps unfinishable, since its subject is the quest for truth.

It is written in the old alliterative metre, and starts 'In a summer season, when soft was the sun', with Will, dressed in rough clothes, like a shepherd, setting off to walk 'wide in the world, wonders to hear'. He remembers how he fell asleep, 'On a May morning, on Malvern hills', and dreamed a marvellous dream. There was a tower, and a deep dungeon, and a 'field full of folk' – merchants, minstrels, beggars, pilgrims and palmers, and some who worked hard at the plough to 'win what wasters with gluttony destroy'.

It is a long, confusing poem, filling (in the B text) twenty books (or 'Passus', meaning steps). Will wakes and sleeps and dreams and wakes and sleeps and dreams. His dominant theme is the contrast between rich and poor. Christ, he reminds us, was poor, 'And in a poor man's apparel pursues us ever'. His disciples had no possessions. He sent them out 'silver-less', 'barefoot and breadless', yet they were 'merry-mouthed men, minstrels of heaven'. Will remembers how the poor suffered in famine years, like 1370, and he prays for them.

> And poor people, thy prisoners, Lord, in the pit of mischief,
> Comfort thy creatures, that much care suffer,
> Through dearth, through drought, all their days here,
> Woe in wintertime, for wanting of clothes,
> And in summer time seldom sup to the full,
> Comfort thy careful, Christ, in thy kingdom.

As for the wealthy, they are, in Will's vision, corrupt, and corruption spreads everywhere. Churchmen absolve the rich of their sins, provided they cough up money to build churches and endow stained glass windows. Lawyers take bribes. Merchants cheat. Brewers and bakers 'poison the people privily and oft'. The dream-figure who represents wealth is called 'Lady Mede' (meaning 'Reward') and she is inseparably betrothed to Falsehood. Go where money is, and you will find crooks, is Will's message.

Will's quest is necessary because the Church is crooked. His poem shows a man trying to construct his own religion, when the Church has failed. He wants to know how to live, and imagines three levels of conduct, 'Dowel', 'Dobet' and 'Dobest'. It is not clear that he ever finds what doing well, better and best involve, but in his dreams he hears various advisers – Reason, Wit, Study, Clergy, Scripture, and others. The most important figure to emerge is Piers, a ploughman, who sets the field full of folk to work, to help him plough his half-acre. One character, Waster, refuses, so Piers sends Hunger to punish him. In a country recovering from the Black Death, Langland seems to be saying, there can be no idlers. It is June, and Piers lists the food he has left until harvest-time – parsley, leeks, a lot of cabbages, two green cheeses, an oaten loaf and two loaves made of beans and bran. But he has a cow and a calf and a horse to draw his dung-cart, so if he works he will survive. The seven deadly sins, redeemed, join Piers's workforce, not as abstractions but as believable men and women. Anger, for example, worked before his redemption in a priory kitchen, and tells how he spread malicious gossip among the nuns that had them at each other's throats ('If they'd had knives, by Christ, they'd have killed one another').

Will is guided by Conscience and Kind Wit (common sense), not theology ('The more I muse therein, the mistier it seemeth'). The primal virtue for him is love, which he describes as coming to earth with Christ:

> For heaven could not hold it, it was so heavy of itself,
> Till it had of the earth eaten its fill,
> And when it had of this fold flesh and blood taken,
> Was never leaf upon linden-tree lighter thereafter,
> And portable and piercing as the point of a needle,
> That no armour could keep it out, nor any high walls.

For Piers, too, love is sovereign. Conscience says of him:

> For one Piers the Plowman has impugned us all,
> And set all sciences at a sop, save love alone.

Towards the end, Will, in his dream, attends the crucifixion.

> The day for dread withdrew, and dark became the sun,
> The wall wagged and cleaved, and all the world quaked,
> Dead men for that din came out of deep graves,
> And told why that tempest so long time endured.

Faith tells Will that Jesus is 'jousting' in Piers's armour, so Piers and Christ seem to have fused.

As a religious poet, Langland is unusual, in that enquiry and questioning dominate in his work, not awe or worship. Unlike, say, Dante, he does not dwell on hell and punishment. Rather, he believes that all are redeemable, and that:

> All the wickedness in the world, that man might work or think.
> Is no more to the mercy of God than in the sea a spark.

CHAPTER 8

Tudor Court Poets
SKELTON, WYATT, SURREY, SPENSER

John Skelton (*c.* 1463–1529) was the first English poet who dared openly to attack those in authority. He wrote blistering satires deriding Cardinal Wolsey, then the most powerful man in the realm, and was imprisoned more than once. As Vicar of Diss, in Norfolk, he caused scandal by marrying (forbidden to priests) and displaying his little son naked from the pulpit, to defy the gossips.

He invented his own helter-skelter kind of poetry, called 'Skeltonics', which can be deliberately repellent, as in *The Tunning of Elinour Rumming*, about drunken women in a Norwich pub, or tender, as in *Philip Sparrow* (loosely based on Catullus' Lesbia and her sparrow), about a tame bird killed by a cat and fondly remembered by its owner, Jane Scrope, a Norwich schoolgirl.

Skelton's most magnificent bird appears in *Speak, Parrot*, a poem put into the mouth – or beak – of a vain, fastidious fowl who describes his luxurious cage, 'curiously carven, with a silver pin', his looking-glass, in which he 'toots', his partiality to almonds and dates, and other parrot matters.

With my beak bent, my little wanton eye,
   My feathers fresh as is the emerald green,
About my neck a circlet like the rich ruby,
   My little legs, my feet both feat and clean,
   I am a minion to wait upon a queen.
'My proper Parrot, my little pretty fool!'
With ladies I learn and go with them to school.

He claims he can speak Latin, Hebrew, Arabic, Chaldean, Greek, French, Dutch, Spanish and Italian, and snippets of several of these languages, plus Welsh and German, appear in the poem (which makes it what is called a 'macaronic' or mixed-language poem).

Though it contains jibes at Cardinal Wolsey, no one has ever discovered what *Speak, Parrot* is really about. Skelton was vain and flamboyant, like his parrot, and in 1512 was appointed King's Orator, with the distinction of wearing a white and green robe, embroidered with the name 'Calliope' (the Muse of Eloquence). Quite possibly *Speak, Parrot* is a mocking self-portrait.

Sir Thomas Wyatt (1504–1542) was no Skelton. A career diplomat under Henry VIII, he changed sides as the wind blew in court. He left his wife, accusing her of adultery, and was imprisoned on suspicion of being Anne Boleyn's lover but escaped execution.

Many of his poems are unremarkable, but a handful are unforgettable. Best known is 'They Flee from Me that Sometime Did Me Seek', where, forsaken, he remembers better times:

Thanked be fortune, it hath been otherwise,
   Twenty times better, but once in special,
In thin array after a pleasant guise,
   When her loose gown from her shoulders did fall,
   And she me caught in her arms long and small,
Therewithal sweetly did me kiss,
And softly said, 'Dear heart, how like you this?'

It was no dream, I lay broad waking . . .

Wyatt's poems are often translations or adaptations of Petrarch, but Petrarch never wrote anything like that.

Even when less good, he can surprise with an arresting phrase – about his last patron, Thomas Cromwell, for example, on the scaffold, who:

> ... much known of other, and of himself, alas,
> Doth die unknown, dazed with dreadful face.

His second Satire, about the town and country mouse, ends in resonant scorn for fools misled by ambition:

> No other pain pray I for them to be
> But, when the rage doth lead them from the right,
> That, looking backward, virtue they may see
> Even as she is, so goodly, fair and bright,
> And whilst they clasp their lusts in arms across
> Grant them, good Lord, as thou mayst of thy might,
> To fret inward for losing such a loss.

Henry Howard, Earl of Surrey (1517–1547) belonged to one of the noblest English families and served as a commander in Henry VIII's French wars, but was beheaded because Henry suspected him of aspiring to the English throne. He is best at sonorous, troubling effects. Gripped by the pain of love, he recalls others' pain.

> I call to mind the navy great
> That the Greeks brought to Troia town,
> And how the boisterous winds did beat
> Their ships, and rent their sails adown,
> Till Agamemnon's daughter's blood
> Appeased the gods that them withstood.

His best love poem ('O Happy Dames'), put into the mouth of a woman grieving for her absent lover, is similarly doom-laden.

When other lovers in arms across
Rejoice their chief delight,
Drowned in tears to mourn my loss
I stand the bitter night
In my window, where I may see
Before the wind how the clouds flee,
Lo, what a mariner hath love made me!

Edmund Spenser (1552–1599) is the only English poet to have written a national epic, *The Faerie Queene*. It represents a new kind of epic, not Homeric but chivalric and romantic, and Spenser's model was the *Orlando Furioso* ('Raving Roland') by the great Italian poet Lodovico Ariosto (1474–1533).

The background to Ariosto's epic is the warfare between Charlemagne and his Christian knights on one side and the Saracens invading Europe on the other. The action is tangled, and there are hordes of characters, but the main story is about a knight, Orlando, whose love for a pagan princess, Angelica, drives him mad. There are many magical and fantastic elements – a sorceress, a wizard, a gigantic sea-monster, a flying horse, and a trip to the moon to recover Orlando's lost wits, which are brought back in a bottle. Spenser was also influenced by a later Christian v. Saracen epic, *Gerusalemme Liberata* ('Jerusalem Delivered'), by another famous Italian poet, Torquato Tasso (1544–1595), who really did go mad and was locked up for seven years.

Spenser wrote his *Faerie Queene* when his country was in peril, and dedicated it to Queen Elizabeth ('Gloriana' in the poem). It proclaims the antiquity and supernatural authority of the Tudor dynasty, as Virgil's *Aeneid* had done for the Augustan line. Its old-world language and invocation of Arthur and his knights are part of this appeal to history.

But in reality Protestant England was new and vulnerable. Henry VIII had made himself, rather than the Pope, head of the Church, which was unheard of. In 1570 Pope Pius V excommunicated Henry's daughter, Elizabeth I, releasing all Catholics from allegiance to her. The Spanish Armada was intended to recapture

England for Catholicism, and was defeated in 1588, two years before the publication of the *Faerie Queene*'s first three books. So Spenser's poem defies the armed might of Catholic Europe. In Book 1, Una, companion of the Red Cross Knight, represents the true (English) Church, while the false Duessa is Roman Catholicism. To understand, we must set aside our image of Anglicanism as a rather tepid branch of the establishment, and see it as a heresy for which foreigners would burn you alive.

Spenser invented a new stanza form for his new poem. It starts as if it is going to be a sonnet, but has a long last line which slows the pace and seals each stanza off from the next. Within this tight rhyme-scheme the sentences can be as loose and fluid as he chooses, following the inflexions of the speaking voice. Here is an example:

> And is there care in heaven? And is there love
> In heavenly spirits for these creatures base
> That may compassion of their evils move?
> There is: else much more wretched were the case
> Of men than beasts. But O the exceeding grace
> Of highest God, that loves his creatures so,
> And all his workes with mercy doth embrace,
> That blessed angels he sends to and fro,
> To serve to wicked man, to serve his wicked foe.
>
> (2.8.1)

This shows how the voice can slip and slide within the walls of the stanza, spilling over the line breaks and introducing its own rhythms that play against the metrical beat. Many poets have used the Spenserian stanza since, for a wide variety of purposes – most famously Keats for *The Eve of St Agnes*.

A Londoner, Spenser went to Ireland in 1580 in the service of Elizabeth's Deputy, Lord Grey de Wilton, and settled at Kilcolman in North Cork. He married an Irish woman Elizabeth Boyle, and addressed his love sonnets, the *Amoretti*, and his wedding poem, the *Epithalamion*, to her. In 1598 his house was burnt down by Irish freedom fighters and he fled with his family to England. Dying soon after, he was buried in Westminster Abbey, near Chaucer. This was the origin of what is now Poets' Corner.

The *Faerie Queene* is a moral allegory and recounts a bewildering series of adventures in which knights, representing different virtues, battle with aliens. But the action is less important than the scenic effects. Many critics have noted that the poem is essentially a series of spectacles – the Cave of Mammon, with its furnaces for melting gold, or the Garden of Proserpina, with its black trees and golden apples (both in Book 2), or the Masque of Cupid (Book 3), where Amoret's 'trembling' heart is carried before her in a basin of steaming blood, and so on. To understand the attraction of this pictorial element we need to remember how rare actual pictures were in Elizabethan England. It is estimated that we see more pictures in a single day than the average Elizabethan would in a lifetime. Wall paintings in their parish church were the only pictures many Elizabethans would ever see. So Spenser's pictorial poem filled a gap in the culture.

Some of the pictorial sequences were, for their time, daringly explicit. In the Bower of Bliss (Book 2) naked maidens jump up and down in a fountain. In Book 6 Serena, naked and bound, is surrounded by cannibals, whetting their knives and deciding which of her 'daintie parts' to eat first. Nothing so sensual had happened in English poetry before. To call these effects 'pictorial' is really too static. Spenser's figures are always in motion. In the Bower of Bliss, for example, he suggests the coming and going of colour in a girl's face.

> Withall she laughed, and she blusht withall,
> That blushing to her laughter gave more grace,
> And laughter to her blushing . . .

He also invents new words to convey motion more forcibly than the existing ones. 'Scruze', for example, meaning 'squeeze', which he uses to describe crushing the juice out of grapes or herbs (2.12.56, 3.5.33). Even when describing a static artwork he puts it into motion. A tapestry in Busirane's house depicts Leda and the swan, but it moves. The swan approaches 'ruffling' its feathers (another Spenserian coinage), and Leda pretends to be asleep but watches, smiling, through half-closed eyelids. 'Scruze' and 'ruffles' are both tactile, invoking the sense of touch, and this is often true of Spenser's coinages. A scorpion's claws become 'craples' (5.8.40), which seems to combine 'crawls' and 'grapples'. From this angle Spenser's moving pictures look forward not just to the cinema but to Aldous Huxley's imaginary 'feelies' in *Brave New World*.

So Spenser was doing new things. But, being a Renaissance poet, he was also looking back to the classics. In one of his best short poems, *The Fate of the Butterfly*, we watch Arachne turning into a spider – her legs becoming 'crooked crawling shankes, of marrow empted', her body a 'bag of venim' – in what could be a scene from Ovid's *Metamorphoses*. In the *Faerie Queene*, as in Ovid, humans turn into plants and interact with the natural world. A bough is torn from a tree, and it bleeds (1.2.30). Chrysogne sunbathes, naked, and (as in D.H. Lawrence's short story 'Sun') the sun makes her pregnant (3.6.7).

Another modern invention Spenser seems to have anticipated is the robot. Talus, Artegall's terrible slave, is a man made of iron. Munera is a woman with hands and feet of gold and silver. The false Florimel is artificial, manufactured out of mercury, snow, wax and wire. When the Elizabethan poets threw their quills and verses into Spenser's grave they were recognising a colossally innovative imagination.

CHAPTER 9

Elizabethan Love Poets
Shakespeare, Marlowe, Sidney

As everyone knows, William Shakespeare (1564–1616) is the world's greatest dramatist. But he wrote non-dramatic poetry too. Best known are his sonnets, published in 1609. It's not known whether he wanted them published, or even wrote all of them. Though they are world famous, they may disappoint modern readers. Some of them consist largely of complicated word-play, and scarcely engage our feelings at all.

They don't tell a coherent story, and how they relate to Shakespeare's life is unclear. Many attempts have been made to identify real-life originals for the young man of Sonnets 1–126, the 'dark lady' of Sonnets 127–52 and the rival poet or poets of Sonnets 78–80. But these attempts are just guesswork. Even if the young man represents, in some way, Shakespeare's patron, the Earl of Southampton, it seems unlikely the love affair the sonnets depict took place anywhere outside Shakespeare's imagination.

However, whether the sonnets represent real life is immaterial. What matters is that they are dramatic. The poet addresses another character – arguing, persuading, blaming. This saves them from the uneventful sameness often found in other Elizabethan sequences.

With so many sonnets to read, a good plan is to concentrate, to start with, on the most famous, numbering about fifteen in all. Which are they and what are they about?

Eight of them are about time and its destructive power. Some critics suggest that this interested Shakespeare's age because clocks and watches became commoner by the late sixteenth century, changing the way time was regarded. Instead of being related to natural things it came to seem mechanical and alien. That may be true. But only one of our eight time-sonnets – 'When I do count the clock that tells the time' (12) – starts with clock time, and it quickly switches to nature and the barley harvest:

> . . . summer's green, all girded up in sheaves,
> Borne on the bier with white and bristly beard.

That is not surprising. Shakespeare's England was agricultural, and the seasons remained its usual time-measure, as in Sonnet 18:

> Shall I compare thee to a summer's day?
> Thou art more lovely and more temperate.
> Rough winds do shake the darling buds of May,
> And summer's lease hath all too short a date . . .

or Sonnet 73:

> That time of year thou mayst in me behold
> When yellow leaves, or none, or few do hang
> Upon those boughs which shake against the cold,
> Bare ruined choirs where late the sweet birds sang . . .

In Sonnet 104, 'To me, fair friend, you never can be old', seasonal time predominates again, though clock time ('a dial hand') briefly intervenes, while Sonnet 60, 'Like as the waves make towards the pebbled shore', turns to another natural rhythm as its starting point.

The other three time-sonnets, 'Devouring Time, blunt thou the lion's paws' (19), 'Not marble, nor the gilded monuments' (55) and 'Since brass, nor stone, nor earth, nor boundless sea' (65) are variations on the boast we saw the Roman poet, Horace, making in his *Odes*, that his poetry would outlast bronze monuments and the pyramids.

Four of the fifteen most famous sonnets are about the joys and sorrows of love, and seem clearly personal. Surely, we think, 'When, in disgrace with Fortune, and men's eyes' (29), and 'When to the sessions of sweet silent thought' (30), must be Shakespeare truly pouring out his heart? Surely, 'Full many a glorious morning have I seen' (33) must recall a particular incident that really happened? Surely the heart-rending 'No longer mourn for me when I am dead' (71) can't be just make-believe? But Shakespeare was a playwright. He spent his life making up speeches for imaginary people, and that is what these probably are.

The same goes for the remaining three of our fifteen sonnets – the defiant declaration of faith in true love (116), the tirade against lust, 'The expense of spirit in a waste of shame' (129), and the strange, difficult comparison of two personality types, 'They that have power to hurt and will do none' (94) with its caustic last line, 'Lilies that fester smell far worse than weeds.' Unlike all the other sonnets in the sequence these three are free-standing, not part of the love story, but apparently Shakespeare expressing his own thoughts. Or that is how it seems, but we cannot possibly know.

Of all the sonnets, 116 is probably most people's favourite, perhaps because it expresses what we want to believe.

> Let me not to the marriage of true minds
> Admit impediment, love is not love
> Which alters when it alteration finds,
> Or bends with the remover to remove.
> O no, it is an ever-fixed mark

That looks on tempests and is never shaken;
It is the star to every wandering bark,
Whose worth's unknown, although his height be taken.
Love's not Time's fool, though rosy lips and cheeks
Within his bending sickle's compass come;
Love alters not with his brief hours and weeks,
But bears it out even to the edge of doom.
    If this be error and upon me proved,
    I never writ, nor no man ever loved.

Some modern readers interpret it as bitterly ironic.

But leaving questions of sincerity aside, is the poet of the sonnets recognisably the Shakespeare who wrote the great tragedies? It seems a foolish question, since the forms are so different. Yet there are links. One feature of Shakespeare's art common to both the poems and the plays is that abstract nouns are made agents, performing real acts, so that, though our imaginations are stirred, we can't exactly visualise what is happening. For example, Lear's:

Take physic, pomp.
Expose thyself to feel what wretches feel,
That thou mayst shake the superflux to them . . .

                                  (*King Lear*, 3.4.33–5)

or Macbeth's:

Pity, like a naked, new-born babe,
Striding the blast . . .

                                  (*Macbeth*, 1.7.19–20)

'Pomp' and 'pity' are abstract nouns, yet seem to behave as if they were not. In the sonnets this pairing of abstract with concrete can happen in just a single phrase: as in 'winter's ragged hand' (6); or 'my tattered loving' (26). Or it can extend over several lines, creating some of Shakespeare's most powerful effects. Writing of 'sad mortality' in Sonnet 65, he asks:

How with this rage shall beauty hold a plea,
Whose action is no stronger than a flower?

The 'flower' seems hopelessly weak, yet it is the only word in the lines that is not abstract, and that foregrounds it. In Sonnet 60 the ages of human life are described in four lines:

Nativity, once in the main of light,
Crawls to maturity, wherewith being crowned,
Crooked eclipses 'gainst his glory fight,
And Time that gave doth now his gift confound.

All the activity here is done by abstract nouns. Yet we have a distinct visual impression of a baby crawling on all fours, and of something dark and sinister in 'Crooked eclipses', and of an ocean of brightness in 'main'.

Some critics have speculated that this interaction between the abstract and the concrete shows Shakespeare connecting two different parts of the brain – the part that deals with concepts and the part that deals with bodily sensations. Perhaps that is what gives such lines their power.

Shakespeare's other non-dramatic poems have never achieved the fame of the sonnets. One, though, is magnificent. Called *The Phoenix and the Turtle* it is a funeral dirge for two dead birds, a phoenix and a turtle dove, who represent love and chastity. No one knows why or for whom it was written or what it means. But the plangent notes of its opening stanzas are unforgettably haunting.

Let the bird of loudest lay,
On the sole Arabian tree,
Herald sad and trumpet be,
To whose sound chaste wings obey . . .

Let the priest in surplice white,
That defunctive music can,

Be the death-divining swan,
Lest the requiem lack his right.

Shakespeare's two longer poems, *Venus and Adonis* and *The Rape of Lucrece*, can seem ornate and slow to modern readers. As a narrative poet he was no match for Christopher Marlowe (1564–1593), whose *Hero and Leander*, though unfinished, is a Renaissance gem. A brilliant young dramatist, Marlowe was stabbed to death in a pub brawl in Deptford. He had been employed in espionage, which may be why he was silenced. Shakespeare had read *Hero and Leander* and it is the only contemporary work quoted in his plays – by Phoebe in *As You Like It*, 3.5.

Dead shepherd, now I find thy saw of might
'Whoever loved that loved not at first sight?'

Shakespeare calls Marlowe a 'shepherd' because his most famous poem, 'Come live with me and be my love', was titled *The Passionate Shepherd to his Love*.

Shakespeare's sonnets are about same-sex love, but he is cautious about how he expresses it. Sonnet 20 states firmly that sex with the young man is not what the poet of the sonnets wants. Marlowe was much less guarded. He was reported to the authorities for making scandalous jokes about sex between males (which was illegal in Elizabethan England), saying that 'All they that love not tobacco and boys are fools', and that Christ and St John were lovers.

Whereas Shakespeare's sonnets omit any extensive description of the young man's physical attractions, *Hero and Leander* does just the opposite. As Leander swims across the Hellespont, shameless old Neptune adoringly accompanies him:

He clapp'd his plump cheeks, with his tresses played,
And smiling wantonly his love bewrayed;
He watched his arms, and as they opened wide
At every stroke betwixt them would he slide,
And steal a kiss, and then run out and dance,

And as he turned cast many a lustful glance,
And threw him gaudy toys to please his eye,
And dive into the water, and there pry
Upon his breast, his thighs, and every limb,
And up again, and close beside him swim,
And talk of love. Leander made reply,
'You are deceived, I am no woman, I',
Thereat smiled Neptune . . .

Nothing in Shakespeare's sonnets matches this for sensuality or wit.

Sir Philip Sidney (1554–1586) cannot compare with Shakespeare or Marlowe as a poet. All the same, his sonnet sequence *Astrophil and Stella* (meaning 'The Star-lover and the Star') was read by Shakespeare, who may have got the idea for his 'dark lady' from Sidney's black-eyed Stella (*Astrophil and Stella*, 7, 20, 48).

Sidney was a nobleman, nephew of the Earl of Leicester, and died gallantly fighting the Spaniards at the Battle of Zutphen. Stella may be based on Penelope Devereux whose father, the Earl of Essex, wanted her to marry Sidney. She actually married Lord Rich – hence Sidney's satirical puns on 'rich' (24, 37). His sonnets, like Shakespeare's, use natural speech rhythms to break up their metrical sameness, as in, 'Fly, fly, my friends! I have my death's wound – fly!' (20). Sonnet 31, among Sidney's finest, is a masterpiece of conversational tone.

With how sad steps, O moon, thou climb'st the skies!
How silently, and with how wan a face.
What, may it be that even in heavenly place
That busy archer his sharp arrows tries?
Sure, if that long-with-love-acquainted eyes
Can judge of love, thou feel'st a lover's case:
I read it in thy looks, thy languished grace,
To me, that feel the like, thy state descries.
Then, even of fellowship, O moon, tell me,
Is constant love deemed there but want of wit?

Are beauties there as proud as here they be?
Do they above love to be loved, and yet
Those lovers scorn whom that love doth possess?
Do they call virtue there ungratefulness?

The last line changes the poem. Up to then the male speaker had complained about how women behave. But the last line does not follow suit. It is men, not women, who accuse virtuous women of ungratefulness for not yielding to their wooing. The poem is spoken by a man, but in the last line a female voice breaks in and puts the woman's point of view. Sidney was used to educated women who spoke their minds, and his niece, Lady Mary Wroth, wrote sonnets herself.

CHAPTER 10

Copernicus in Poetry
JOHN DONNE

In the hundred years before John Donne's birth in 1572, the world changed. A vast new continent came to light when Christopher Columbus made landfall in the Americas in 1492. In 1543 a Polish astronomer called Nicolaus Copernicus published his theory that the earth was not the centre of the universe, as had always been thought, but orbited the sun. Both the Catholic and the Protestant Churches dismissed the idea as ridiculous and also damnable, for the Bible says the earth does not move and the sun does. So it was not just the solar system but God's word that was called into question.

Donne eagerly absorbed both novelties in his poems. Undressing his mistress, he reimagines her as the new continent that the Spanish colonists were, as he wrote, ransacking for treasure:

> O my America! my new-found-land,
> My kingdom, safeliest when with one man manned,
> My mine of precious stones, My Empirie,
> How blest am I in this discovering thee!

That is in 'To His Mistress Going to Bed'.

In 'An Anatomy of the World' he turns his attention to Copernicus. The 'new philosophy', he writes, has overthrown the old certainties. It 'calls all in doubt', and we no longer know where we are:

> The sun is lost, and the earth, and no man's wit
> Can well direct him where to look for it.

Donne sounds excited rather than worried by the prospect, and that is natural, because he is in the business of upsetting expectations himself. His contemporaries called him 'Copernicus in poetry', recognising his newness.

What makes him new is that he is always arguing. He used to be called a 'metaphysical' poet. But that implies he was interested in propounding abstruse philosophy, and he was not. What does interest him, persistently, is argument. In his poems he often uses it to get his way with women (or imaginary women). A notorious example is 'The Flea', where the lovers are in bed and he tells her that since a flea, which has bitten them both, has already mixed their bloods there can be no harm in having sex. She threatens to kill the flea, but he argues against it:

> O stay, three lives in one flea spare,
> Where we almost, nay more than married are,
> This flea is you and I, and this
> Our marriage bed and marriage temple is;
> Though parents grudge, and you, we are met
> And cloistered in these living walls of jet,
>   Though use make you apt to kill me,
>   Let not to that self-murder added be,
>   And sacrilege, three sins in killing three.

Nevertheless she goes ahead and kills it, and boasts that she feels no different now it's dead. Exactly so, Donne retorts, that proves he's right:

'Tis true, then learn how false fears be,
Just so much honour, when thou yield'st to me,
Will waste, as this flea's death took life from thee.

You could say the poem is a joke. But it is not just a joke. The description of the flea ('these living walls of jet') is tender and beautiful. No one had written about a flea like that before. T.S. Eliot (who was largely responsible for reviving Donne's reputation after two centuries of neglect) said, 'a thought to Donne was an experience, it modified his sensibility', and in 'The Flea' we can see what he means.

It may be wrong to call the woman in 'The Flea' imaginary. How far Donne's love poems reflect his real life is not known. He had a reputation as a rake, and in his Love Elegies he boasts of his goings-on about town – cuckolding husbands, seducing daughters and (in 'To His Mistress Going to Bed') ordering a woman to strip while he watches. They may be just make-believe. Or not.

Donne was ambitious, and rose high in what we should now call the civil service. But in 1601 he secretly married a young heiress, Anne More, without her parents' permission. When the secret was discovered he lost his job. For years he and Anne lived in poverty in the country, with a rapidly expanding family of children. Perhaps that is why the love poems are so scornful of worldly success – 'The Anniversary', for example:

All kings, and all their favourites,
All glory of honours, beauties, wits,
The sun itself, which makes times as they pass,
Is older by a year now than it was
When thou and I first one another saw.
All other things to their destruction draw,
Only our love hath no decay,
This no tomorrow hath, nor yesterday.
Running, it never runs from us away,
But truly keeps his first, last, everlasting day.

Along with argumentativeness and contempt for worldly success, Donne is singular because he changes his viewpoint from poem to poem. Sometimes he is shamelessly promiscuous, as in 'The Indifferent', or cynical, as in 'Farewell to Love'. Set against these are poems such as 'The Ecstasy', which situate love in the soul, and proclaim that, though lovers are parted, their souls are not, but span the space between them. In 'The Funeral' he imagines how, when he is dead, a twist of his mistress's hair, bound round his arm, will act like a soul and stop his body from decaying:

> Whoever comes to shroud me, do not harm,
> > Nor question much,
> That subtle wreath of hair which crowns my arm;
> The mystery, the sign, you must not touch,
> > For 'tis my outward soul,
> Viceroy to that, which then to heaven being gone,
> > Will leave this to control,
> And keep these limbs, her provinces, from dissolution.

In 'A Valediction, Forbidding Mourning' he tells his mistress (or, some think, his wife) that he must go on a journey. But he assures her that they are 'refined' by love and so, though their bodies are separated, they will still be together:

> Our two souls, therefore, which are one,
> > Though I must go, endure not yet
> A breach, but an expansion,
> > Like gold to airy thinness beat.

In 'The Relic' he claims that his love and the loved woman's was so pure it was like angels' love, not sexual at all. They did not even know they were a male and a female. The poem starts with the twist of hair from 'The Funeral'. He imagines those who dig up his skeleton finding 'A bracelet of bright hair about the bone', and taking it for a miracle. But he will tell them, he says, 'What miracles we harmless lovers wrought':

First, we loved well and faithfully,
Yet knew not what we loved, nor why;
Difference of sex no more we knew
Than our guardian angels do;
    Coming and going, we
Perchance might kiss, but not between those meals,
    Our hands ne'er touched the seals,
Which nature, injured by late law, sets free;
These miracles we did, but now alas,
All measure and all language I should pass,
Should I tell what a miracle she was.

The 'seals' are their genitals, which in the state of nature were not restricted by recent ('late') man-made laws, such as the laws relating to marriage. But Donne says they never even touched them. That may seem strange to some, but not knowing exactly what it is you love in another person (not knowing 'what we loved, nor why') is something every lover will recognise. Donne writes about it again in 'Negative Love', where he says it is not the woman's body, nor her 'virtue', nor her 'mind' that he loves. But what it is he can't say. Donne enjoys argument, even when it is argument for argument's sake. But he is a thinker too, and knows that some things are mysterious beyond the reach of argument, and love is one.

It is for poems like these that Donne is celebrated as the greatest English love poet. No other poet has so expressed the desolation of bereavement as he does in 'A Nocturnal Upon St. Lucy's Day', or the strange mystery of love at first sight, as in 'Air and Angels':

Twice or thrice had I loved thee
Before I knew thy face or name,
So in a voice, so in a shapeless flame,
Angels affect us oft, and worshipped be;
Still when, to where thou wert I came,
Some lovely glorious nothing I did see . . .

After reading that, it's a shock to come upon one of the cynical poems like 'Love's Alchemy', which warns:

Hope not for mind in women, at their best
Sweetness and wit, they are but mummy possessed.

'Mummy' means 'mummified corpses'; 'possessed' means 'once you have made love to them'. How could the same poet write this and the 'soul' poems?

One answer is that Donne was, as he frequently admits, hopelessly changeable. ('Oh, to vex me contraries meet in one,' he laments in Holy Sonnet 19, 'I change in vows and in devotion'). But another is that he was, we know, a keen theatre-goer, and he lived in the great age of English drama when Shakespeare's plays were being staged for the first time. His poems are often in effect dramatic monologues, trying out different voices and different speakers.

He argues with women in his love poems, and in his religious poems he argues with God. Why should only humans be damned, he demands, when plants, minerals and animals are not (Holy Sonnet 9)? Why doesn't God make more effort to save him (Holy Sonnet 14)?

In Donne's day many people worried whether they were damned (it was their equivalent of our searching the internet to see what our symptoms mean we are suffering from). But he had a special reason. He feared he was damned because, though brought up as a Roman Catholic, he had forsaken the faith and joined the Protestant Church. In Elizabethan England he could not have had a civil service career otherwise. But to his family and Catholic friends his apostasy meant he belonged to Satan, and, as he tells God in Holy Sonnet 2, he fears they may be right:

O I shall soon despair, when I do see
That thou lov'st mankind well, yet wilt not choose me,
And Satan hates me, yet is loth to lose me.

Sometimes he feels he would just like to get it over, and know the worst. So, he says, bring on the end of the world and the Last Judgment now, immediately:

> At the round earth's imagined corners, blow
> Your trumpets angels, and arise, arise
> From death you numberless infinities
> Of souls, and to your scattered bodies go.
> All whom the flood did, and fire shall o'erthrow,
> All whom war, dearth, age, ague, tyrannies,
> Despair, law, chance hath slain, and you whose eyes
> Shall behold God and never taste death's woe.

Those last two lines (from Holy Sonnet 7) refer to St Paul's declaration (1 Corinthians 15.51) that we shall not all die, but that those still alive at the end of the world will be changed 'in a moment, in the twinkling of an eye, at the last trumpet'. Donne hoped he would be one of these, for he hated the idea of the grave and bodily corruption. But then, half way through the sonnet, he changes his mind – mutable, as ever:

> But let them sleep, Lord, and me mourn a space,
> For if above all these my sins abound,
> 'Tis late to ask abundance of thy grace
> When we are there; here on this holy ground
> Teach me how to repent, for that's as good
> As if thou hadst sealed my pardon with thy blood.

Donne never outgrew the terror that he might be damned. In 'A Hymn to God the Father' he confessed:

> I have a sin of fear, that when I have spun
> My last thread, I shall perish on the shore . . .

That was written in 1623, eight years after he had become a clergyman in the Anglican Church, and two years after he had been appointed Dean of St Paul's Cathedral.

CHAPTER 11

An Age of Individualism
Jonson, Herrick, Marvell

The seventeenth century was an age of astonishing diversity in English poetry. Donne dominated at the start, Milton towards the end. As poets they are different from each other in every possible way, and the poets who emerged in the intervening years are wholly and unmistakably individual too. This is a great change from the Elizabethan age, when one sonneteer or song-writer can easily be mistaken for another. Where did the new sense of individuality come from? One suggestion is Protestantism, which frees the individual believer from conformity and encourages self-examination. Another suggestion is London. It was the first metropolitan culture England had known, and city life, which surrounds you with strangers, intensifies your sense of difference.

Ben Jonson (1572–1637) was a Londoner, and also a Protestant (though, anxious about his own salvation, he converted to Catholicism for a while). He was an unruly character from a rough background. Over the course of his life he served several spells in prison. His stepfather was a bricklayer and young Jonson learned the trade too. But a rich relative paid for him to go to Westminster school where he flourished and developed a deep love and knowledge of Greek and Latin literature. He fought as a soldier in the Netherlands and boasted of killing an enemy soldier and plundering his body. Working as an actor, he killed a fellow actor in a duel, saved his neck by pleading 'benefit of clergy' (proving he could read Latin), and was branded 'F' for 'felon' on his thumb instead.

He was a keen observer of city life, and wrote great satirical dramas (*Volpone* and *The Alchemist* are his masterpieces). We know a lot, too, about his opinion of other poets, because in 1618 he walked from London to Edinburgh (400 miles) to stay with the Scots poet William Drummond of Hawthornden (1585–1649). Drummond kept notes on Jonson's talk, and they are the earliest record of literary gossip to survive. Jonson reckoned Donne, 'the first poet in the world for some things', but also said that Donne 'for not being understood would perish'. His own poetry avoids Donne's obscurity. It is lucid and elegant, often following classical models.

His epigrams satirise modern vice and luxury. But, more positively, his long poem, 'To Penshurst', praises the old-world hospitality and graciousness of the Sidney family, idealising their country estate where even the fruit trees are decorous and obliging.

> The early cherry with the later plum,
> Fig, grape and quince, each in his time doth come,
> The blushing apricot and woolly peach
> Hang on thy walls, that every child may reach.

Though he wrote elaborate, extravagant court masques for James I and his queen, in his poetry he is suspicious of show.

> Still to be neat, still to be dressed,
> As you were going to a feast.
> Still to be powdered, still perfumed,
> Lady, it is to be presumed,

Though art's hid causes are not found,
All is not sweet, all is not sound.

Give me a look, give me a face,
That makes simplicity a grace,
Robes loosely flowing, hair as free,
Such sweet neglect more taketh me
Than all the adulteries of art,
They strike mine eyes, but not my heart.

His most moving poems are those on the deaths of his son, Benjamin (who died of bubonic plague, aged seven), and his daughter, Mary (aged six months). Trying to explain Benjamin's death, Jonson writes, 'My sin was too much hope of thee, loved boy'. To us it seems monstrous to believe in a God who would kill a child because of a father's excessive love. But it indicates the sternness of religious belief at the time. Besides, belief had its comforting side, for Mary is not really dead:

At six months' end she parted hence
With safety of her innocence,
Whose soul heaven's Queen, whose name she bears,
In comfort of her mother's tears,
Hath placed amongst her virgin train;
Where, while that severed doth remain,
This grave partakes the fleshly birth,
Which cover lightly, gentle earth.

Jonson can also write with majestic moral authority, as in his ode for two friends who had died young:

It is not growing like a tree
    In bulk, doth make man better be,
Or standing long, an oak, three hundred year,
To fall a log at last, dry, bald and sere.
    A lily of a day

Is fairer far in May,
Although it fall and die that night,
It was the plant and flower of light;
In small proportions we just beauties see,
And in short measures life may perfect be.

He wrote one of the best-known love songs in English ('Drink to Me Only with Thine Eyes'), but he cannot match Donne's passion as a love poet. His love poetry, even when exquisite, is relatively detached:

Have you seen but a bright lily grow,
    Before rude hands have touched it?
Have you marked but the fall of the snow,
    Before the soil hath smutched it?
Have you felt the wool o' the beaver?
        Or swan's down ever?
Or have smelt o' the bud of the briar?
        Or the nard i' the fire?
    Or have tasted the bag o' the bee?
O so white, O so soft, O so sweet is she.

But he can be winningly down to earth about himself and his ageing body. In love with a younger woman, he complains that she is deaf to the beauty of his poetry. Then he has second thoughts:

Oh but my conscious fears,
    That fly my thoughts between,
    Tell me that she hath seen
My hundred of grey hairs,
    Told seven and forty years,
Read so much waist as she cannot embrace,
    My mountain belly and my rocky face,
And all these, through her eyes, have stopped her ears.

Among the poets who used to be thought of as Jonson's followers
the most original is Robert Herrick (1591–1674), who is in fact a
quite different kind of poet. He is a miniaturist. Most of his poems
are very short, some only two lines long, and they give significance
to small things:

> She by the river sat, and sitting there
> She wept, and made it deeper by a tear.

Small words can bear unusual weight, as in 'Lovers How They
Come and Part':

> They tread on clouds, and though they sometimes fall,
> They fall like dew, but make no noise at all.

The second line would be quite different if he had written 'and' for
'but'. 'But' implies that even dew is noisy compared to lovers. It is
really a poem that tries to express an almost inexpressible lightness
of touch. Another poem with a similar aim is 'The Coming of
Good Luck':

> So good luck came, and on my roof did light
> Like noiseless snow, or as the dew of night:
> Not all at once, but gently, as the trees
> Are, by the sun-beams, tickled by degrees.

The transience of beauty is a common Herrick theme ('Gather ye
rosebuds while ye may' is one of his most famous poems), and in
'To Dianeme' he links it with sensitivity to touch:

> Be you not proud of that rich hair
> Which wantons with the love-sick air,
> Whenas that ruby which you wear
> Sunk from the tip of your soft ear,
> Will last to be a precious stone
> When all your world of beauty's gone.

'Sunk', with its suggestion of oceanic depths, accentuates the elasticity of the earlobe that the ruby weighs down. The feel of fabrics attracts Herrick too:

Whenas in silks my Julia goes,
Then, then, methinks, how sweetly flows
The liquefaction of her clothes.

'Liquefaction' means turning to liquid, and suggests that Julia's skin-clinging silk seems to have been poured over her.

Writing so much about women's clothes and underclothes was obviously unseemly in an ordained clergyman. It may have been done partly to annoy the Puritans, who had turned Herrick out of his vicarage at Dean Prior in Dorset during the Civil War (though he got back again at the Restoration).

Andrew Marvell (1621–1678) was, like Donne, rescued from oblivion by, among others, T.S. Eliot. In the eighteenth and nineteenth centuries he was remembered, if at all, as a political satirist. His lyrics were neglected. But Eliot rated them highly, noticing 'a tough reasonableness beneath the slight lyric grace'.

Marvell sees inner conflict as basic to our human make-up. In 'A Dialogue between the Soul and the Body', the soul complains that the body imprisons it in 'fetters' of feet and 'manacles' of hands. The body replies that it is plagued by all kinds of torments – hope, fear, love, hate, sin – because the soul won't let it live in its simple naturalness:

So architects do square and hew
Green trees, that in the forest grew.

But are trees superior to architecture, or architecture to trees? Marvell does not decide. A teasing, intriguing doubleness permeates this poem, and all his poetry.

For the body, a way out of the dilemma would be to become a tree, and in 'Appleton House' he begs the plants to reclaim him as one of themselves:

Bind me ye woodbines in your twines,
Curl me about ye gadding vines,
And O so close your circles lace
That I may never leave this place.

If they just turned him on his head they would see, 'I was but an inverted tree'.

In 'The Garden', the plants welcome his body back:

The luscious clusters of the vine
Upon my mouth do crush their wine,
The nectarine and curious peach
Into my hands themselves do reach,
Stumbling on melons as I pass
Ensnared with flowers, I fall on grass.

Meanwhile his mind escapes into intellectual happiness:

Annihilating all that's made
To a green thought in a green shade.

Marvell's doubleness makes his tone hard to judge. Poems that seem funny or slight, such as 'The Mower to the Glow-worms' or 'The Nymph Complaining for the Death of her Fawn', reveal serious depths as you read them.

His most famous poem, 'To his Coy Mistress', is often read as a love poem, but it is not, or not just. It starts like a love poem. The lover urges his mistress to yield. If they had limitless time her 'coyness' might make sense.

But at my back I always hear
Time's winged chariot hurrying near,
And yonder all before us lie
Deserts of vast eternity.
Thy beauty shall no more be found,
Nor in thy marble vault shall sound

My echoing song; then worms shall try
That long-preserved virginity,
And your quaint honour turn to dust,
And into ashes all my lust.
The grave's a fine and private place,
But none I think do there embrace.

Worms eating her 'quaint' (meaning vagina) sour the tone, and it gets worse:

Now let us sport us while we may
And now, like amorous birds of prey,
Rather at once our time devour,
Than languish in his slow-chapped power . . .
Thus, though we cannot make our sun
Stand still, yet we will make him run.

With the birds-of-prey image the lovers become a horror – two raptors armed with beaks and claws – and their attempt to slow time only speeds it up.

That is a common pattern in Marvell's poetry. Life is a trap. Deeds rebound on their doer. In 'Damon the Mower', the scythe slips:

And there among the grass fell down
By his own scythe, the mower mown.

'An Horatian Ode Upon Cromwell's Return from Ireland' warns Cromwell to keep his sword 'erect'. For:

The same arts that did gain
A power, must it maintain.

Deeds rebound on their doer. If you win power by the sword you must live by the sword. But though the poem addresses Cromwell, Marvell's doubleness reserves its noblest lines for the doomed king:

He nothing common did or mean
Upon that memorable scene,
    But with his keener eye
    The axe's edge did try:
Nor called the gods with vulgar spite
To vindicate his helpless right,
    But bowed his comely head
    Down, as upon a bed.

CHAPTER 12

Religious Individualists
HERBERT, VAUGHAN, TRAHERNE

The individual differences encouraged by Protestantism domi-
nated seventeenth-century Britain's religious turmoil. Charles I's
marriage to a Catholic, Henrietta Maria, alarmed Protestants,
while Charles's Archbishop of Canterbury, William Laud, enforced
'High Anglican' rituals ('Papist' according to Puritans) and perse-
cuted nonconformists. After Parliament's victory in the Civil War,
Protestant sects multiplied. Ministers who had accepted Laud's
reforms (like Robert Herrick) were turned out of their vicarages,
and religious statues and stained glass windows, considered idola-
trous by Puritans, were smashed.

The three poets in this chapter – leaders in what is often called
the 'Golden Age' of English religious poetry – were all nominally
Anglican. But they were so different they could almost have been
worshipping different Gods. George Herbert (1593–1633) was
born into a wealthy and influential family. His brother was Lord
Herbert of Cherbury. But three years before his early death (of
tuberculosis) he took holy orders and became rector of two small

Wiltshire villages. It was a humiliating come-down for someone of his social class, and seems to have been the result of intense inner struggle. On his deathbed he entrusted his poems to a friend (Nicholas Ferrar, head of a High Anglican spiritual community in the village of Little Gidding, Huntingdonshire), saying that they were 'a picture of the many spiritual conflicts that have passed betwixt God and my soul, before I could subject mine to the will of Jesus, my Master'.

Several poems seem to re-enact moments in these conflicts. The most famous is 'The Collar', which starts in rebellion:

I struck the board, and cried, No more,
   I will abroad.
What? Shall I ever sigh and pine?
My lines and life are free, free as the road . . .

The 'board' means the communion table, and furious complaints about what he has given up for God follow, until God intervenes:

But as I raved, and grew more fierce and wild
   At every word,
Methought I heard one calling *Child*!
   And I replied *My Lord*.

In 'Dialogue' it is the poet who intervenes. He is complaining about his lot, as usual, and God, in reply, reminds him of what he, God, has given up for man:

. . . I did freely part
With my glory and desert,
Left all joys to feel all smart –
   Ah! No more: thou break'st my heart.

Sometimes the soul's meeting with God is presented as a sort of parable. In 'Redemption' the poet imagines himself a tenant, leasing a piece of land from a 'rich lord', and wanting his rent lowered. The hidden meaning is that he is a sinner seeking redemption. He searches for the rich lord in heaven, but is told he has gone down to earth, so the tenant looks for him there:

> . . . and knowing his great birth,
>   Sought him accordingly in great resorts,
>   In cities, theatres, gardens, parks and courts:
> At length I heard a ragged noise and mirth
>   Of thieves and murderers: there I him espied,
>   Who straight, *Your suit is granted,* said, and died.

It takes the reader a moment to understand that what has been described is the crucifixion, and that jolt of newness is the poem's point.

Another new take on God comes in 'Love Bade Me Welcome', where the poet remembers how Love asked him to dinner. When he arrived, 'quick-eyed Love' noticed him and:

> Drew nearer to me, sweetly questioning,
>   If I lacked anything.
>
> A guest, I answered, worthy to be here.
>   Love said, You shall be he.

It is a witty exchange, and we gather that we are listening to two seventeenth-century gentlemen behaving courteously to each other. Then – astonishingly (and we may think, from our modern perspective, rather absurdly) – we realise that these witty, polite, upper-class personages represent the soul confronting Almighty God.

In 'Dullness' the poet's relationship with God is altered again, to that of a lover:

> Thou art my loveliness, my light, my life,
>   Beauty alone to me . . .

Then we learn that this is horribly unlike the usual love-poetry mistress:

> Thy bloody death, and undeserved, makes thee
> Pure red and white.

In 'The Flower', God has yet another new disguise. He becomes the weather, first afflicting the poet with frost and storms, then reviving him, like springtime:

> And now in age I bud again,
> After so many deaths I live and write;
> I once more smell the dew and rain,
>   And relish versing: O my only light,
>   It cannot be
>   That I am he
> On whom thy tempests fell all night.

The simplicity of Herbert's poetic language acts as a kind of guarantee, assuring us of his sincerity and humility. But there are occasional riddles and enigmas, as if to remind us of his intelligence. 'The Answer', one of his greatest poems, ends in a riddle:

> My comforts drop and melt away like snow,
> I shake my head, and all the thoughts and ends,
> Which my fierce youth did bandy, fall and flow
> Like leaves about me, or like summer friends,
> Flies of estates and sunshine. But to all,
> Who think me eager, hot, and undertaking,
> But in my prosecution slack and small,
> As a young exhalation, newly waking,
> Scorns his first bed of dirt, and means the sky,
> But cooling by the way grows pursy and slow,
> And settling to a cloud doth live and die

In that dark state of tears: to all that so
  Show me, and set me, I have one reply,
  Which they that know the rest, know more than I.

The amazing metaphoric flow – falling hair, snow, thoughts, leaves, flies, estates, sunshine, an exhalation (mist) – reads like Shakespeare, not Herbert, and perhaps he was deliberately writing a pastiche Shakespeare sonnet. But the baffling final line is not Shakespearean, and points to something known only to Herbert – and God.

Henry Vaughan (1621–1695) was a Welsh doctor whose poetry, unlike Herbert's, shows no sign of struggle but soars straight to mystical transcendence, as in 'The World':

I saw eternity the other night:
Like a great ring of pure and endless light,
  All calm, as it was bright . . .

He seems to exist in another reality, where the human soul is like a plant:

O joys! Infinite sweetness! With what flowers
And shoots of glory my soul breaks and buds!
  All the long hours
  Of night and rest,
  Through the still shrouds
  Of sleep and clouds,
This dew fell on my breast;
  O how it bloods
And spirits all my earth . . .

That is from 'The Morning-watch', and it gains wonder and intensity by using common words – 'blood', 'spirit' – as verbs, not nouns. 'Dew' is also a mystical word for Vaughan. In Welsh, 'Duw' means 'God', and it seems to have that meaning, among others, in another of his greatest poems, 'The Seed Growing Secretly':

My dew, my dew! My early love,
My soul's bright food, thy absence kills.
Hover not long, eternal dove,
Life without thee is loose and spills . . .

Here, too, the words are usual – 'loose', 'spills' – yet transcend their normal meaning when applied to 'Life'.

Vaughan's twin brother, Thomas, was an alchemist who wrote learned treatises on 'natural magic'. His theories enter Henry Vaughan's poetry – the idea, for example, that the natural world is conscious, as in 'Rules and Lessons':

There's not a spring
Or leaf, but hath his morning-hymn; each bush
And oak doth know I AM . . .

Thomas's belief that God has placed a 'seed' of light in all creatures inspires Henry Vaughan's 'Cock-crowing':

Father of lights! What sunny seed,
What glance of day hast thou confined
Into this bird? To all the breed
This busy ray thou hast assigned:
  Their magnetism works all night,
  And dreams of paradise and light.

Their eyes watch for the morning hue,
Their little grain, expelling night,
So shines and sings, as if it knew
The path unto the house of light.
  It seems their candle, howe'er done,
  Was tinned and lighted at the sun.

'Tinned' means 'kindled', and Thomas Vaughan, writing of the 'secret candle of God', had used the same word.

Unlike Herbert, Vaughan lived through the English Civil War, and was on the losing side, serving briefly in the Royalist army. In his poem, 'They Are All Gone into the World of Light', he envisions the dead – 'I see them walking in an air of glory' – who may include friends killed in the fighting. The sorrows of the war may lie behind his idealisation of childhood, as in 'The Retreat', which seems to anticipate Wordsworth and Blake.

Happy those early days, when I
Shined in my angel-infancy.
Before I understood this place
Appointed for my second race,
Or taught my soul to fancy ought
But a white, celestial thought.
When yet I had not walked above
A mile or two from my first love,
And looking back, at that short space,
Could see a glimpse of his bright face,
When on some gilded cloud or flower
My gazing soul would dwell an hour,
And in those weaker glories spy
Some shadows of eternity.

Thomas Traherne (1636–1674) was the son of a shoe-maker in Hereford, studied at Brasenose College, Oxford, and became an ordained clergyman. His prose *Meditations* contain the first realistic attempt in English to describe the world as seen by a child. They were lost for two centuries and published only in 1908. His poems were lost, too, and rediscovered on a street-barrow in 1896.

A few of the poems remember childhood realistically, as the *Meditations* do. In 'Shadows in the Water', for example, Traherne recalls thinking, as a child, that reflections in puddles were real people. But childhood in the poems is usually more idealised. In 'The Preparative' he remembers, or imagines himself remembering, a time when, new-born, he was pure consciousness, free of self, not even aware of his body.

> Then was my soul my only all to me,
> > A living, endless eye,
> > Far wider than the sky,
> Whose power and act and essence was to see.
> > I was an inward sphere of light,
> Or an interminable orb of sight,
> > An endless and a living day,
> A vital sun that round about did ray
> > All life and sense,
> A naked, simple, pure intelligence.

In 'Dreams' (as in the *Meditations*) he develops the idea that reality exists only in our thoughts, not in the material world.

> Thoughts! Surely Thoughts are true;
> They please as much as Things can do:
> > Nay, Things are dead,
> And in themselves are severed
> From souls, nor can they fill the head
> Without our Thoughts. Thoughts are the real things
> From whence all joy, from whence all sorrow springs.

This line of reasoning leads Traherne to the theory, apparently original (and in his day dangerously unorthodox), that God can enjoy his creation only through seeing it reflected in the thoughts of humans. The *Meditations* develop this at length, but it is also spelt out in poems, such as 'Thoughts II':

> A delicate and tender thought
> The quintessence is found of all he wrought,
> > It is the fruit of all his works,
> > > Which we conceive,
> > > Bring forth, and give . . .

'Amendment' develops the same daring idea – daring, because it makes God dependent on humans, a suggestion that would have been thought blasphemous in Traherne's day:

> The Godhead cannot prize
> The sun at all, nor yet the skies,
> Or air, or earth, or tree, or seas,
> Or stars, unless the soul of man they please.

So in Traherne's theory there is a kind of reciprocity. God creates the world; mankind finds joys in it, and:

> These are the things wherewith we God reward.

Like Vaughan, Traherne looks back on childhood, in his poems, as a time of perfection:

> How like an angel came I down!
>
> ('Wonder')

As a child he was unfallen, like Adam in Paradise:

> I was an Adam there,
> A little Adam in a sphere
> Of joys . . .

But as he grew up adults taught him to value worthless things – money, toys, hobby-horses or 'some useless gaudy book'. In this way, as he recounts in 'Apostasy', his soul 'was quickly murdered':

> Drowned in their customs, I became
> A stranger to the shining skies,
> Lost as a dying flame.

CHAPTER 13

Poetry from the World Beyond
JOHN MILTON

John Milton (1608–1674) is usually reckoned the greatest English poet after Shakespeare. His father was a 'scrivener', preparing legal documents, and a money-lender. But he was also a musician and composer. Milton was a musician too, and music is everywhere in his poetry. Educated at St Paul's School, London, and Christ's College, Cambridge, he did not have to get a job after university but embarked on a further-education programme. He also travelled to Italy, where he met the astronomer, Galileo, and heard early operas, perhaps by Monteverdi.

His first book of poems, published in 1645, included a masque called *Comus*, written to be acted by the children of a noble family. Milton did not know them personally, but his father's friend, the composer Henry Lawes, was their music teacher.

Perhaps mischievously, young Milton gives the best poetry not to the noble children but to the wicked tempter, Comus. He is a fairy-tale character out of Homer's *Odyssey*, son of the enchantress

Circe, and he remembers how his mother used to sing so beauti-
fully it charmed even the sea-monsters:

> ... Scylla wept,
> And chid her barking waves into attention,
> And fell Charybdis murmured soft applause.

Poetically responsive to the natural world (which the children
think of as just a horrid wood they get lost in) he fantasises about
fish doing Morris dances:

> The sounds and seas, with all their finny drove,
> Now to the moon in wavering morris move ...

– and about Nature's busy band of workers, including:

> millions of spinning worms,
> That in their green shops weave the smooth-haired silk.

Worms, even silk-worms, seldom get honoured in poetry, but
young Milton takes the trouble to imagine the spaces they work in.

Another famous poem in the 1645 book *Lycidas*, mourns a
college acquaintance drowned in a shipwreck. Milton probably did
not know him well, and adopts the artificial form of a pastoral, with
attendant nymphs and shepherds. The great eighteenth-century
critic Dr Johnson, disliking pastorals, condemned it as 'easy, vulgar
and therefore disgusting', whereas for Tennyson it was 'the touch-
stone of poetic taste'. Despite Johnson, *Lycidas* has a grandeur that
prefigures *Paradise Lost*, as in its passing glance at the Cornish
coastline:

> Where the great vision of the guarded mount
> Looks toward Namancos and Bayona's hold.

Comus's attention to the minuscule is replicated just once in
Lycidas, where the mourning flowers include 'the pansy freaked

with jet'. Milton is credited with coining more new words even than Shakespeare (630 to Shakespeare's 229), and 'freaked' is one of them, denoting the untidy-looking black blotch on a pansy's petals.

Also in the 1645 book are Milton's famous 'Nativity Ode', written on Christmas day 1629, in which the usual gentle Jesus is replaced by a sort of infant Hercules defeating a 'damned crew' of pagan gods, and two poems in short-lined, light-hearted couplets, *L'Allegro* ('The Joyful Man') and *Il Penseroso* ('The Pensive Man'). Expectably, the second seems the more Miltonic, imagining an ideal life of solitary country walks and sitting up late reading:

> ... let my lamp at midnight hour
> Be seen in some high lonely tower ...

Milton believed in liberty. He thought that hereditary monarchy was ridiculous, and that the Church was a racket, with its bishops decked out in absurd finery living off the 'tithes' or taxes paid by the workers, and running special church courts to punish those with whom they disagreed. He wrote several tracts against the bishops, full of disgust and contempt, and when the English Civil War broke out he sided with the Parliamentarians.

Unfortunately he had recently married sixteen-year-old Mary Powell, who came from a Royalist family, and after a month of marriage she returned home. So Milton left off attacking the bishops and wrote pamphlets demanding that divorce should be legalised. They caused a rumpus, so he wrote his most famous pamphlet, *Areopagitica* (1644), championing freedom of the press.

All this left little time for poetry, and he soon had less. When the Royalists were defeated, Mary and the Powells came crawling back, and Milton generously took them in. Mary bore him two daughters, in 1646 and 1648. Meanwhile the Parliamentarians, noting his brilliance as a pamphleteer, appointed him Cromwell's secretary, with the job of publicly justifying the execution of Charles I.

The 1650s were disastrous for Milton. Mary and the son she had recently borne him both died. He married again, but his second

wife and her baby daughter died too. His sight had been failing for
some years and in 1652 he became completely blind. It seemed he
would never write the great poem he had set his heart on. In his
sonnet, 'When I consider how my light is spent', he tells how he
cried out against God's injustice, but how he then reminded
himself that he and his ambitions meant nothing to God:

> . . . God doth not need,
> Either man's work or his own gifts, who best
> Bear his mild yoke, they serve him best; his state
> Is kingly. Thousands at his bidding speed
> And post o'er land and ocean without rest;
> They also serve who only stand and wait.

So he waited, and a miraculous thing happened. He found that a
supernatural female, whom he called his 'heavenly muse', spoke his
poem to him night by night while he slept. She delivered it in
sections of about forty lines, and when he woke he dictated them
to whoever was there to write them down. In this way, gradually,
over several years, his great poem accumulated.

To us it seems obvious he was mistaken about the heavenly
muse, and that the poem came from his own mind – some would
say his unconscious. However, he believed otherwise. At the start
of *Paradise Lost* he states that the same muse who is dictating his
poem inspired Moses to write the biblical Book of Genesis. In
other words *Paradise Lost*, with its many additions to scripture, has
the same authority as the Bible. Or so Milton thought.

For many of its readers Satan is the hero. At the poem's start he
is chained down on a burning lake in hell, cast out from heaven by
God's invincible power. But he will not admit defeat.

> . . . What though the field be lost?
> All is not lost; the unconquerable will,
> And study of revenge, immortal hate,
> And courage never to submit or yield.

(1.105–8)

We can all recognise that as heroism, and the poem teaches us that heroism can be evil.

Escaping from hell, Satan flies up to the earth, and finds Adam and Eve in Eden. Their beauty astonishes him, and their innocence makes him weep. Yet he determines to destroy them:

And should I at your harmless innocence
Melt, as I do, yet public reason just,
Honour and empire, with revenge enlarged,
By conquering this new world, compels me now
To do what else, though damned, I should abhor.

(4.388–92)

So Satan, disguised as a snake, talks Eve into eating the forbidden fruit, knowing it means that she, and the whole human race descended from her, will die. Adam eats the fruit too, because he knows Eve will die, and cannot bear to lose her:

How can I live without thee, how forgo
Thy sweet converse and love so dearly joined,
To live again in these wild woods forlorn?

(9.908–10)

Why does God let it happen? He knows everything, including the future, so why doesn't he step in and stop it? Milton needs to answer these questions, since his aim is to 'justify the ways of God to men' (1.26). His answer is that God had to give Adam and Eve free will, otherwise they would not have been humans but robots (or puppets in a fairground, as Milton puts it when pondering the same question in *Areopagitica*).

While he was writing his poem, the political tide turned. Cromwell died, the republic collapsed, Charles II was restored. Retribution followed. Those who had signed Charles I's death warrant were barbarously executed. Milton, surrounded by gleeful Royalists, was briefly imprisoned, and must have feared the worst. Invoking his muse in Book 7, he begs her to protect him, comparing himself to the mythical poet Orpheus, who was torn to pieces by a drunken mob, even though his mother was the Muse Calliope.

> But drive far off the barbarous dissonance
> Of Bacchus and his revellers, the race
> Of that wild rout that tore the Thracian bard
> In Rhodope, where woods and rocks had ears
> To rapture, but the savage clamour drowned
> Both harp and voice, nor could the Muse defend
> Her son. So fail not thou who thee implores
> For thou art heavenly, she an empty dream.
>
> (7.32–9)

A possible criticism of *Paradise Lost* is that God and his Son conquer Satan and his army just by military might, not by any more spiritual means. *Paradise Regained*, his next poem, could almost have been written to correct that. It is about Satan's temptations of Jesus in the wilderness, as told in the gospels – or, rather, not as told in the gospels, but completely rewritten by Milton, who nevertheless insists that the events he describes really did happen, but were somehow omitted from the biblical account. They were:

> in secret done,
> And unrecorded left through many an age,
> Worthy t' have not remained so long unsung.
>
> (1.15–17)

Jesus, in this poem, has no military might at all. He is just a man, alone in the wilderness, keeping his nerve and trusting in God. He does not use any divine powers, nor does he have any memory of his previous existence as the Son of God in heaven.

Satan has no idea who Jesus is. He was present at his baptism, and heard him proclaimed the Son of God, but he does not know what that means. The aim of his temptations – the biblical ones, plus additions of Milton's own – is to find out.

However, he fails, and, losing patience, he carries Jesus to the highest pinnacle of the temple and places him there, expecting him to topple off. Mockingly he quotes from Psalm 91, where it is said that God will send angels to 'bear thee up lest thou dash thy foot against a stone'. Calmly, Jesus quotes scripture back at him:

> 'Also it is written,
> Tempt not the Lord thy God', he said and stood.
> But Satan smitten with amazement fell.

(IV.460–62)

Satan falls because he takes Jesus's biblical quotation (from Deuteronomy 6.16) to mean that he is alone on the pinnacle with God, who defeated him in the war in heaven. But whether Jesus meant his quotation to be a claim to godhead, we cannot tell. He has not laid a finger on Satan, and he is able to stand on the giddy height because he has complete faith in God, which Adam and Eve lacked.

Samson Agonistes, Milton's second masterpiece, was published with *Paradise Regained* in 1671, but may have been written earlier. It is based on the Samson story in the biblical book of Judges, but follows the rules of a Greek tragedy. The action is restricted to the last day in Samson's life, which culminates in his pulling down the amphitheatre, killing himself and the Philistines who have enslaved and blinded him.

Milton puts into Samson's mouth the most searing of all his laments about blindness:

> O dark, dark, dark, amid the blaze of noon.
> Irrecoverably dark, total eclipse
> Without all hope of day . . .
> The sun to me is dark
> And silent as the moon,
> When she deserts the night
> Hid in her vacant interlunar cave.

(80–82, 86–9)

Samson's slaughter of the Philistines used to be read as Milton's surrogate revenge on the triumphant Royalists, and maybe it is. But at the end of the drama Samson's father Manoa's glee over the massacre is set against the horrified report of an eye-witness:

> O whither shall I run, or which way fly
> The sight of this so horrid spectacle . . .

Perhaps that should warn us against rejoicing in the slaughter even of enemies, and remind us, rather, of Milton's warning in his sonnet to the Parliamentarian general Fairfax:

> For what can war but endless war still breed?

CHAPTER 14

The Augustan Age
DRYDEN, POPE, SWIFT, JOHNSON, GOLDSMITH

The so-called Augustan age lasted from the 1680s to the 1740s, or later, depending on whose estimate you accept. By the end of the seventeenth century England's power-base had shifted from the royal court to Parliament, and the new age saw political parties forming and political vendettas flourishing. At the same time, novels were being written and circulating libraries starting up. In the coffee-houses (also new), newspapers and magazines were argued over. This appetite for reading-matter meant that writers could live by their pens. 'Grub Street' was born, and cartoonists depicted poets starving in garrets.

The two leading Augustan poets, John Dryden (1631–1700) and Alexander Pope (1688–1744) did not starve, however. They both wrote political satires, which was risky. Dryden was beaten up in Covent Garden by thugs hired by John Wilmot, Earl of Rochester. Pope took a pair of loaded pistols and his Great Dane, Bounce, with him on walks. As poets they were completely dissimilar, though they both wrote mostly in 'heroic couplets' (ten-syllable lines, rhymed in pairs). They were also, despite their Augustan label, completely unlike the Augustan poets of ancient Rome.

Dryden's best-known poem, *Absalom and Achitophel* (1681), was a satirical rejoinder to Parliament's attempt to get Charles II's brother James, a Roman Catholic, debarred from succession to the English throne. So it was a direct intervention into public debate, intended to change the nation's future, and in that respect it has no counterpart in English poetry before or since.

Dryden based his satire on an Old Testament story, with Charles II as King David, and Charles's illegitimate son, the Duke of Monmouth, as Absalom. Achitophel is the Earl of Shaftesbury, a leading anti-Catholic who wanted to put Monmouth, a Protestant, on the throne. Dryden makes him dangerous and complex, a bit like Milton's Satan in heroic couplets:

> Of these the false Achitophel was first,
> A name to all succeeding ages cursed,
> For close designs and crooked counsels fit,
> Sagacious, bold, and turbulent of wit,
> Restless, unfixed in principles and place,
> In power unpleased, impatient of disgrace,
> A fiery soul which, working out its way,
> Fretted the pygmy body to decay,
> And o'er informed the tenement of clay.

Greatly gifted, Dryden became the first Poet Laureate, and would be better known today if he had not written mostly about current affairs, now forgotten.

Pope wrote about current affairs too, but he tended to create universal types that we still recognise. He was also more sensuous and more resentful than Dryden. From the age of twelve he suffered from tuberculosis of the bone, which deformed his body and stunted his growth. He had to be laced into a corset to stand upright, and suffered chronic pain. His enemies openly mocked his disabilities. As his parents were Catholic, the law prevented him from attending a normal school or going to university.

Suffering made him pity suffering. He mourns for skylarks, shot by trigger-happy sportsmen: 'They fall, and leave their little lives in air.' He is filled with wonder by things Dryden would never have noticed:

The spider's touch, how exquisitely fine!
Feels at each thread, and lives along the line.

Or, recalling Milton's worms in *Comus*:

So spins the silkworm small its slender store,
And labours, 'till it clouds itself all o'er.

But he could be savage. His most brutal portrait is of a courtier called Lord Hervey whom he depicts as 'Sporus' in *An Epistle to Dr Arbuthnot*. He makes it more damning by pretending that his friend, John Arbuthnot, butts in to stop him wasting his satire on such an insignificant creature:

Let Sporus tremble – 'What? That thing of silk?
Sporus, that mere white curd of ass's milk?
Satire, or sense, alas, can Sporus feel?
Who breaks a butterfly upon a wheel?' –
Yet let me flap this bug with gilded wings,
This painted child of dirt that stinks and stings,
Whose buzz the witty and the fair annoys,
Yet wit ne'er tastes and beauty ne'er enjoys . . .

It was inaccurate as well as malicious, for Hervey married and fathered eight children, as well as having several affairs.

In Pope's masterpiece, *The Rape of the Lock*, satire and sympathy mix. In 1711, an impetuous beau, Lord Petre, then aged twenty-one, caused a scandal by snipping off a lock of a young society beauty's hair. In the poem she is 'Belinda', but in real life she was Arabella Fermor, aged sixteen. Wishing to calm hurt feelings and put things in perspective, Pope wrote his poem in the mock-heroic mode. Belinda is guarded by an entourage of fairy-beings, called sylphs, and her dressing table is a treasury of exotic marvels:

> This casket India's glowing gems unlocks,
> And all Arabia breathes from yonder box,
> The tortoise here and elephant unite,
> Transformed to combs, the speckled and the white.

It is a hymn to wealth, luxury and the expansion of England's trading empire – all subjects that would normally attract Pope's censure, but here charm him.

His attitude to Belinda's frivolity seems divided, too. Slipping 'bibles' into the jumble on her dressing table – 'Puffs, powders, patches, bibles, billets-doux' – seems to criticise her negligence of sacred things. Yet he makes a joke of sacred things himself when describing Belinda's imperious supervision of a card game. '"Let spades be trumps", she said, and trumps they were', is a parody of Genesis 1.31, 'And God said, "Let there be light", and there was light.' The mock-heroic design of the poem itself ridicules seriousness, with the sylphs, whose airy bodies heal themselves when wounded, resembling the angels in Milton's *Paradise Lost*.

Belinda does not seem to care much about chastity either. Chiding Petre, she is sexually suggestive, even inviting:

> Oh hadst thou, cruel, been content to seize
> Hairs less in sight, or any hairs but these!

Pope offers this as part of her charm. But his view of young flirts and their futures, in the *Epistle of the Characters of Women*, was less indulgent:

> See how the world its veterans rewards!
> A youth of frolics, an old age of cards,
> Fair to no purpose, artful to no end,
> Young without lovers, old without a friend,
> A fop their passion, but their prize a sot,
> Alive, ridiculous, and dead, forgot.

A death scene in the *Epistle to Cobham* (based, Pope said, on fact) represents vanity as women's guiding principle and the last thing they relinquish:

> 'Odious! In woollen! 'Twould a saint provoke!'
> Were the last words that poor Narcissa spoke,
> 'No! Let a charming chintz, and Brussels lace,
> Wrap my cold limbs and shade my lifeless face:
> One would not, sure, be frightful when one's dead –
> And – Betty – give this cheek a little red.'

Was Pope ever in love? Yes, it seems, with Martha Blount. She came from a family of Catholic gentry and they first met in 1705 when they were both teenagers. She had been educated in Paris, and one poem he wrote for her he sent with a copy of Voiture's works. He also sent her *The Rape of the Lock*. In his *Epistle to Miss Blount on her Leaving the Town after the Coronation*, he calls himself her 'slave' and describes how he stands 'abstracted' in London's bustle, thinking of her. In his will he left her his books and £1,000 – a great deal in those days. Whether they were lovers is not known.

Pope considered himself a moralist:

> Ask you what provocation I have had?
> The strong antipathy of good to bad.
> When truth or virtue an affront endures,
> The affront is mine, my friend, and should be yours . . .
> Yes, I am proud, I must be proud to see
> Men not afraid of God, afraid of me.

Perhaps that was how he justified, to himself, the cruelty of some of his satires.

But though he was a moralist, he was a poet first, and as a poet he can be captivated by what we expect him to condemn. It happens in *The Rape of the Lock*, and it happens again in *The Dunciad*. Planned as a satire on 'dullness', Pope's mock-epic gathers a host of contemporary writers – real, living people, whom he knew and despised – and embroils them in an obscene parody of epic-heroic games. They slither about in ordure, compete at sending 'smoking' streams of urine into the air, and take part in a diving-contest in the Thames's foully polluted mud,

Pope describes it with gusto, and it has been plausibly suggested that *The Dunciad* should be seen not as a critique of contemporary writers, but as an escape from the proprieties of Augustan culture. It allows Pope to access a childhood world where ordure and physicality are free from shame or inhibition. His return to pre-literate infancy brings him close to Bedlam and madness, which always fascinated him, and to the Freudian unconscious,

The same mixture of repulsion and fascination with bodily functions has often been noted in the writings of Jonathan Swift (1667–1745), and is savagely evident in a poem like 'A Beautiful Young Nymph Going to Bed'. Two of Swift's poems that stand out, though, are 'A Description of the Morning' and 'A Description of a City Shower'. In both he notices everyday things. In the morning scene, street vendors cry their wares, 'Moll' dexterously whirls her mop, 'Prepared to scrub the entry and the stairs', and:

. . . Betty from her master's bed has flown,
And softly stole to discompose her own.

In the second poem, cats, sensing that rain is coming, grow 'pensive', 'Brisk Susan whips her linen from the rope', and a seamstress, with her skirts tucked up, walks with 'hasty strides', while 'streams run down her oiled umbrella's sides'.

Samuel Johnson (1709–1784) came to London as a poor, unknown country boy in 1737, and his poem *London* (1738) describes the contempt, abuse and physical danger the poor suffer in a big city, where 'All crimes are safe but hated poverty'. It was based on Juvenal, and so is Johnson's *The Vanity of Human Wishes* (1749), which satirises hope. For Johnson, hope is not a virtue but a curse, because it tricks its victims into grand ambitions. Suffering is universal, he warns, even if you prosper:

Yet hope not life from grief or danger free,
Nor think the doom of man reversed for thee!

His (very English) dislike of pride and grandeur found personal expression in *On the Death of Dr Robert Levett*. It mourns a shy, obscure physician who worked among London's poor, often for no fee. Johnson's deep Christian faith is reflected in its closing reference to the parable of the talents.

His virtues walked their narrow round,
  Nor made a pause, nor left a void,
And sure the Eternal Master found
  The single talent well employed.

Pride and grandeur are targeted, too, by Oliver Goldsmith (1728–1774). An Irish parson's son, he belonged to Johnson's circle, and wrote a famous comedy, *She Stoops to Conquer*. His poem *The Deserted Village* takes a critical look at the eighteenth-century craze for landscape gardening among the super-rich – the craze that produced National Trust showpieces we are now invited to admire. To create these huge, useless pleasure grounds, Goldsmith reminds us, ancient villages were torn down, the gentle rhythms of rural life were snuffed out, and the survivors joined hordes of emigrants facing an uncertain future in the wilds of America. The village ('Auburn') he had in mind may have been Nuneham Courtenay, near Oxford, which was destroyed and removed to another site by the 1st Earl Harcourt in 1756, so that he could build a Palladian villa with parkland designed by 'Capability' Brown.

Yet, while sympathising with the victims, Goldsmith cannot resist joking about the limitations of rustic life, which he captures in a few cutting phrases – 'The loud laugh that spoke the vacant mind', or the villagers wondering, as they listen to their schoolmaster, 'That one small head could carry all he knew'. By retaining this element of ridicule, the poem combines mockery with morality – the twin mainstays of 'Augustan' poetry.

CHAPTER 15

The Other Eighteenth Century
MONTAGU, EGERTON, FINCH, TOLLET, LEAPOR,
YEARSLEY, BARBAULD, BLAMIRE, BAILLIE,
WHEATLEY, DUCK, CLARE, THOMSON,
COWPER, CRABBE, GRAY, SMART

Accounts of Augustan literature often omit women writers, but more women published in the eighteenth century than ever before. The most famous in Britain was Lady Mary Wortley Montagu (1689–1762). Born into an aristocratic family, she taught herself Latin as a child and by the age of fifteen had already filled two albums with poems. Her husband became British Ambassador to Constantinople and her graphic *Embassy Letters* describe the beauty and hospitality of Ottoman women, and her own experience of a Turkish bath, where her corset caused great hilarity and was taken to be a cage in which Western males kept their women.

She learned about smallpox inoculation from the Turks, had her own children inoculated, and persuaded Caroline, Princess of Wales, to do the same. In one of Montagu's *Town Eclogues* 'wretched

Flavia', a smallpox victim, laments her ruined beauty. But though she had caught smallpox herself when young, Montagu's portraits, perhaps flatteringly, show no scars. In later life she travelled around Europe, took a lover, Count Francesco Angarotti, and lived with him in Venice.

Sarah Fyge Egerton (1668–1723) first became known at the age of fourteen when she wrote *The Female Advocate*, a spirited reply to a satire against women by the minor Restoration poet Robert Gould. Rejecting Gould's account of female pride, lust and inconstancy, she asserts that women are superior, and that males by themselves are 'A barren Sex and insignificant'. Later poems such as 'Emulation' denounce 'tyrant Custom' which denies women education and makes them 'in every state a slave'.

Other women poets who endorsed the feminist case, and argued for the mental and spiritual equality of women, included Anne Finch, Countess of Winchelsea (1661–1720), and Elizabeth Tollet (1694–1754), who wrote religious and philosophical poems, as well as translations from the classics, and derides males for their fear of educated women. Mary Leapor (1722–1746) argues the same case, though she had almost no formal schooling herself. A gardener's daughter, she worked as a kitchen maid, and picked up knowledge where she could. One employer sacked her for reading and writing in working hours. Her *Essay on Women* observes how an educated woman is shunned by both sexes:

> The damsels view her with malignant eyes,
> The men are vexed to find a nymph so wise.

Leapor died young, of measles, and her poems were published posthumously by a woman friend. A working-class woman writer who lived to publish four volumes of poetry, as well as *A Poem on the Inhumanity of the Slave Trade* (1788), was the Bristol milkmaid Ann Yearsley (1752–1806). In her 'The Indifferent Shepherdess to Colin' the speaker reprimands her lover for imagining that she will fall into the trap of marriage:

My heart shall sooner break
Than I a minion prove,
Nor care I half a rush,
No snare I spread for thee;
Go home, my friend, and blush
For love and liberty.

Yearsley did, however, marry a yeoman farmer and they raised six children.

Accounts of the Romantic movement, as of the Augustan age, often omit women writers, but their role was vital. Anna Laetitia Barbauld (1743–1825) travelled with her husband to revolutionary France in 1785, and her enthusiastic response helped to inspire Wordsworth and Coleridge, though they later turned against her. Her poem *Eighteen Hundred and Eleven* (1812), a satire in the manner of Juvenal, denounced the war against France, and warned that Britain faced imminent catastrophe ('Ruin, as with an earthquake shock, is here'). This did not happen, but the poem's prophecy that the United States would replace Britain as a world power, which seemed ridiculous at the time, has been proved true. Now reckoned her masterpiece, the poem attracted such savage criticism that she published nothing else in her lifetime.

Romanticism is torn between a demand for revolutionary change and a desire for the constancy of nature. In the Cumbrian poet Susanna Blamire (1747–1794) nature prevails. She has been judged the greatest female poet of the Romantic age, but she published little, preferring to circulate her poems privately. She liked to write out of doors beside the stream in her garden, sometimes playing the guitar or flageolet (a woodwind instrument), and pinning the poems to trees. Her most admired work, *Stoklewath*, records life in a Cumbrian village and links it to life in a Native American community (recounted by an old soldier, back from the American war), which is similarly in harmony with nature. *The Nun's Return* (1790) expresses enthusiastic support for the French Revolution, and the much earlier 'Lament for the Happy Swain', written when she was twenty, after a disappointment in love, has been seen as anticipating the Romanticism of Wordsworth and Coleridge before either was born.

A younger Romantic, the poet and playwright Joanna Baillie (1762–1851), created her imaginative world from memories of her childhood roaming the Scottish countryside, before her family moved to London. The daughter of a Church of Scotland minister, she could be stern. A memorable poem is 'A Mother to Her Waking Infant', in which the mother berates the infant for its regrettable lack of all the higher human capacities, including thought, speech and consideration for others. It is a powerful antidote to sentimentality about babies.

Feminist poets like Yearsley campaigned against the slave trade, but Phillis Wheatley (1753–1784) was an ex-slave herself, and became the first known African-American woman poet. Born in West Africa, she was sold into slavery at the age of seven, and shipped to America where a wealthy Boston family bought her as a servant and educated her. She was reading Greek and Latin classics by the age of twelve, and started writing poetry at fourteen. In 1773, aged twenty, she travelled to London with a member of the Boston family and published *Poems on Subjects Religious and Moral*, for which she could not find a publisher in Boston. Welcomed by leading figures in the English establishment, she was granted an audience with George III, but returned to America before it could happen. She had become a devout Christian while living with the Boston family, and in her poem 'On Being Brought from Africa to America', she admonishes her co-religionists:

Remember, Christians, Negroes, black as Cain,
May be refined, and join the angelic train.

No male poet can match Wheatley's extraordinary story. But one who climbed through the barriers of the eighteenth-century class structure was Stephen Duck (1705–1756). Born into a family of Wiltshire agricultural labourers, he left charity school at thirteen to start work in the fields. His poem *The Thresher's Labour* (1730), powerfully describes his brutal working conditions. It was hailed as the product of natural untaught genius, and became the model for a new genre in which working-class writers recounted their daily experiences. He gained the patronage of Queen Caroline, was ordained, and became the pastor of Byfleet in Surrey.

Duck would be better known if his standing as a 'peasant poet' had not been eclipsed in the following century by a greater poet, John Clare (1793–1864). A labourer's son, Clare became an agricultural labourer himself while still a child. Writing in his Northamptonshire dialect, with non-standard grammar and spelling, he observes nature and wild life – birds, insects, animals – more keenly and knowledgably than any Romantic poet. His best-known poem, 'I am – yet what I am none cares or knows', was written in his final years when he was a patient in the Northampton General Lunatic Asylum.

It seems strange that a poet as distinctive as Clare should have been drawn to poetry by reading *The Seasons* by James Thomson (1700–1748), with its ill-judged imitation of Milton's blank verse and convoluted poetic diction. Yet Thomson's poem was extremely popular, and inspired, besides Clare, Joseph Haydn and the painters Thomas Gainsborough and J.M.W. Turner.

A more original poet, William Cowper (1731–1800) gave poetry a new direction with his rambling, conversational, almost stream-of-consciousness, six-book, blank verse poem *The Task* (1785). It is a medley of his opinions on various subjects, including the evils of slavery, the cruelty of blood sports, gardening, divine providence, and the pleasures of country life ('God made the country, and man made the town'). Jane Austen quotes it frequently in her novels, and its informality fed into Romantic poetry. Coleridge admired its 'divine Chit-chat'.

A clergyman's son, Cowper endured two periods of insanity, during which he was tormented by the belief that he was singled out for eternal damnation. This is the subject of his poem 'The Castaway'. It is based on a real-life event that Cowper had read about, in which a sailor was swept overboard and, after agonising struggles and cries for help, drowned. Most of the poem is about the doomed man's horrifying ordeal. But at the end Cowper compares the sailor's fate with his:

We perished, each alone,
But I beneath a rougher sea
And whelmed in deeper gulfs than he.

The self-pity is breath-taking, yet it shows the intensity of Cowper's delusion.

George Crabbe (1754–1832) found another direction for poetry in *The Village* (1783). He was a surgeon, and became a clergyman, so he saw life at its most basic. He addresses his poem sarcastically to 'gentle souls, who dream of rural ease', and gives them a more realistic account of middle- and lower-class provincial life. Byron called him 'nature's sternest painter, yet the best'. Crabbe writes, in effect, short stories in heroic couplets, and this turn to narrative reflects the new age of novel-reading and the lending library which was to deplete poetry's readership.

But the eighteenth-century poet who has embedded himself most deeply in the thought and language of later generations is Thomas Gray (1716–1771). He was a perfectionist, published only thirteen poems, and spent his life quietly in a Cambridge college reading the classics. His *Elegy Written in a Country Churchyard* has remained one of the most popular poems in the language since its publication in 1751. Its theme is universal and timeless – the vanity of grandeur:

The boast of heraldry, the pomp of power,
And all that beauty, all that wealth e'er gave,
Await alike the inevitable hour,
The paths of glory lead but to the grave.

It was part of Gray's genius, probably derived from classical study and the terse, gnomic capacity of Latin, to coin phrases that have become familiar quotations. Some have acquired an almost prover-bial ring – 'where ignorance is bliss / 'Tis folly to be wise', for example, from his *Ode on a Distant Prospect of Eton College* (where his milliner mother worked hard to send him to school), or 'Far from the madding crowd's ignoble strife', from the *Elegy*. But the

Elegy is not just a collection of truisms. It has an argument, which is that seemingly insignificant people deserve respect because they are innocent of the crimes world leaders commit.

The eighteenth century is known as the Age of Reason, so it might not be expected to produce a great religious poem, still less one written in a lunatic asylum, however this was the achievement of Christopher Smart (1722–1771). A Cambridge graduate, he scraped a living as a hack journalist, but in 1757 was admitted to St Luke's hospital for incurable pauper lunatics in London's Bethnal Green. While there he wrote his masterpiece, *Jubilate Agno* ('Rejoice in the Lamb'), which was not published until 1939, and gloriously overflows the usual strict forms of Augustan verse. It describes, among many other creatures (a mouse, birds, insects, flowers, particles of matter), his cat, who was his sole companion in the asylum:

> For I will consider my Cat Jeoffry.
> For he is the servant of the Living God, duly and daily serving him.
> For at the first glance of the glory of God in the East he worships
>   in his way.
> For is this done by wreathing his body seven times round with
>   elegant quickness.

This may seem whimsical, but is firmly biblical, based on Psalm 148, which calls on all creatures to worship God in their own way, like Jeoffry.

CHAPTER 16

Communal Poetry
Popular Ballads and Hymns

Ballads and hymns combine music with words, so you might say they belong in a book about songs but not in a history of poetry. On the other hand, many of the people who, in earlier centuries, listened to ballad singers or, in later centuries, sang hymns in church, would very likely have had no other contact with poetry throughout their lives. So ballads and hymns constitute their poetry, and have a place here.

It is hard to date ballads, but many seem to have been composed in the seventeenth and eighteenth centuries. Some became international, spreading to different European countries, as well as to America where they were brought by immigrants. Many survive in multiple versions, because they were passed on by oral transmission and individual ballad singers made their own changes. The standard collection is Francis James Child's *English and Scottish Popular Ballads* (1882–98), which contains 305 ballads.

All ballads tell a story, and often it is about unhappy love. In 'Bonny Barbara Allen', for example, a woman scorns her lover, who dies heartbroken. Then she repents, and dies heartbroken too. Most ballads are less gentle than this, however. Their usual subjects are sex and violence. Rape, murder, incest and the 'honour-killing' of women by vengeful brothers or fathers happen a lot. The characters are often upper-class – kings, earls, lords, knights – but they almost never represent real historical figures. They are like the fictional grandees in fairy tales.

A ballad that combines several of these motifs is 'Lady Maisry', which was evidently very popular as it survives in multiple versions with alternative names for the heroine. The basic story is that a woman becomes pregnant and refuses to renounce her true love, who is a knight. Her family disapprove of him, so they burn her alive. His page tells the knight what is happening, and he rides to the rescue, too late:

And boots and spurs, all as he was,
　　Into the fire he leapt,
Gave one kiss to her comely mouth
　　While her body gave a crack,
O I'll gar burn for thee, Maisry,
　　Your sister and your brother,
And I'll gar burn for thee, Maisry,
　　Your father and your mother,
And I'll gar burn for thee, Maisry,
　　The chief of all your kin,
And the last bonfire that I'll come to,
　　Mysel' I will cast in.

Ballad stories are often supernatural. Elves and other fairy folk appear regularly, often in disguise. In the popular 'riddle ballads', where one character sets riddles for the other to answer (sometimes with fearsome forfeits, such as losing your child, if you guess wrongly), the riddler is likely to turn out to be some magical being, or occasionally the Devil himself. Mermaids and other semi-humans are also frequent participants, but they are never introduced as mere poetic ornaments, as they might be in more upmarket kinds of poetry. Ghosts appear too, and are sometimes sinister but sometimes quite harmless, as in 'The Wife of Usher's Well', where a mother hears that her sons are dead and prays for their return. They come, but ask her to stop praying and let them rest in peace.

Witches also play a part in ballad stories and are generally wicked, unlike the 'wise women' (that is, dispensers of folk medicines) who provided a useful service in rural communities but were often burnt as witches. Stepmothers are nearly always wicked too, and are sometimes witches, as in the ballad 'The Laily Worm and the Machrel of the Sea', which seemingly originated in Orkney. 'Laily' means 'loathsome' and 'worm' means 'snake', and 'machrel' means 'mackerel', and the ballad, spoken by a bewitched boy, tells how his stepmother put a spell on him and his sister:

> She turned me to the laily worm,
>   That lies at the foot of the tree,
> And my sister Maisry
>   To a machrel of the sea,
>
> And every Saturday at noon
>   The machrel comes to me,
> And she takes my laily head
>   And lays it on her knee,
> And combs it with a silver comb,
>   And washes it in the sea.

The poet who dreamed up this surreal and poignant fantasy surely deserved to be remembered but, like all ballad poets, is forgotten.

Though the supernatural attracts ballad composers, the natural world and its wild creatures are of little interest to them. The Romantics' joy in the countryside would have seemed ridiculous to an audience that had to subsist on what the countryside yielded. An exception to the exclusion of wild creatures is 'The Twa Corbies' (meaning 'The Two Ravens'), one of the most widespread ballads. In spirit it harks back to Anglo-Saxon poetry, with its carrion birds wheeling over battlefields, only here the birds are given voices and personalities. They find a dead knight, and one addresses the other ('hause' means 'neck'):

> Ye'll sit on his white hause bane,
>   And I'll pike out his bonny blue e'en,
> With ae lock of his gowden hair
>   We'll theek our nest when it grows bare.

A remarkable feature of ballads is that they show almost no interest in religion. One or two, such as 'Judas' and 'Dives and Lazarus', are loosely based on biblical stories, and characters in ballads fairly often pronounce curses on each other. Otherwise they seem untouched by Christianity.

Hymns, on the other hand, have been part of religious life for centuries, and it is possible that communal singing or chanting to foster the unity of a human group goes back to prehistory. Singing hymns in church was a Protestant development. In the pre-Reformation Catholic Church the choir sang and the congregation remained silent. It was Martin Luther who changed this. He wrote 'chorales', translating passages from scripture into rhyming verse for the congregation to sing, so that even the uneducated could carry texts from scripture in their hearts and heads. His most famous chorale, 'A Mighty Fortress Is Our God', written in 1529, and based on Psalm 46, came to be known as 'The Battle Hymn of the Reformation', and has been translated into more languages than any other hymn.

The earliest hymns sung in English churches were also based on psalms, for example George Herbert's rendering of Psalm 23, 'The God of Love My Shepherd Is'. Isaac Watts (1674–1748), a noncon-formist preacher, wrote several hundred hymns, and many of them are still sung. Some are psalm-translations. 'O God Our Help in Ages Past', for example, is based on Psalm 90. But Watts also wrote original hymns, such as:

> When I survey the wondrous cross
> On which the prince of glory died,

My richest gain I count but loss,
And pour contempt on all my pride.

The fourth stanza, the most personal, passionate and poetic, is now excluded when the hymn is sung in churches, perhaps because its intensity is considered unseemly:

His dying crimson, like a robe,
Spreads o'er his body on the tree,
Now I am dead to all the globe,
And all the globe is dead to me.

Charles Wesley (1707–1788), the younger brother of John Wesley who founded the Methodist Church, was also a prolific writer of hymns, among them 'Jesus, Lover of My Soul', 'Come, Thou Long-expected Jesus', and the Christmas carol, 'Hark, the Herald Angels Sing'. Methodist preachers reached out to the working class and to criminals. They taught that salvation was assured for all believers, and that perfection was attainable in this life. This belief was not acceptable to Anglicans, so some of Wesley's hymns had to be altered before being allowed into Anglican hymn-books. His most famous hymn, 'Love Divine, All Loves Excelling', is a Christian version of a song by John Dryden, 'Fairest Isle, All Isles Excelling', which is sung by Venus in Henry Purcell's opera *King Arthur* (1691).

An early convert to Methodism was Augustus Toplady (1740–1778). He is said to have been walking in the Mendip Hills when he was caught in a sudden storm and sheltered in a gap in the rocks. While there he scribbled down the opening of a poem, which he continued to think about later in a nearby teashop. It became one of the best-loved of all hymns, turning the rock that sheltered Toplady into Christ's side, wounded by a spear as he hung on the cross.

Rock of ages, cleft for me,
Let me hide myself in thee,

Let the water and the blood,
From thy riven side which flowed,
Be of sin the double cure,
Save me from its guilt and power.

The English poet William Cowper and a clergyman, John Newton (1725–1807), published their *Olney Hymns* in 1778. Cowper's contributions included 'O for a Closer Walk with God', but the hymn that was destined to become world-famous was Newton's 'Amazing Grace'. Newton had been engaged in the Atlantic slave trade, but underwent a spiritual conversion during a storm at sea in 1748. He became a curate at Olney, Buckinghamshire, and wrote 'Amazing Grace' in 1773. It was adopted as the anthem of emancipation in the American Civil War, and is sung by Uncle Tom in Harriet Beecher Stowe's anti-slavery novel, *Uncle Tom's Cabin* (1852).

Amazing grace. How sweet the sound
That saved a wretch like me.
I once was lost but now am found,
Was blind but now I see.

The nineteenth-century Oxford Movement aimed to bring the Anglican Church closer to Roman Catholicism. John Keble (1792–1866), one of its leaders, was Professor of Poetry at Oxford and his book of poems, *The Christian Year* (1827), contained several hymns, including 'New Every Morning Is the Love'. But the most famous hymn to emerge from the Movement was by John Henry Newman (1801–1890), who later converted to Catholicism and became a Cardinal. As a young man, travelling in Italy, he was taken ill, but managed to get aboard a sailing ship carrying a cargo of oranges to Marseilles. He wrote 'Lead, Kindly Light' while it was becalmed in the straits between Corsica and Sardinia. The hymn asks for guidance, but also looks forward to reunion with lost loved ones after death

So long thy pow'r hath blest me, sure it still
Will lead me on,

O'er moor and fen, o'er crag and torrent, till
The night is gone,
And with the morn those angel faces smile
Which I have loved long since, and lost awhile.

In 1909 an explosion in the West Stanley Colliery, Durham, killed 166 men and boys. But twenty-eight survivors found a pocket of air and were sitting in almost total darkness when one of them began to hum 'Lead Kindly Light', and the rest joined in with the words. One boy died of his injuries while the hymn was being sung, but, after fourteen hours, the remainder were rescued.

Another hymn that people turn to in times of stress and danger is 'Abide with Me'. Unlike Newman, its author was not famous but an obscure country clergyman, Henry Francis Lyte (1793–1847), who underwent an evangelical conversion when attending a dying priest. He wrote other hymns, among them 'Praise My Soul the King of Heaven', based on Psalm 103. But 'Abide with Me' is his masterpiece. He suffered from tuberculosis, and moved to the south of France in search of a climate in which he might survive, but 'Abide with Me' was written on his deathbed. It is said to have been played by the band aboard the *Titanic* while the ship sank. Since 1927, the first and last verses are traditionally sung before kick-off at the FA Cup Final.

Abide with me, fast falls the eventide,
The darkness deepens, Lord with me abide.
When other helpers fail and comforts flee,
Help of the helpless, Lord, abide with me . . .

Hold thou thy cross before my closing eyes,
Shine through the gloom and point me to the skies,
Heaven's morning breaks, and earth's vain shadows flee,
In life, in death, O Lord, abide with me.

CHAPTER 17

Lyrical Ballads, and After
WORDSWORTH AND COLERIDGE

William Wordsworth (1770–1850) grew up in the Lake District, and it had a profound influence on him and his poetry. He went to Hawkshead Grammar School and St John's College, Cambridge, and after leaving university he travelled to France, where the Revolution had begun. He was converted to the revolutionary cause, and in his autobiographical poem, *The Prelude*, he recalled the hopes of a new world that the future seemed to promise: 'Bliss was it in that dawn to be alive, / But to be young was very heaven!'

He fell in love with a young French woman, Annette Vallon, and their daughter, Caroline, was born in 1792. But, short of money, he had to return to Britain in 1793, and the political situation prevented him re-joining Annette and Caroline. They never lived together as a family, and in 1802 he married a childhood friend Mary Hutchinson.

In 1795 he met Samuel Taylor Coleridge (1772–1834), a brilliant but unstable young man, also Cambridge-educated, and in 1798 they published, anonymously, *Lyrical Ballads, With a Few Other Poems*. It changed the course of English poetry.

All but four of the twenty poems in it were by Wordsworth. He also wrote a Preface for the second edition in which he defines poetry as 'the spontaneous overflow of powerful feelings', and sets out the aims of his new poetry. It will use 'the real language of men', and will avoid the 'poetic diction' common in the eighteenth century.

He takes as his subjects the poor, the old and the outcast. 'Goody Blake and Harry Gill' is about an old woman who has to steal firewood to survive the winter; 'Her Eyes Are Wild', about a vagrant woman suckling her child:

> Suck, little babe, oh suck again,
> It cools my blood, it cools my brain,
> Thy lips I feel them, baby, they
> Draw from my heart the pain away.

A beggar in 'The Old Cumberland Beggar' sits among 'wild unpeopled hills' eating, and his 'palsied hands' scatter crumbs while the 'small mountain birds' surround him, waiting warily for their 'destined meal'. In 'The Idiot Boy' a poor countrywoman, Betty Foy, is the mother of a disabled son who gets lost and spends a night in the open air. When she finds him he speaks wonderingly of the owls and the moon, without realising what they were: 'The cocks did crow to-whoo, to-whoo, / And the sun did shine so cold!' No one had written poems about such people before.

Also new in *Lyrical Ballads* are poems about children and how adults fail to understand them. In 'Anecdote for Fathers', a boy resists adult logic, and in 'We Are Seven', a small girl, whose brother has died, insists that he still counts as one of the family. Wordsworth's belief in the superiority of childhood is expressed most challengingly in the 'Immortality Ode' (1802) where he remembers his own early years:

> There was a time when meadow, grove and stream,
>   The earth, and every common sight
>   To me did seem,

> Apparelled in celestial light,
> The glory and the freshness of a dream.

But as he grew up the 'visionary gleam' faded and this, the poem explains, is because our souls have existed elsewhere before our birth, and we remember it:

> Our birth is but a sleep and a forgetting,
> The soul that rises with us, our life's star,
>   Hath had elsewhere its setting,
>   And cometh from afar.
>   Not in entire forgetfulness,
>   And not in utter nakedness,
>   But trailing clouds of glory do we come
>   From God who is our home.
> Heaven lies about us in our infancy!
> Shades of the prison house begin to close
>   Upon the growing boy . . .

Wordsworth's sympathy with the poor in *Lyrical Ballads* reflects his experiences in France. He recalls in *The Prelude* how a revolutionary friend pointed to an emaciated girl they met on a walk and declared:

> 'Tis against *that*
> That we are fighting.

In the 'Residence in London' book of *The Prelude*, he remembers seeing a poor man with a sick child in his arms, who:

> Bending over it,
> As if he were afraid both of the sun,
> And of the air which he had come to seek,
> Eyed the poor babe with love unutterable.

The griefs of the poor continued to haunt him, and inspired some of his greatest poems. 'The Ruined Cottage' is about a woman who has lost her husband in the wars and hopes, for years, for his return. 'Michael', included in the 1800 edition of *Lyrical Ballads*, tells of a shepherd whose son goes off to seek his fortune in the city. Before he leaves he puts in place the first stone of a sheepfold that Michael continues to build during his absence. But the boy is corrupted by city life and never returns. Years later the country-folk remember how Michael would still go up to work at the sheepfold: 'And 'tis believed by all / That many and many a day he thither went, / And never lifted up a single stone.'

'Lines Written in Early Spring', included in *Lyrical Ballads*, expresses Wordsworth's belief that nature is conscious: ''Tis my faith that every flower / Enjoys the air it breathes.'

Only one poem in the volume draws on his power as a nature poet, but it is one of his greatest: 'Tintern Abbey', written, he records, on 13 July 1798 when he was on a walking tour with his sister Dorothy. In it he recalls how, when he was a child, nature was 'all in all' to him:

> I cannot paint,
> What then I was. The sounding cataract
> Haunted me like a passion . . .

But now the time of 'thoughtless youth' has passed and, he says, he can hear in nature 'the still, sad music of humanity':

>   And I have felt
> A passion that disturbs me with the joy
> Of elevated thought, a sense sublime
> Of something far more deeply interfused,
> Whose dwelling is the light of setting suns,
> And the round ocean and the living air,
> And the blue sky, and in the mind of man;
> A motion and a spirit that impels
> All living things, all objects of all thought,
> And rolls through all things.

With this awareness, he recognises:

> In nature and the language of the sense
> The anchor of my purest thoughts, the nurse,
> The guide, the guardian of my heart and soul,
> Of all my moral being.

The belief that nature is a moral educator is stated with breath-taking simplicity in another *Lyrical Ballads* poem, 'The Tables Turned':

> One impulse from a vernal wood,
> May teach you more of man,
> Of moral evil and of good,
> Than all the sages can.

A famous passage from *The Prelude* gives an instance of nature acting as a moral guardian. One summer evening, young Wordsworth takes a boat without its owner's permission, and as he rows:

> A huge peak, black and huge,
> As if with voluntary power instinct,
> Upreared its head.

It seems to stride after him and, trembling, he returns the boat to where he found it. Even when not guilt-ridden, the boy Wordsworth in *The Prelude* is aware of nature as a living presence:

> I heard among the solitary hills
> Low breathings coming after me, and sounds
> Of indistinguishable motion, steps
> Almost as silent as the turf they trod.

The belief in nature as an educator is one idea that lies behind the Lucy poems, which Wordsworth wrote in the winter of 1798

when he was living in Germany with his sister Dorothy. She was
very close to him, and some of his poems, for example the famous
'Daffodils' ('I wandered lonely as a cloud'), are based on passages
in her journals. He may have been thinking of Dorothy and her
sensitivity to nature when he wrote, of Lucy:

> The stars of midnight shall be dear
> To her, and she shall lean her ear
> In many a secret place,
> Where rivulets dance their wayward round,
> And beauty born of murmuring sound
> Shall pass into her face.

But Dorothy outlived Wordsworth, whereas the imaginary Lucy
dies, and becomes part of nature:

> No motion has she now, no force,
> She neither hears nor sees,
> Rolled round in earth's diurnal course,
> With rocks, and stones, and trees.

Together Wordsworth and Coleridge evolved a new kind of
blank verse, more like everyday speech than the blank verse of
Shakespeare or Milton. Wordsworth uses it in 'Tintern Abbey' and
The Prelude (which was provisionally titled 'Poem to Coleridge').
Coleridge, who may have been its originator, uses it in his 'conver-
sation poems' such as 'This Lime-tree Bower, My Prison' (written
when he had to stay at home, having spilt boiling milk on his foot),
and 'Frost at Midnight', which is addressed to his little son, whom
he imagines as a future nature-lover:

> Therefore all seasons shall be sweet to thee,
> Whether the summer clothe the general earth
> With greenness, or the redbreast sit and sing
> Betwixt the tufts of snow on the bare branch
> Of mossy apple-tree, while the nigh thatch

Smokes in the sun-thaw; whether the eave-drops fall,
Heard only in the trances of the blast,
Or if the secret ministry of frost
Shall hang them up in silent icicles,
Quietly shining to the quiet moon.

It would be hard to tell, if you did not know, that that was not written by Wordsworth.

But Coleridge's greatest poems lie far outside Wordsworth's scope. 'The Rime of the Ancient Mariner' is one of the best-known poems in the language, and having an albatross round your neck has become almost proverbial. The poem appeared in *Lyrical Ballads*, but Wordsworth nearly cut it from the second edition, and its Gothic-horror goings-on (still more spookily intrusive in Coleridge's unfinished 'Christabel') jar with the rest of the volume.

On the other hand, the simplicity of its language, as in 'As idle as a painted ship / Upon a painted ocean', or 'Water, water every-where, / Nor any drop to drink', fits Wordsworth's demands for the new poetry. The poem's moral climax accords, too, with his rever-ence for nature. The mariner watches the water-snakes – 'Blue, glossy green and velvet black' – swimming in the ship's shadow, and: 'A spring of love gushed from my heart, / And I blessed them unaware'. Immediately the albatross drops from his neck and sinks 'Like lead into the sea'.

'Kubla Khan', Coleridge's other masterpiece, would be selected by many as the greatest English poem, partly on the grounds that, though it makes grammatical sense, attempts to paraphrase it look ridiculous. Coleridge once said that it would be as possible to push out a stone from the pyramids with the bare hand as to alter one word in Shakespeare or Milton, at any rate in their best passages, without making them say something different and something worse than they had done. That applies to 'Kubla Khan'.

As is well known, Coleridge had been reading in a travel book about the Mongol emperor Kublai Khan, and the poem was the result of an opium dream, which he had started to write down when he was interrupted by 'a person on business from Porlock' (a nearby village). All that can be said with certainty about the unfinished poem's meaning is that it links creativity with violence, danger and bliss, and that danger and bliss predominate at the end:

Could I revive within me
　Her symphony and song,
　　To such a deep delight 'twould win me,
That with music loud and long,
I would build that dome in air,
That sunny dome! Those caves of ice!
And all who heard should see them there,
And all should cry, Beware! Beware!
His flashing eyes, his floating hair!
Weave a circle round him thrice,
And close your eyes with holy dread,
For he on honey-dew hath fed,
And drunk the milk of paradise.

CHAPTER 18

Second-Generation Romantics
KEATS AND SHELLEY

John Keats (1795–1821) was a London boy from a poor background. His father hired out horses for a living. After leaving school he became a medical student and 'dresser' (surgeon's assistant) at Guy's Hospital. He fell in love with a local young woman, Fanny Brawne, and his passionate, desperate letters to her are now classics. In 1818 his brother, Tom, died of tuberculosis and Keats, who nursed him, contracted the disease himself. His greatest poems, including the Odes ('To Autumn', 'On a Grecian Urn', 'To a Nightingale', 'On Melancholy', 'On Indolence' and 'To Psyche'), were written in a single year, 1819. He died in Rome, where he had gone in hope of recovery, in a house overlooking the Spanish Steps, now a pilgrimage site.

His poems were cruelly mocked by critics, partly on grounds of his social class (he was called a 'cockney' poet), and he wanted his gravestone to bear no name or date but only the words, 'Here lies One whose Name was writ in Water'. It is in the Protestant Cemetery in Rome, and also attracts many pilgrims.

Discussing poetry in his letters he praises sensation – 'O for a life of sensation rather than of thoughts!' – and sees the poet as a 'chameleon' who can take on the feelings of others: 'if a sparrow come before my window, I take part in its existence and pick around the gravel'. In *The Eve of St Agnes*, the greatest of his narrative poems, these qualities are evident from the start as he registers the effect of a winter night in the wild: 'The owl for all his feathers was a-cold'; 'The hare limped trembling through the frozen grass'.

The poem is about two lovers, Porphyro and Madeline, who, like Romeo and Juliet, are separated by family enmity. Daringly, Porphyro enters the enemy castle, gains admission to Madeline's bedroom and, in hiding, watches her undress. Keats registers not just sights and sounds, but temperatures. Madeline unclasps her 'warmed jewels', and as her dress slips down to her knees she stands, chillily, 'like a mermaid in seaweed', before getting into bed.

While she sleeps, Porphyro heaps the room with sensuousness:

> . . . candied apple, quince, and plum, and gourd,
> With jellies soother than the creamy curd,
> And lucent syrops tinct with cinnamon,
> Manna and dates, in argosy transferred
> From Fez, and spiced dainties, every one,
> From silken Samarcand to cedar'd Lebanon.
>
> These delicates he heap'd with glowing hand
> On golden dishes and in baskets bright
> Of wreathed silver, sumptuous they stand
> In the retired quiet of the night,
> Filling the chilly room with perfume light.

Then he wakes her. She has been dreaming of him, but the living man seems 'pallid, chill, and drear' compared to her dream. She begs him not to leave her, and their love-making is like two fragrances mingling:

Into her dream he melted, as the rose
Blendeth its odour with the violet,
Solution sweet . . .

Keats's most famous poem, 'To Autumn', is as densely sensuous, conveying not just how things feel (the 'moss'd' apple trees; the bees' 'clammy cells') but how they move. In 'sometimes like a gleaner thou dost keep / Steady thy laden head across a brook', we feel the gleaner's momentary unsteadiness as we cross the line-break.

The sensory power of Keats's poetry extends not just to sight and hearing but to touch. He can make us feel the difference between two kinds of metallic friction. Compare the dockyard scene in 'Lamia':

    . . . his galley now
Grated the quay-stones with her brazen prow
In port Cenchreas from Egina isle . . .

with the ending of the sonnet 'To Sleep':

Turn the key deftly in the oiled wards,
And seal the hushed casket of my soul.

But the other pressure in Keats's poetry, pulling him away from sense perception, is imagination. He declares in his letters: 'I am certain of nothing but of the holiness of the heart's affections and the truth of imagination. What the imagination seizes as Beauty must be truth, whether it existed before or not.' Imagination takes him beyond the bodily senses, and we can see it happening in, for example, the 'Ode on a Grecian Urn'. Looking at the figures depicted on the urn, he wonders who they are:

Who are these coming to the sacrifice?
    To what green altar, O mysterious priest,

Lead'st thou that heifer, lowing at the skies,
    And all her silken flanks with garlands dressed?

This leads to a further thought. He wonders not who these people are but where they have come from, and that thought passes beyond the sensory to pure imagination:

What little town, by river or sea-shore,
    Or mountain-built, with peaceful citadel,
      Is emptied of its folk, this pious morn?
And, little town, thy streets for evermore
    Will silent be, and not a soul to tell
      Why thou art desolate, can e'er return.

But there is no little town, and never was. Yet, because Keats's imagination has created it, with its emptiness and its silence, it does – for us as readers – exist, 'whether it existed before or not'. The 'Ode to a Grecian Urn' is not singular in this respect. All the odes fluctuate between sensory acuteness and an imaginative drive that outsoars the senses.

Percy Bysshe Shelley (1792–1822) was the son of a baronet. He was brutally bullied at Eton, which may explain his lifelong hatred of violence and of authority based on violence. He was expelled from Oxford for publishing a pamphlet entitled *The Necessity of Atheism*, and, aged nineteen, eloped with a sixteen-year-old school-friend of his sisters, Harriet Westbrook, who bore him a son and daughter. In 1814 he visited the radical philosopher, William Godwin, author of *Political Justice*, and fell in love with his sixteen-year-old daughter, Mary, later the author of *Frankenstein*. Abandoning Harriet, Shelley moved with Mary to Switzerland, where they met Byron. In 1816 Harriet drowned herself in the Serpentine in Hyde Park. Shelley and Mary married three weeks later and joined Byron in Venice, later moving to Florence. In July 1822 Shelley's sailing boat, the *Don Juan*, sank in a sudden storm on the Gulf of Spezia, and he drowned. A copy of Keats's poems was found in his pocket.

Shelley was an idealist, that is, he had aims and ideas that he believed could make the world a perfect place. ('Poets', he wrote, were 'the unacknowledged legislators of the world'.) So sense perception, responding to the world as it is, mattered less to him than to Keats. In 'To a Skylark' the bird is deprived of its physical being in the first two lines: 'Hail to thee, blithe spirit, / Bird thou never wert'. In 'Adonais', his poem in memory of Keats, colour, which meant so much to Keats, is banished from eternity's perfection: 'Life, like a dome of many-coloured glass, / Stains the white radiance of eternity'.

The symbols Shelley uses again and again – the moon, stars, the wind, clouds – all represent eternity. They persist, even when not seen or felt. 'The Cloud' spells this out: 'I pass through the pores of oceans and shores: / I change, but I cannot die'. So, too, in 'Ode to the West Wind', the wind scatters seeds in autumn but they will be eternally reborn each spring, and Shelley wants his ideas to have similar immortality: 'Drive my dead thoughts over the universe / Like withered leaves, to quicken a new birth!'

His ideals included free love, sexual equality ('Can man be free if woman be a slave?' he asks in 'The Revolt of Islam'), the abolition of marriage and the abolition of Christianity. He believed that Jesus had been a perfect man, but not divine, and he detested the cruelties done in Jesus's name. The Chorus in Shelley's imitation Greek tragedy, *Prometheus Unbound*, voice this with bitter terseness:

One came forth of gentle worth,
Smiling on the sanguine earth.
His words outlived him, like swift poison
   Withering up truth, peace and pity.

Shelley hated tyranny and his most famous poem, 'Ozymandias', scorns the pride and futility of tyrants. It was written in 1818 when he heard that a huge fragment of a statue of Rameses II, ruler of ancient Egypt, was being brought to the British Museum. In the poem a traveller tells how he saw, in the desert, the remains of a colossal statue, just the legs and the face:

And on the pedestal these words appear:
'My name is Ozymandias, king of kings,
Look on my works, ye mighty, and despair!'
Nothing beside remains. Round the decay
Of that colossal wreck, boundless and bare,
The lone and level sands stretch far away.

Shelley soon heard of an example of tyranny nearer home – the Peterloo Massacre. In St Peter's Field, Manchester, on 16 August 1819, 50,000 people gathered to demand parliamentary reform. The magistrates ordered the Manchester Yeomanry to disperse the crowd; they charged, and eighteen protesters were killed. Shelley's 'The Mask of Anarchy' blames the nation's rulers – Leader of the House of Commons, Lord Castlereagh:

I met Murder on the way –
He had a mask like Castlereagh –

and Eldon, the Lord Chancellor, who had refused to give Shelley custody of his two children by Harriet, and who was said to weep when pronouncing harsh sentences:

Next came Fraud, and he had on
Like Eldon, an ermined gown:
His big tears, for he wept well,
Turned to millstones as they fell,
And the little children, who
Round his feet played to and fro,
Thinking every tear a gem,
Had their brains knocked out by them.

The poem does not cry for revenge. Shelley advises meeting force with passive resistance (his idea of civil disobedience influenced Tolstoy and Gandhi):

With folded arms, and steady eyes,
And little fear, and less surprise,
Look upon them as they slay,
Till their rage has died away.

Shelley's 1819 sonnet, beginning 'An old, mad, blind, despised and
dying king', is a shattering indictment of George III's England.

But Shelley can be less wrought-up. Remembering his friendship
with Byron in 'Julian and Maddalo', he finds an amiably relaxed voice:

I rode one evening with Count Maddalo
Upon the bank of land which breaks the flow
Of Adria towards Venice . . .

In 'Peter Bell the Third' he is wickedly funny about Wordsworth's
sexless account of Nature:

He touched the hem of Nature's shift,
Felt faint – and never dared uplift
    The closest, all-concealing tunic.

Despite his own eager advocacy of love as life's ideal, Shelley
writes more powerfully of its pains than its joys. In 'Hymn of Pan',
Pan remembers how the nymph Syrinx changed into a reed to
escape his pursuit:

I pursued a maiden, and clasped a reed,
Gods and men, we are all deluded thus;
It breaks in our bosom, and then we bleed . . .

The lyric 'When the Lamp is Shattered' is about how, when two
people love and one of them stops loving, the other is left desolate,
and still in love:

    Its passions will rock thee
As the storms rock the ravens on high;

Bright reason will mock thee,
Like the sun from a wintry sky,
    From thy nest every rafter
Will rot, and thine eagle home
    Leave thee naked to laughter,
When leaves fall and cold winds come.

CHAPTER 19

Romantic Eccentrics
BLAKE, BYRON, BURNS

William Blake (1757–1827) was a mystic and a graphic artist as well as a poet. The son of a London hosier, he was trained as an engraver. Prior to photography, engraving was the usual way of reproducing images commercially. But Blake experimented with engraving techniques and hand-coloured his prints, producing original artworks to illustrate his poems.

From childhood on he had visions of God, angels and other supernatural beings. He once told a friend that the books and pictures he had produced 'in ages of eternity', before his mortal life, were studied by archangels in heaven. Many thought him insane, including Wordsworth. However, his works have inspired count-less writers and artists from the Pre-Raphaelites to the 1960s beat poets and beyond.

His ideas, like those of other Romantics, centre on freedom. He was inspired by the American and French revolutions, and campaigned against slavery. In obscure and often lengthy poems, now known as the 'Prophetic Books', he worked out a new morality and a new religion, using a cast of invented mythological figures. Scholars still debate the meaning of these writings.

However, some things are clear. Blake sees Reason and Energy as opposites. He associates Reason with the tyrannical, Old Testament God of Milton's *Paradise Lost*, and Energy with Milton's Satan. Energy is good; Reason is evil. Energy expresses itself in sexual desire and sexual gratification:

> What is it men in women do require?
> The lineaments of gratified desire.
> What is it women do in men require?
> The lineaments of gratified desire.

But God and his church condemn sexual desire. So, in 'The Garden of Love', the poet sees:

> ... priests in black gowns were walking the rounds,
> And binding with briars my joys and desires.

So, too, in 'Ah, Sunflower', the 'youth pined away with desire' and the 'pale virgin shrouded in snow' exemplify life-blighting chastity. 'The Sick Rose' shows the unhealthy effect of chastity too. In Blake's illustration the rose is defended with thick thorns and a caterpillar is eating its leaf:

> O rose, thou art sick,
> The invisible worm
> That flies in the night,
> In the howling storm,
>
> Has found out thy bed
> Of crimson joy;
> And his dark secret love
> Does thy life destroy.

Self-restraint is, for Blake, destructive. 'A Poison Tree' shows its deadly effect:

> I was angry with my friend,
> I told my wrath, my wrath did end,
> I was angry with my foe,
> I told it not, my wrath did grow . . .
>
> And it grew both day and night
> Till it bore an apple bright –
> And my foe beheld it shine,
> And he knew that it was mine,
>
> And into my garden stole,
> When the night had veiled the pole.
> In the morning glad I see
> My foe outstretched beneath the tree.

The opposition of reason and energy is replaced in *The Marriage of Heaven and Hell* by balance. Reason and energy are both 'necessary to human existence'. But the work gains its power from the daring paradoxes of the 'Proverbs of Hell': 'One law for the lion and ox is oppression'; 'Sooner murder an infant in its cradle than nurse unacted desires.' Such maxims shock and horrify us. But that, Blake might reply, is because we are being reasonable, and his God in *The Marriage of Heaven and Hell* is, unlike Milton's, not reducible to reason. He is fierce, cruel and lustful: 'The lust of the goat is the bounty of God. The wrath of the lion is the wisdom of God.' In 'Tiger, tiger, burning bright', the answer to 'Did he who made the lamb, make thee?' is 'Yes.' God can be both tigerish and lamb-like: 'Without contraries is no progression.' But God cannot be simply reasonable, because he is wise: 'The tigers of wrath are wiser than the horses of instruction.'

Since Blake distrusted pure reason, he also distrusted the Enlightenment and science, believing them hostile to the power imagination gives you:

To see a world in a grain of sand
And a heaven in a wild flower,
Hold infinity in the palm of your hand
And eternity in an hour.

In 'Mock On, Mock On, Voltaire, Rousseau', he dismisses Enlightenment values and Newton's theories about 'particles of light'. He blamed them for the industrial revolution's 'dark, Satanic mills' that blight England in 'Jerusalem' – and must be swept away:

I will not cease from mental fight,
Nor shall my sword sleep in my hand,
Till we have built Jerusalem,
In England's green and pleasant land.

George Gordon, Lord Byron (1788–1824), was as unlike Blake as it is possible to be. The son of a dissolute father and an unstable mother, he was born with a club foot, which always made him self-conscious. He inherited his title, 'Lord Byron', aged ten, from an uncle. Bisexual, he had countless affairs with both males and females, starting at school, and scandal buzzed around him wherever he went.

After Harrow and Cambridge University, he travelled abroad, where gay sex was easier to find, visiting Portugal, Spain, Albania, Greece and Constantinople (where he famously swam across the Hellespont). The first two books of *Childe Harold's Pilgrimage*, published in 1812, caused a sensation. 'I awoke one morning and found myself famous,' he recalled.

In fashionable London between 1811 and 1816, he lived with extravagant abandon, had an affair with Lady Caroline Lamb (who called him 'mad, bad and dangerous to know') and married an heiress for her money. She soon left him, taking their daughter with her, and he quitted England for good in 1816, amid rumours (correct) of an incestuous affair with his half-sister. He wrote *Don Juan* when he was living in Italy with the young Countess Guiccioli, who left her husband to join him. He volunteered to fight for the

Greeks in their War of Independence, but died of a fever in Missolonghi without seeing any action.

In the first two cantos of *Childe Harold* the hero, recognisably Byron, laments the lost glories of classical civilisation. Advice on how to deal with women is included:

> Brisk confidence still best with woman copes:
> Pique her and soothe in turn, soon passion crowns thy hopes.

He adds that the 'paltry prize' is not worth having.

The later cantos have the famous passage on the Battle of Waterloo, and the dramatic scene on the eve of battle with Wellington and his officers at the Duchess of Richmond's ball: 'There was a sound of revelry by night'. Byron admired Napoleon, regretted his defeat, and deplored the restoration of the old order. Also famous are the stanzas about a gladiator dying in the Colosseum, 'Butchered to make a Roman holiday' – another example of pointless slaughter applauded by an ignorant mob.

In *Beppo* (1817) Byron tried out a new stanza form (called *ottava rima* in Italian), which is a perfect medium for seemingly offhand mockery:

> 'Tis true, your budding Miss is very charming,
>   But shy and awkward at first coming out,
> So much alarmed that she is quite alarming,
>   All giggle, blush; half pertness and half pout,
> And glancing at *Mamma*, for fear there's harm in
>   What you, she, it, or they, may be about,
> The nursery still lisps out in all they utter –
> Besides, they always smell of bread and butter.

This is the form he uses for *Don Juan*.

At the start Juan is a boy living in Lisbon with his parents. He is sexually precocious, and is sent abroad out of harm's way. Shipwrecked, he finds himself in an open boat surrounded by starving mariners, who, after drawing lots, eat his tutor, Pedrillo.

Captured by pirates and sold into slavery, he is smuggled into the Sultan's harem disguised as a girl, escapes, joins the Russian army, witnesses slaughter and rapine at the fall of a Turkish fortress, attends the court of Catherine the Great (who lusts for him), is sent as envoy to England, and is cavorting with various aristocratic ladies when the narrative is cut short by Byron's death.

Byron relates these adventures with dazzling panache. He pours out epigrams:

> What men call gallantry, and gods adultery,
> Is much more common where the climate's sultry.

He observes his characters' behaviour with witty detachment:

> A little while she strove, and much repented,
> And whispering, 'I will ne'er consent' – consented.

He issues (very male) generalisations about human nature:

> Man's love is of man's life a thing apart,
> 'Tis woman's whole existence.

But it is hard, in this medium, not to sound callous. When the sailors have eaten Juan's tutor, they die from hunger and thirst:

> But chiefly from a species of self-slaughter,
> In washing down Pedrillo with salt water.

Tenderness is difficult, too. Juan's love for Haidee, the daughter of an Aegean pirate, keeps sounding almost comic. They embrace passionately:

> And thus they form a group that's quite antique,
> Half-naked, loving, natural and Greek.

When Haidee dies, she is pregnant, and Byron arouses pity, as he seldom does elsewhere:

> She died, but not alone, she held within
>   A second principle of life, which might
> Have dawned a fair and sinless child of sin,
>   But closed its little being without light.

Robert Burns (1759–1796) is known as Scotland's national poet. But he was also a Romantic poet of European stature. The son of a chronically indebted Ayrshire tenant farmer, he spent his early life labouring to support his family of siblings. His lack of education has been exaggerated. He learned French, Latin and mathematics at school, and started writing poetry aged fifteen.

He was highly sexed, and had at least two illegitimate children by servant girls. Jean Armour, whom he wed in 1788, and who bore him nine children, was pregnant before their marriage. The church took a dim view of these activities, and Burns did public penance in the kirk. He planned to emigrate to Jamaica, where he had accepted a job as a book-keeper on a slave plantation, but could not raise money for the passage.

His *Poems*, published in 1786, were an immediate success, and he was feted in Edinburgh, where he met Walter Scott. As well as writing, he collected Scots folksongs and music. Some of his best-known poems, including 'Auld Lang Syne', were written to fit traditional melodies.

His great gift is authenticity. Other Romantics sympathised with the working class; he belonged to it. His use of Scots dialect is almost like a passport, identifying him as of the people. 'The Twa Dogs' takes a cheerfully sardonic view of persons of Byron's class:

> At operas and plays parading,
> Mortgaging, gambling, masquerading.

'Honest poverty', that laughs at titles and dignitaries, is like the gold in a gold coin:

> The rank is but the guinea's stamp,
> The man's the gowd for a' that.

His satire in, for example, 'Holy Willie's Prayer', can be devastating, exposing his victim's bluster and hypocrisy with what seems like casual good humour, as if Willy were not worth getting angry about.

Mostly he treats other creatures gently, especially the helpless, as in 'The Poet's Welcome to his Love-begotten Daughter':

> Thou's welcome, wean, mishanter fa' me,
> If aught of thee, or of thy mammy
> Shall ever daunton me, or awe me,
>   My sweet wee lady
> Or if I blush when thou shalt ca' me
>   Tit-ta or daddy.

Even disregarding the dialect, you can't imagine Byron or any other Romantic poet writing that.

Tenderness towards other living things also impels 'To a Mouse on Turning Her Up in Her Nest with the Plough, November 1785':

> Wee, sleekit, cow'rin', tim'rous beastie,
> O what a panic's in thy breastie.

And sympathy broadens into folk-wisdom:

> The best laid schemes o' mice an' men
> Gang aft a-gley.

Calm moral authority sounds again in 'To a Louse':

> O wad some pow'r the giftie gie us
> To see oursels as others see us.

His poems flow so naturally that his art is easy to miss. His greatest love poem starts with almost incompetent simplicity:

> My love is like a red, red rose

But with the start of the second stanza it gathers earth-shaking force:

> Till a' the seas gang dry, my dear,
>   And the rocks melt wi' the sun,
> And I will luve thee still, my dear,
>   While the sands o' life shall run.

CHAPTER 20

From Romanticism to Modernism in German Poetry
GOETHE, HEINE, RILKE

Germany did not become a nation until 1871. But German poetry had spread its influence through Europe long before that. Asked who 'invented' Romanticism, many would reply Johann Wolfgang von Goethe (1749–1832). He was a scientist, writing treatises on botany, anatomy and colour theory, as well as a novelist, cultural critic and poet. Born in Frankfurt, and trained as a lawyer, he moved to the duchy of Saxe-Weimar in 1775, serving in many offices of state and becoming virtual prime minister. As director of the theatre he produced the romantic dramas of his friend Friedrich von Schiller (1759–1805).

His first novel, *The Sorrows of the Young Werther*, written in 1774, brought him instant fame. It recounts (in a series of letters) how a sensitive young artist, Heinrich Werther, falls in love with beautiful, kind Charlotte, who is engaged to, and marries, an older man, Albert. Despairing, Werther borrows Albert's pistols and shoots himself. In the 'Werther fever' following its publication there was an epidemic of suicides. Some dressed up as Werther and acquired pistols similar to his before killing themselves, and the book was banned in several countries. Like Schiller's *The Robbers* (1781) it came to be seen as part of the proto-Romantic, *Sturm und Drang* movement, which cultivated wild emotion and violent action as a reaction against Enlightenment reason.

Goethe's most famous poetic work is his two-part tragedy *Faust*. At the start God bets Mephistopheles, an agent of Satan, that he will not be able to lead Faust astray. Faust, however, agrees to sell his soul provided Mephistopheles can give him such delight that he wishes a moment would last for ever:

> If I say to the moment,
> 'Stay! You are so beautiful!',
> Then you can lock me in fetters.

In their ensuing adventures Faust seduces an innocent young girl, Margaret (Gretchen), and kills her brother in a sword fight. She goes mad, drowns her new-born son, is condemned to death, and refuses to save herself by fleeing with Faust. However, at the end of the first part, a voice from on high pronounces her 'redeemed'.

Faust, Part Two (published after Goethe's death) is a five-act poetic fantasia, scarcely related to Part One. In a fairy vision of the imperial court, Faust conjures up Helen of Troy, the 'ideal form' of beauty, and falls in love with her. With Mephistopheles, he encounters gods and monsters from Greek myth, and visits the underworld. In the last act Faust, old and powerful, experiences a moment of bliss when planning how to better the lives of his subjects, and drops dead. Mephistopheles claims his soul. But angels drop burning rose-petals on the demons, and take Faust's soul to heaven, where it is received by various sanctified females, including Gretchen. In conclusion, a 'mystical chorus' assures us that:

> Eternal Womanhood
> Leads us above.

The best-known of Goethe's shorter poems is the 'Erlking', based on a traditional ballad and set to music by Schubert. In it a father rides through the night clasping in his arms his little son, who sees phantoms, which the father explains away as fog or rustling leaves. At the end the child shrieks that the 'Erlking' is harming him, and dies.

More remarkable, though, are the twenty-four *Roman Elegies*. Magnificently sensuous and elegant, they imitate classical love-elegists, like Ovid, and ingeniously preserve the Latin metre. Recalling Goethe's Italian journey (1786–8), they describe his amorous encounters:

We are content with Cupid's delights, authentic and naked –
And with the exquisite creak-crack of the bed as it rocks.

They were considered too indecent to publish in Goethe's lifetime.

Heinrich Heine (1797–1856), like Goethe, began as a Romantic but forsook Romanticism. Born in Dusseldorf, into a Jewish family, he converted to Protestantism as a 'ticket of admission to European culture', since Jews were debarred from most professions. Even with this ticket he could not earn a living, however, but was luckily supported by a millionaire banker uncle. He is best known for his early lyrics about love and its sorrows, set to music by Schumann, Schubert and others. Like most Romantics he responds profoundly to the natural world. In his *North Sea* poems the 'mysterious thrill' of the sea makes him feel that his 'scarcely-healed heart' is being kissed open by 'dear lips'. His *Harz Mountains* poems romanticise the peasant folk – a bewitching little girl, scared of the snow, a shepherd boy dozing and dreaming in the sun.

But his mature work is distinguished by satire and irony. His targets are Prussian militarism, nationalism and xenophobia, and the greed of the ruling class. At the same time he despairs of the political apathy of the German people, interested only in sauer-kraut and sausage. He admired Napoleon as a liberator and, like Byron, lamented his downfall (as in his poem 'The Grenadiers').

His opinions riled the authorities, so he moved, for safety, to Paris in 1831, where he met and lived with a child-like, illiterate nineteen-year-old, Mathilde, whom he eventually married in 1841.

In Paris he also met Karl Marx, a distant relative, who published Heine's poem 'The Silesian Weavers', about a weavers' strike, in his journal *Forwards*. However, Heine distrusted Communism and feared the proletariat, foreseeing that their 'raw fists' would destroy his 'beloved world of art'. This ambivalence is expressed in his masterpiece, the twenty-seven-canto lyric-satire *Atta Troll*. The 'hero', a huge polar bear, representing the populace, shakes off his fetters and escapes to the mountains, where he preaches equality – all animals are equal, and just as good as humans. Anyone should be able to become prime minister, and the lion must carry corn to the mill like the ox. While satirising leftist rant through his bear, though, Heine, also detests the bear's foe, a wraith-like figure called Lascaro, the son of a witch who renews his strength at night with magic ointment. Lascaro, we gather, represents the dying spirit of autocratic government, propped up by superstition. He is the villain of the poem, but Heine also condemns the bear's ideal of complete equality as 'high treason against the majesty of humanity'. In this respect *Atta Troll* expresses the eternal quandary of the liberal intellectual.

Heine was partially paralysed eight years before his death (from, it is thought, lead-poisoning), and wrote the 'Lazarus poems', questioning God's justice. To a friend who praised them he said, 'Yes, I know. They are frighteningly beautiful. They are like a lament from the grave.'

The poet who took German poetry to another plane, however, was not Goethe or Heine but Rainer Maria Rilke (1875–1926). Born in Prague, of Austrian parents, he studied philosophy and literature in Prague and Munich, where he met and fell in love with the married Russian psychiatrist and author, Lou Andreas-Salomé, who had studied with Freud and introduced Rilke to psychoanalysis. He travelled with her to Italy and Russia, where he met Tolstoy. In 1901 he married the sculptor Clara Westhoff and their daughter Ruth was born later that year. In Paris from 1902 to 1910, he acted briefly as secretary to the sculptor August Rodin. This period produced his *New Poems* (1907–8). In 1912, staying in Duino Castle, near Trieste, he began his *Duino Elegies* (which are not really elegies but meditative philosophical poems). In Munich at the outbreak of the First World War, he was called up for military service, but basic training shattered him. Though friends soon secured his release, he wrote no poetry for several years. After the war he moved to Switzerland where, in a brief period of intense activity in 1922, he finished the *Duino Elegies* and wrote, in three weeks, the fifty-five *Sonnets to Orpheus*. He died of leukaemia.

His poetry is difficult, and that is because it tries to express the inexpressible. Ordinary language cannot do this, and he considers it shallow and reductive. The way people use words frightens him, he says ironically in an early poem, because 'Everything they pronounce is so clear'.

What he wanted to express was an idea of a consciousness purer, deeper and richer than we can imagine, and he calls the beings who possess this consciousness 'angels'. They are not like biblical angels, he explained, but what they are like is problematic. They are beyond the limitations of time and physicality, and in them, he said, 'the transformation of the visible into the invisible' is 'completed'. He says, too, that they are frightening (*schrecklich*), and that:

> At the back of the stars, if an Archangel now, dangerous, took even
> one step down to us, our own heart, wound upward,
> beating in leaps, would beat us to death.

Unlike angels, we live in an 'interpreted' world, diminished and protected by reason and understanding. It shuts us off from full consciousness, and he asks us to imagine what it would be like to leave this world:

> . . . to let go even the use
> of one's own name, as if dropping a broken toy.

Since human life is, in Rilke's vision, inadequate and inferior, death takes on a special meaning for him, though what that meaning is remains obscure:

> For we are only rind of fruit, and leaf.
> The great death, which each of us contains,
> is that fruit round which the world turns.

Obscure or not, Rilke writes with great power about death, as in the poem 'Orpheus Eurydice Hermes', where Eurydice, being led up from the underworld by Orpheus, is abstracted and 'hampered by her long grave-wrappings'. Seemingly she does not want to return to life:

> . . . her being-dead
> was filling her like fullness.
> For like a fruit all of sweetness and dark
> she too was full of her immense death,
> which was so new she could not take it in.

In the private symbolism of Rilke's poems certain beings, though not 'angels', have consciousness superior to the normal. These include the unborn, people who die young, unrequited lovers, heroes and saints. Animals, too, belong to this group. Their minds, unlike ours, are not 'traps', capturing the world and reducing it to order, but completely open. They are:

> . . . Free of death.
> That, only we can see. The free animal
> has its decline perpetually behind it
> and God before, and in its movement moves
> within eternity, like welling springs.
> Never, for a day, do *we* have
> pure space before us for the opening
> of endless flowers.

That is from the eighth Duino Elegy. Earlier, in Paris, Rilke had written about animals more objectively, perhaps, it is thought, under the influence of Rodin. His best-known and most translated poem is about the panther in the Paris zoo, pacing up and down its cage:

> His eyes have grown so tired with the passing
> of bars that their reservoirs can hold
> no more. There seem a thousand bars, and in
> the drowse beyond a thousand bars, no world.

The mythical Orpheus made trees, rocks and rivers come to life with his song, and Rilke places him at the centre of the *Sonnets to Orpheus*. His poetry escapes the confines of human language, and we are urged to follow:

> Dare to say just what you mean by apple.
> Speak the sweetness that intensifies
> only to rise in taste and clarify
>
> tranquilly, awake, transparent.
> Ambiguously sunny, earthy, present –
> O feeling, joy, experience – immense!

Language alone will not be enough to accomplish this:

> dance the taste discovered in fruit! . . .
>
> Dance the orange. Thrust warmer landscape
> out of yourselves, that it may gleam
> ripe in home breezes!

The mythical Orpheus was torn to pieces by a drunken mob of women, worshippers of Bacchus, and the *Sonnets* record this:

> but your sound lingered on in the lions and in the rock face,
> and in the trees and the birds. You are singing there still.

The poem Rilke chose as his epitaph uses another of his symbols, the rose. It compares rose-petals to eyelids, as he often does, and it praises contradiction, which is central to his poetry. As usual, it is hard to say quite what it means:

> Rose, oh pure contradiction, delight,
> in being no one's sleep under so many
> eyelids.

CHAPTER 21

Making Russian Literature
PUSHKIN, LERMONTOV

Before Alexander Pushkin (1799–1837), there was virtually no Russian literature. Upper-class Russians spoke French and despised their native language. Pushkin was born into an aristocratic family, and went to school at the Imperial Lyceum. But he was drawn to the movement for social reform. Compared to most of Europe and America, Russia was still in the Middle Ages. The Tsar was a dictator, and serfdom, a kind of nationwide slavery, was still in force.

Pushkin circulated his early political poems in manuscript, but they were intercepted by the Tsar's intelligence network and he was exiled from the capital, St Petersburg, first to the Crimea and the Caucasus, and later to his mother's estate north of Moscow. In 1825 several of his associates were involved in the Decembrist uprising, which had aimed to prevent the reactionary Nicholas I from becoming tsar, but was brutally suppressed. In 1831 he married Natalia Goncharova, a court beauty, much admired by the Tsar and others, and they had four children. But Pushkin, offended by rumours that were circulating about his wife's infidelity, challenged a French officer, said to be her lover, to a duel, and was fatally wounded.

He was a novelist, playwright and short-story writer as well as a poet, and his subjects and manner of writing influenced all the great Russian authors who followed him, including Dostoyevsky, who said, 'everything we have comes from Pushkin'. Pushkin, in turn, was heavily influenced by Byron, particularly *Don Juan*. In poetry he cultivated a concrete descriptive style that was intensely visual but sometimes almost prosaic, using metaphor and figurative language only sparingly, and imitating ordinary speech rhythms. 'Listen to the speech of the people', was his advice. This affected his vocabulary too, and critics complained of his 'vulgarisms'.

A reckless womaniser, he left many discarded women in his wake. Yet his writing is profoundly responsive to women's feelings, depicting them, and his own, with a psychological realism and honesty rare in love poetry. Hearing, for example, that a woman he was once madly in love with has died of tuberculosis in Italy, he is shocked to find he feels no grief, and writes a poem admitting it. His wife was, apparently, cold and unloving, and he writes a poem telling her that this is what turns him on, rather than women who writhe around in his arms with passionate yelps.

A blasphemous poem called *The Gavriliad*, which he always denied writing, though everyone knew he had, depicts God (in the shape of a dove), the Devil (in the shape of a snake) and the angel Gabriel (in the shape of a beautiful young man), all making love with the Virgin Mary, who much enjoys it. Despite the flippant obscenity, her pleasure and her pride in her naked loveliness are beautifully and tenderly conveyed.

His old nurse (who also gets a poem to herself) told him about Russian folktales, and he weaves them into his poems. *Rusalka* is about a malign water-nymph who avenges herself on a prince who seduced and deserted her when she was a human. At the other end of the scale is a witty modern tale, *Count Nulin*. A bored young wife watches her husband and his friends ride off to the hunt. She longs for a visitor – any visitor. Then she hears the sound of a carriage overturning down by the bridge, and cheers up immediately at the prospect of welcoming the survivors.

Sure enough, a count and his servants soon arrive at her front door, all quite unharmed. He is a young dandy, just back from foreign travels, and chatters at dinner about what's on at the Paris theatres. After retiring to bed, it occurs to him his hostess might welcome his advances, so he feels his way along the dark corridor to her room, and Pushkin slips in a reference to the dreaded Tarquin in Shakespeare's *The Rape of Lucrece*. But this is a joke. No old-style melodrama is in store. The young wife, startled from sleep, slaps 'Tarquin's' face soundly and he creeps back to bed. Next morning he leaves early in his repaired carriage, but she tells all her friends about her adventure. The one who laughs loudest, Pushkin adds, is the twenty-four-year-old owner of the neighbouring estate – evidently the young wife's current lover.

The contrast between the wild and the civilised, a key Romantic topic, underlies Pushkin's *The Gypsies*. We start in the Roma encampment – firelight, supper cooking, horses grazing, a tame bear dozing. Zemfira, a Roma girl, arrives with a stranger, Aleko, a city man fleeing the law. As the carefree days pass, he and Zemfira become lovers. But she tires of him (women's incalculable changeability is a favourite Pushkin theme) and takes another lover. Wildly jealous, Aleko kills them both. The Old Man, Zemfira's father, responds with dignified restraint:

> Leave us, proud man! We are wild, we have no laws,
> we do not torture men, we do not put men to death –
> we have no need of blood and groans –
> but with a murderer we do not wish to live.

In an Epilogue, though, Pushkin recalls his own days among Roma in the Caucasus, and warns that even life in the wild cannot escape tormenting dreams and fateful passions.

Boris Godunov, Pushkin's attempt at Shakespearean tragedy, is chaotic, and not remotely Shakespearean. But his 'Little Tragedies' are studies in psychological realism and much more successful. In the best-known, *Mozart and Salieri* (which inspired Peter Shaffer's *Amadeus*), Salieri's motive for murdering Mozart is not envy (or so he tells himself, though he admits he is envious), but concern for the dignity of art, which is threatened when genius alights on a buffoon like Mozart.

Pushkin's most famous poem, *The Bronze Horseman*, presents readers with a problem. It is set in the 1820s in St Petersburg, a city built on marshes beside the River Neva – at the expense of thousands of workers' lives – on the orders of Tsar Peter the Great (1672–1725). Pushkin praises the city's glittering beauty, but then tells the story of a poor clerk, Yevgeni, whose home is destroyed when the city floods (as it often did). Worse, Yevgeni finds that his girlfriend's house has also been destroyed, and she and her family have drowned. He goes mad with grief, and becomes a down-and-out. But one day, seething with resentment, he wanders into St Peter's Square, looks up at the bronze equestrian statue of Tsar Peter – 'lord of half the world' – and utters wild threats through clenched teeth. Then he runs away, scared at his own temerity. Behind him he hears the clatter of bronze hooves, and later his body is found in a ramshackle hut on a desolate island.

How should we interpret the poem? The modern Russian poet, Joseph Brodsky (1940–1996), believed that it criticises Peter as the heartless arbiter of the common man's fate, and some take it to be Pushkin's protest at the repressive regime of Nicholas I. But in the Soviet era it was read as praise for a strong leader such as Stalin, who placed the advance of society before individual suffering.

Pushkin's masterpiece, the verse-novel *Eugene Onegin*, is in 389 complicated 14-line stanzas, mingling 'masculine' or single-syllable rhymes (e.g. slam/cram) with 'feminine' (e.g. middle/riddle), and it defies translation even more than most of his poetry. The story is relatively simple. Onegin, a selfish, cynical dandy, inherits a country estate. In the country he makes friends with an idealistic young poet, Lensky. Tatyana, a shy but passionate seventeen-year-old, the daughter of a landowner, falls in love with Onegin and writes to tell him so. But he reproaches her for her rashness, and tells her that marriage would bore him. Lensky invites Onegin to a country dance. But Onegin, irritated by the unsophisticated company, deliberately annoys Lensky by flirting with Tatyana's younger sister Olga, Lensky's fiancée. Lensky challenges Onegin to a duel. Onegin feels obliged to accept, for form's sake, and shoots Lensky dead.

Afterwards he travels abroad, and Tatyana, visiting his empty mansion, goes through his books and papers and concludes that Eugene Onegin is really a kind of composite Byronic invention rather than a real person. Years pass. Onegin returns. At a grand ball in Moscow he catches sight of Tatyana, now married to a prince. Smitten with love, he secures a private audience and begs her to elope with him. But she refuses to ruin her life, though she admits she still loves him.

Even more than the dramatic action, it is the taut storytelling and the sharp, realistic details that make *Eugene Onegin* so dazzling. In the duel scene, for example, everything is picked out with unsparing precision, from the pouring of the thin, greyish stream of powder into the pistols, and the insertion of the bullets in the faceted barrels, to the moment when Lensky quietly puts his hand to his breast, and falls, as a heap of snow falls slowly down a mountain slope with sparks flashing in the sun.

Mikhail Lermontov (1814–1841) was, like Pushkin, born into an aristocratic family. His mother died when he was three and his indulgent, wealthy grandmother brought him up. He was well educated, fluent in French, German and English, and a gifted painter, but any control irked him, and he left Moscow University after two years, enrolling as a cadet in the Cavalry School. As a Hussar officer in the Imperial Guard he led a life of luxury and dissipation, famed as a womaniser, and for his cruel, sardonic wit.

Pushkin was his idol, and within days of the fatal duel in January 1837, a poem called 'The Poet's Death' was circulated in hand-written copies. It laid the blame for the catastrophe, as many did, on Tsar Nicholas's inner circle, 'The greedy pack who swarm around the throne.' Lermontov was the author and, accused of incitement to rebellion, he was arrested, briefly imprisoned, then sent to join a dragoon regiment in the Caucasus.

However, that was no punishment for Lermontov. He loved the mountains and their rugged inhabitants, remembering them from happy childhood holidays. In conflict, he distinguished himself by reckless bravery, and was popular with his Cossack troopers. After the Battle of the Valerik River in 1840, official dispatches commended his 'outstanding courage'. But Nicholas I refused to decorate him. The following year he was killed in a duel with a brother officer who could not stand his biting sarcasm any longer. Like John Keats, he died at twenty-six.

It is as a war poet, describing his own battle-experience in 'Valerik', that he makes his closest approach to Pushkin's graphic authenticity. He remembers the waiting-time before battle – the Cossack horses huddled in a row, with lowered heads, the soldiers talking of old times, their bright bayonets gleaming in the sun. His account of the hand-to-hand fighting matches the official record, but the pointless slaughter disgusts him:

> We killed in silence, breast to breast, like beasts,
> In fury, piles of bodies choked the stream.
> I tried, because of heat and weariness,
> To drink – the stream was muddied, warm and red.

For the most part, however, Lermontov's poetry alternates between the Romantic pathos of dying gladiators (following Byron) or children weeping for a lost paradise, and the Romantic grandeur of Caucasian peaks. In his prison cell in 1837 he seems about to break away from egocentric posturing:

> Dear lonely neighbour whom I cannot know,
> My prison friend in suffering and woe . . .

But increasingly he indulges himself in lonely heroes – a prophet stoned and derided, an ostracised coward, a novice monk (in 'The Novice') who escapes into the countryside and slays a panther single-handed, and a demon (in 'The Demon') who manages to seduce a nun, only to be foiled at the last moment by a redeeming angel.

Lermontov, it should be added, is remembered as much for his pioneering psychological novel, *A Hero of Our Time* (1839–40), as for his poetry. It is about a bored, disenchanted young nobleman, rather like Lermontov.

CHAPTER 22

Great Victorians
Tennyson, Browning, Clough, Arnold

Alfred, Lord Tennyson (1809–1892), was the son of a Lincolnshire vicar. He went to Trinity College, Cambridge. His early poems were ridiculed for what was seen as their femininity, but in 1850 he succeeded Wordsworth as Poet Laureate. 'The Charge of the Light Brigade', probably his best-known poem, honours the courage of a cavalry unit that, because of a mistaken order, charged the Russian guns during the Battle of Balaclava:

> Theirs not to reason why,
> Theirs but to do and die:
> Into the valley of Death
>   Rode the six hundred.

He can still be heard intoning it, indistinctly, in a wax-cylinder recording.

He was subject to depression, and also bore a grudge because his father had been disinherited, the estate going to the Tennyson d'Eyncourt branch of the family. This was all the more hurtful as he believed himself of royal descent, and used to visit Westminster Abbey to identify his likeness in the Plantagenet tombs. In 1884 he accepted a peerage – the first (and, so far, only) poet to be ennobled for writing poetry.

His poetry is noted for its melodiousness, but his brilliance goes far beyond that. He is a master of perspective and precision, both evident in 'The Eagle':

> He clasps the crag with crooked hands,
> Close to the sun in lonely lands,
> Ring'd with the azure world he stands.
>
> The wrinkled sea beneath him crawls,
> He watches from his mountain walls,
> And like a thunderbolt, he falls.

Grief and loss are persistent themes:

> Tears, idle tears, I know not what they mean,
> Tears from the depth of some divine despair.

He finds outward emblems for inner desolation:

> Break, break, break,
> On thy cold gray stones, O sea!

In 'Tithonus', the speaker, doomed to immortality, watches the world wither:

> The woods decay, the woods decay, and fall,
> The vapours weep their burthen to the ground,
> Man comes, and tills the field, and lies beneath,
> And after many a summer dies the swan.

In 'Ulysses', Homer's old hero, back in Ithaca, longs for one last voyage:

To sail beyond the sunset, and the baths
Of all the western stars, until I die.

More than any other English poet, Tennyson was inspired by the *Odyssey*. 'The Lotos-eaters' is a marvel of dreamy forgetfulness:

In the afternoon they came unto a land
In which it seemed always afternoon . . .

Tennyson imagines, too, the sufferings of women, in a society that condemned them to watching and waiting, and men stole all the action. 'The Lady of Shallot', 'half sick of shadows', breaks out of her restricted life, and dies. 'Mariana' waits for a lover who never comes, while her surroundings fall into ruin:

The rusted nails fell from the knots
That held the pear to the gable-wall,
The broken sheds looked sad and strange . . .

In 1833 a college friend of Tennyson's, Henry Hallam, died of a stroke aged twenty-two, and Tennyson mourned him in a long poem, 'In Memoriam', often thought his masterpiece:

He is not here, but far away
    The noise of life begins again,
    And ghastly thro' the drizzling rain
On the bald street breaks the blank day.

It was not just Hallam that 'In Memoriam' mourned. In the early nineteenth century geologists revealed that the earth was millions of years older than the Bible suggested, that the land-masses were constantly changing, and that not only the human race, but every trace of its existence, would one day be obliterated. 'In Memoriam' records this fearful discovery:

The hills are shadows, and they flow
    From form to form, and nothing stands,

They melt like mist, the solid lands,
Like clouds they shape themselves and go.

Many, including it seems Tennyson, found that their Christian
faith could not survive such knowledge.

In his last great poem, 'Maud' (1855), his fury over the d'Eyncourt
disinheritance and his bitter memory of a banker's daughter, Rosa
Baring, who had once rejected him, erupt in a murderous tirade
against the upstarts who were making their fortunes in Victorian
commerce and industry. Its intensity is almost maniacal. Waking
from a dream of Maud's 'Cold and clear-cut face', the speaker
strides through the night:

Listening now to the tide in its broad-flung ship-wrecking roar,
Now to the scream of a maddened beach dragged down by the wave,
Walked in a wintry wind by a ghastly glimmer, and found
The shining daffodil dead, and Orion low in his grave.

Its passionate sexuality belies received notions about Tennyson and
Victorian poetry:

She is coming, my own, my sweet,
    Were it ever so airy a tread,
My heart would hear her and beat,
    Were it earth in an earthy bed;
My dust would hear her and beat,
    Had I lain for a century dead;
Would start and tremble under her feet,
    And blossom in purple and red.

Robert Browning (1812–1889) came from a nonconformist
family, so was barred from attending university. But his father was
prosperous and had an extensive library, so Robert was educated at
home and, like Tennyson, did not need to get a job. He fell in love
with Elizabeth Barrett, who was six years older and already well
known as a poet, and in 1846 she eloped with him from her father's

house in Wimpole Street. They settled in Florence. Browning immersed himself in Renaissance art and history, and described Italy as his 'university'.

His favourite poet was John Donne, and like Donne he wrote dramatic monologues – imagined speeches by imagined characters. Often the speakers have twisted, malevolent psyches and betray themselves by their talk. In 'Soliloquy of the Spanish Cloister' the speaker is poisoned by hatred:

> Gr-r-r – there go, my heart's abhorrence!
>   Water your damned flower-pots, do!
> If hate killed men, Brother Lawrence,
>   God's blood, would not mine kill you!

Brother Lawrence, it becomes clear, is blameless, cares for the monastery garden, and grows fruits for all to share. It is the very thought of his virtues that torments his hater. Vice cloaked as religion also inspires 'The Bishop Orders his Tomb at Saint Praxed's Church', where a great Catholic dignitary, nearing death, instructs his sons (which, as a celibate cleric, he should not have) on the glorious memorial they are to build, incorporating:

> Some lump, ah God, of *lapis lazuli*,
> Big as a Jew's head cut off at the nape,
> Blue as a vein o'er the Madonna's breast.

Lascivious and brutal, the similes betray their speaker.

'My Last Duchess' is more complicated and sinister. A nobleman is showing a visitor round his art gallery and draws a curtain to reveal the portrait of a young woman. She was, he explains, his last duchess. Her fault was that she was too nice. She smiled at everyone:

> . . . as if she ranked
> My gift of a nine-hundred-years-old name
> With anybody's gift.

So he had her murdered:

> . . . I gave commands,
> Then all smiles stopped together.

As they leave the gallery he points out another artwork:

> . . . Notice Neptune, though,
> Taming a sea-horse, thought a rarity,
> Which Claus of Innsbruck cast in bronze for me.

This art-lover, we realise, prefers a painted wife to a living one, because a living one has a will of her own. He is drawn to Neptune taming a sea-horse because taming deprives it of its natural vitality – as does casting it in bronze. The mock-modesty of 'thought a rarity' (meaning 'actually unique and priceless') is perfectly in character. How people speak, move, dress and look are vital for Browning's art – even their proneness to catarrh:

> A-babble in the larynx while he laughs,
> As he had fritters deep-down frying there.

That is from *The Ring and the Book*, Browning's epic about a Roman murder case, which shows how conflicting views of an event blur the concept of truth. Not much read now, it is one of the all-time wonders of verbal art.

'Fra Lippo Lippi' is spoken by the fifteenth-century Florentine painter whom Browning saw as, like himself, a pioneer of realism, depicting living people as opposed to the stereotypes of religious art. In the poem, Fra Lippo, arrested by the watch (local police), asks for a bit of chalk or charcoal so that he can make a quick sketch of one of their faces. It will be perfect, he explains, for the oafish brute who is holding up John the Baptist's head by the hair in a painting of the Saint's execution he is working on.

Browning's psychological insight and self-revealing speakers perhaps influenced Arthur Hugh Clough (1819–1861). The son of a Liverpool cotton merchant, he spent his childhood in South Carolina, but returned to England to be educated. For a time he worked as unpaid secretary to his wife's cousin, Florence Nightingale. His best-known poem is the lyric 'Say not the Struggle nought Availeth', which Winston Churchill quoted when broadcasting to the nation in the dark days of the Second World War. But his masterwork is *Amours de Voyage*, a novella in verse, consisting mainly of letters sent home to a friend in England by Claude, a sensitive, supercilious young man holidaying in Rome (a city he finds '*rubbishy*').

He meets, and is attracted by, a young English girl – and she by him. But, partly through ill luck, partly through Claude's indecisiveness, nothing comes of it. Poignant, subtle and incisive, it is surprisingly modern, and gives a vivid impression of street-life in Rome in 1849 when Mazzini and Garibaldi set up their short-lived Roman republic. At the end, Claude determines to be more resolute in future:

> I will look straight out, see things, not try to evade them;
> Fact shall be fact for me, and the Truth the Truth, as ever
> Flexible, changeable, vague, and multiform, and doubtful.

The wry third line suggests that the geological discoveries that so upset Tennyson were part of a wider loss of certainty at the heart of what was, at the time, the greatest empire on earth.

Matthew Arnold (1822–1888) was the son of a famous educational reformer and headmaster of Rugby School (described in Thomas Hughes's 1857 novel, *Tom Brown's School Days*). He was close to Clough at Rugby and Oxford, and when his friend died of malaria in Florence in 1861 he wrote an elegy for him, 'Thyrsis'. Like Arnold's other poem about the countryside around Oxford, 'The Scholar Gipsy', it places happiness in the past, when:

> . . . life ran gaily as the sparkling Thames,
>   Before this strange disease of modern life,
> With its sick hurry, its divided aims.

Arnold was a cultural critic, widely read in several literatures. His tragic poem, 'Sohrab and Rustum', in which a father unknowingly kills his son, is based on an episode in an epic by the Persian poet Firdawsi (940–1020). Tragic, too, 'The Forsaken Merman' is about a mortal mother who has children by a sea-king, but returns to human life, forsaking her sea-family. The little mer-children creep up on land at night and climb on gravestones to peep in at the church window and see their mother praying. But she does not return.

The sadness that permeates Arnold's poetry is most memorably felt in 'Dover Beach', which contemplates the nineteenth century's gradual loss of religious faith. It was probably written in 1851, eight years before the publication of Darwin's *The Origin of Species* was to accelerate the process it laments.

Ah love, let us be true
To one another, for the world which seems
To lie before us like a land of dreams,
So various, so beautiful, so new,
Hath really neither joy, nor love, nor light,
Nor certitude, nor peace, nor help for pain,
And we are here as on a darkling plain,
Swept with confused alarms of struggle and flight,
Where ignorant armies clash by night.

CHAPTER 23

Reform, Resolve and Religion:
Victorian Women Poets
Elizabeth Barrett Browning,
Emily Brontë, Christina Rossetti

Elizabeth Barrett Browning (1806–1861) was a child prodigy. She began writing poetry at four, and at twelve wrote an epic on the Battle of Marathon. She learned Greek and Hebrew, and translated Aeschylus' *Prometheus Bound*.

Her commitment to social justice was unflinching. Her father's wealth came from Jamaican sugar plantations, but she campaigned resolutely against slavery. In her poem 'A Curse for a Nation', an angel commands her to curse those who, like her family, live by exploitation. She pleads that ties of gratitude and blood prevent her, but the angel insists and she writes the curse. When slavery was abolished in Britain's dominions in 1833 her family's fortunes were severely affected.

Her 1842 poem 'The Cry of the Children' was part of a successful campaign to restrict the use of child labour in mines and factories.

She was inspired, too, by Mary Wollstonecraft's *A Vindication of the Rights of Woman*, and in her verse-novel *Aurora Leigh* (1856) her heroine, angered by a male cousin's assertion that women cannot write poetry, goes off to London and earns her living as a poet. This was not fanciful. Aurora's success mirrors Barrett Browning's own. Her poems were acclaimed, and on the death of Wordsworth she, rather than Tennyson, was widely expected to become Poet Laureate.

Feminist critics have revived her reputation after a period of neglect, but some of her poems have never gone out of currency. Sonnet 43 of 'Sonnets from the Portuguese', 'How do I love thee? Let me count the ways', is regularly read at weddings. (The sonnets were not really 'from the Portuguese', but original love poems written by her to Robert. Publishing them, they agreed to conceal their private nature.) Her religious poems (such as 'Speak low to me, my Saviour, low and sweet') are also love poems of a kind. Even Sonnet 43 ends on a religious note:

> . . . if God choose,
> I shall but love thee better after death.

For many, her most powerful poem is 'A Musical Instrument'. It was also her last, and published only after her death. It reads like a critique of almost everything she had written before, or, alternatively, like a defence of her gentler kind of poetry against the cruelty and violence of the male muse:

> What was he doing, the great god Pan,
>   Down in the reeds by the river?
> Spreading ruin and scattering ban,
> Splashing and paddling with hoofs of a goat,
> And breaking the golden lilies afloat
>   With the dragon-fly on the river.
>
> He tore out a reed, the great god Pan,
>   From the deep, cool bed of the river;

The limpid water turbidly ran,
And the broken lilies a-dying lay,
And the dragon-fly had fled away
    Ere he brought it out of the river.

High on the shore sat the great god Pan,
    While turbidly flowed the river,
And hacked and hewed as a great god can
With his hard, bleak steel at the patient reed,
Till there was not a sign of a leaf indeed,
    To prove it fresh from the river.

He cut it short, did the great god Pan,
    (How tall it stood in the river),
Then drew the pith, like the heart of a man,
Steadily from the outside ring,
And notched the poor, dry empty thing
    In holes, as he sat by the river.

'This is the way', laughed the great god Pan,
    (Laughed as he sat by the river),
'The only way, since the gods began
To make sweet music, they could succeed.'
Then, dropping his mouth at a hole in the reed,
    He blew in power by the river.

Sweet, sweet, sweet, O Pan!
    Piercing sweet by the river!
Blinding sweet, O great god Pan!
The sun on the hill forgot to die.
And the lilies revived, and the dragon-fly
    Came back to dream on the river.

Yet half a beast is the great god Pan
    To laugh as he sits by the river,
Making a poet out of a man,

The true gods sigh for the cost and pain,
For the reed which grows nevermore again
  As a reed with the reeds in the river.

Emily Brontë (1818–1848) was the fifth of the six Brontë chil-
dren and grew up with them at Haworth vicarage where her father,
Patrick, was curate. Her mother died when she was three, and two
sisters died in childhood. She briefly attended the school at Cowan
Bridge, described by her sister Charlotte in *Jane Eyre*, and in 1842
she spent a short time with Charlotte at Constantin Heger's school
in Brussels. Heger remarked on her 'stubborn tenacity of will', and
thought 'she should have been a man'. Though she lacked formal
schooling she taught herself to read German and play the piano,
and even tried teaching for a few months, but could not bear the
routine or the homesickness.

The Brontë children led a fantasy life, describing in prose and
verse the histories of two imaginary realms, Angria and Gondal,
with characters based on their brother Branwell's box of toy
soldiers. Some of Emily's seemingly autobiographical poems relate
to Gondal characters. In 1846 Charlotte, Emily and Anne published
their poems in a joint volume. Using male pseudonyms, they enti-
tled it *Poems by Currer, Ellis and Acton Bell*. It is said to have sold
two copies.

Stories told after Emily's death recalled her wildness and her
closeness to nature. She had been known to bring back a fledgling
or young rabbit from walks on the moors, talking to it and confi-
dent that it understood. She was also capable of rage. When her
bull mastiff cross-breed, Keeper, disobeyed her by lying on a white
counterpane, she pummelled the animal so fiercely with her fists
that it was left 'half-blind'. Dying of tuberculosis in the winter of
1848, she refused to take medicine or allow any 'poisoning doctor'
near her.

Her poems express her courage and her religious faith:

No coward soul is mine,
No trembler in the world's storm-troubled sphere,

I see heaven's glories shine,
And faith shines equal, arming me from fear.

Charlotte later said that this was Emily's last poem, but apparently that is not so. Modern critics have accused Charlotte of 'mythologising' Emily, and even rewriting some of her poems. All the same, the personality reflected in the poems is what one would expect from the author of *Wuthering Heights*. The lure of the wild moors and the ache of lost love are persistent:

Cold in the earth, and the deep snow piled above thee,
Far, far, removed, cold in the dreary grave!
Have I forgot, my only Love, to love thee,
Severed at last by Time's all-severing wave?

Now, when alone, do my thoughts no longer hover
Over the mountains, on that northern shore,
Resting their wings where heath and fern leaves cover
Thy noble heart forever, ever more?

The homesickness which overcame her when she was away from Haworth is expressed in 'A Little While' – all the more powerfully because home does not sound particularly attractive:

The mute bird sitting on the stone,
The dark moss dripping from the wall.
The thorn-trees gaunt, the walks o'ergrown,
I love them – how I love them all!

There is, too, a devastating sense of being alone and unloved:

I am the only being whose doom
No tongue would ask, no eye would mourn,
I never caused a thought of gloom,
A smile of joy, since I was born.

But the loneliness is chosen:

> I'll walk where my own nature would be leading,
> It vexes me to choose another guide,
> Where the grey flocks in ferny glens are feeding,
> Where the wild wind blows on the mountain side.

Christina Rossetti (1830–1894) was born into a literary family. Her father was a poet and a political exile from Italy. Her mother's brother was John William Polidori, Byron's friend, who wrote the first vampire novel. Her brother was the Pre-Raphaelite poet and painter Dante Gabriel Rossetti (1828–1882), and Christina was his model for some of his most famous paintings. At fourteen she suffered a nervous breakdown, and later developed a thyroid condition that altered her appearance. She was deeply religious, turning from poetry to devotional prose in her later years. From 1859 to 1870 she worked as a volunteer at a refuge for former prostitutes.

Her masterpiece is 'Goblin Market', published in 1862. It is like no other English poem, lavishly sensuous and technically brilliant, with its intricate, though seemingly simple, variations of line-length, rhyme and rhythm. Guilefully unpretentious, it seems at first like a fairy tale for children. That alone distinguishes it from anything a male Victorian could have written.

It is about two young women, Laura and Lizzie, and a troop of fruit-vending goblins who cry their wares enticingly:

> Come buy, come buy,
> Apples and quinces,
> Lemons and oranges,
> Plump unpecked cherries,
> Melons and raspberries,
> Bloom-down-cheeked peaches,
> Swart-headed mulberries,
> Wild free-born cranberries,
> Crab-apples, dewberries,
> Pine-apples blackberries . . .

So it goes on, a relentless battery of lusciousness. Lizzie warns, 'Their evil gifts would harm us', and on closer inspection the goblins do look sinister. One has a cat's face, another has a tail, one is like a rat, another like a snail. But heedless Laura buys some fruit with a lock of her golden hair, and sucks and sucks the glorious juice, sweeter than honey, stronger than wine.

Lizzie is alarmed. She remembers a friend, Jeanie, who bought the goblin fruit and pined away and died. Sure enough, Laura soon pays for her rashness. Next time the goblins appear, Lizzie can hear their song, but Laura can't, so she can't buy any more fruit. Her withdrawal symptoms are alarming. She dwindles, and her hair turns grey. Brave Lizzie resolves to save her, and tries to buy fruit for Laura with a silver penny. But the goblins insist it must be eaten on the spot, and when she refuses it they beat and scratch her and tear her gown. They also try to force her mouth open, and squash fruit all over her face and neck, drenching her in juice.

This is what clever Lizzie had planned. She runs home to Laura and cries, 'Kiss me, suck my juice . . . Eat me, drink me, love me.' So Laura kisses and sucks, but the juice now tastes bitter and horrible. She falls asleep in a fever, and Lizzie watches over her. In the morning Laura wakes, cured and innocent, with her hair gleaming gold again. Years later, when they are both wives with children of their own, Laura sometimes gathers the little ones together and tells them about the wicked goblins and Lizzie's saving love.

'Goblin Market' has many meanings, but, whatever else, it is obviously a feminist poem, teaching how love between women can save them from the wicked temptations of men, and Lizzie's 'Eat me, drink me, love me' clearly relates love between women to Christ and the bread and wine of the Eucharist. It seems likely, too, that the poem reflects what Rossetti saw and heard at the refuge for former prostitutes.

Rossetti's best-known poem, aside from 'Goblin Market', is entitled simply 'Song':

When I am dead, my dearest,
Sing no sad songs for me,

Plant thou no roses at my head,
Nor shady cypress tree.
Be the green grass above me,
With showers and dewdrops wet;
And if thou wilt, remember,
And if thou wilt, forget.

I shall not see the shadows,
I shall not feel the rain,
I shall not hear the nightingale
Sing on, as if in pain;
And dreaming through the twilight
That doth not rise nor set,
Haply I may remember,
And haply may forget.

Rossetti scholars insist that the doubt in the second stanza is only about whether the soul is conscious between death and the resurrection, and that Rossetti's Christian faith would have forbidden any wider doubt. Non-Christian readers may find the poem speaks to them just as powerfully without that assurance.

CHAPTER 24

American Revolutionaries
WALT WHITMAN, EMILY DICKINSON

The earliest American poets were English immigrants. Among them were the Puritan poet Anne Bradstreet (1612–1672), and another Puritan poet, Edward Taylor (*c.* 1642–1729), whose poems were not discovered and published until the twentieth century. American-born poets included the philosopher and religious thinker Ralph Waldo Emerson (1803–1882), Henry Wadsworth Longfellow (1807–1882), whose tragic epic, *The Song of Hiawatha*, was based on legends of the Ojibwe people, and Edgar Allan Poe (1809–1849). Poe was a many-sided genius. His 'The Murders in the Rue Morgue' was the first detective story, and was published posthumously with other stories of his in *Tales of Mystery & Imagination*. He was also an outstanding critic. Famous among his poems are 'The Raven', and gorgeously mellifluous love poems like 'Annabel Lee' and 'To Helen':

Helen, thy beauty is to me
  Like those Nicean barks of yore,

That gently o'er a perfumed sea,
   The weary, way-worn wanderer bore
   To his own native shore.

But the two American poets who broke all the old moulds were Whitman and Dickinson.

Walt Whitman (1819–1892) grew up in Brooklyn. His family was poor and he was largely self-educated, leaving school at eleven. He was gay, or possibly bisexual, forming intense relationships with men and boys throughout his life, but also claiming he had six illegitimate children. He worked as a typesetter and printer, then a newspaper editor. In the American Civil War he served as a volunteer nurse in an army hospital. He published his poetry collection, *Leaves of Grass*, in 1855, at his own expense. In the preface he describes himself as 'one of the roughs, a kosmos, disorderly, fleshly and sensual'.

The book scandalised some. One critic dismissed it as 'trashy, profane and obscene', and its author as a 'pretentious ass'. But it is now recognised as a foundational text of American literature. Its longest poem, 'Song of Myself', is an epic of the new America, written in long, dynamic lines of free verse that liberate it from traditional stanzas and metrical rules. It is voiced by a giant consciousness that spans the whole continent and all the spaces beyond, and tells its readers that they are part of him:

   I celebrate myself, and sing myself,
   And what I assume you shall assume,
   For every atom belonging to me as good belongs to you.

He remembers passionate love:

   How you settled your head athwart my hips and gently turn'd over
      upon me,
   And parted the shirt from my bosom-bone, and plunged your
      tongue to my bare-stript heart.

But he also weaves into his song, as part of himself, a vast swathe of American life – trappers and Native Americans in the far west, the runaway slave that he succours, 'men that live among cattle and taste of the ocean and woods', a prostitute, new immigrants crowding the wharves. 'Of every hue and caste am I, of every rank and religion.' If this sounds impossible, he does not care:

> I do not trouble my spirit to vindicate itself or be understood,
> I see that the elementary laws never apologize.

Consistency is of no concern to him either:

> Do I contradict myself?
> Very well then I contradict myself,
> (I am large, I contain multitudes.)

He is at one with the sea, 'scooper of storms', and the winds rub their 'soft-tickling genitals' against him. He believes in 'the flesh and the appetites'. 'Copulation is no more rank to me than death is.' The scent of armpits is 'aroma finer than prayer'. His faith is in nature, not logic or learning:

> I believe a leaf of grass is no less than the journey-work of the stars,
> And the pismire is equally perfect, and a grain of sand, and the
>   egg of the wren,
> And the tree-toad is a chef d'oeuvre for the highest,
> And the running blackberry would adorn the parlors of heaven,
> And the narrowest hinge in my hand puts to scorn all machinery,
> And the cow crunching with depress'd head surpasses any statue,
> And a mouse is miracle enough to stagger sextillions of infidels.

He feels that he could happily live with animals:

> They do not sweat and whine about their condition,
> They do not lie awake in the dark and weep for their sins,
> They do not make me sick discussing their duty to God.

He has witnessed everything. He walked 'the old hills of Judaea with the beautiful gentle God by my side'. He has known battles and shipwrecks, martyrdoms and witch-burnings and disasters, and accepts them all:

> All this I swallow, it tastes good, I like it well, it becomes mine,
> I am the man, I suffered, I was there.

At the end (though such a poem could never really end) a hawk swoops by and 'complains of my gab':

> I too am not a bit tamed, I too am untranslatable,
> I sound my barbaric yawp over the roofs of the world.

Almost all Whitman's poems share the dynamism and exuberance of 'Song of Myself' along with its beliefs and its boundless optimism. Addressing his partner in 'A Woman Waits for Me', he hymns the act of sex and its immeasurable results:

> Through you I drain the pent-up rivers of myself,
> In you I wrap a thousand onward years,
> On you I graft the grafts of the best-beloved of me and America,
> The drops I distil upon you shall grow fierce and athletic girls,
>   new artists, musicians and singers.

'Crossing Brooklyn Ferry' (which plied where Brooklyn Bridge is now, and was an everyday trip for Whitman), he feels countless crowds of the future jostling among the passengers:

> I am with you, you men and women of a generation, of ever so many
>   generations hence.

He is the poet of limitlessness, but also of despair, because he knows the self he sings cannot be limited in a song. He is:

Aware now that amid all the blab whose echoes recoil upon me I
    have not once had the least idea who or what I am,
But that before all my arrogant poems the real Me stands yet
    untouch'd, untold, altogether unreach'd.
Withdrawn far, mocking me with mock-congratulatory signs and
    bows,
With peals of distant ironical laughter at every word I have written.

That is from 'As I Ebb'd with the Ocean of Life'. He did not stop
writing poetry, of course, but kept adding to and emending succes-
sive editions of *Leaves of Grass* until his death.

A poem that recalls his experiences as an army nurse is 'The
Wound-dresser':

On, on I go (open doors of time! open hospital doors!)
The crush'd head I dress, (poor crazed hand tear not the bandage
    away,)
The neck of the cavalry man with the bullet through and through
    I examine,
Hard the breathing rattles, quite glazed already the eye, yet life
    struggles hard,
(Come sweet death! be persuaded O beautiful death!
In mercy come quickly.)

On Good Friday, 14 April 1865, as the Civil War was drawing to
a close, Abraham Lincoln was assassinated. Whitman wrote two
elegies for him. The first, 'O Captain, My Captain', is in rhymed
stanzas and relatively conventional. The second, in free verse, 'When
Lilacs Last in the Dooryard Bloom'd', is among his best-known
poems. It does not mention Lincoln, but merges his death with the
deaths of the fallen and with the life that is going on, 'the fields of
spring, and the farmers preparing their crops', the song of the hermit
thrush and the flowering of the lilac.

Emily Dickinson (1830–1886) was extremely unlike Whitman,
except that they both invented a new kind of poetry. She was born

into a prosperous family in Amherst, Massachusetts, where she lived all her life. She attended Amherst Academy and then Mount Holyoake Seminary. Her reading included Wordsworth, *Jane Eyre*, and Shakespeare's works ('Why is any other book needed?' she asked). She was reclusive, tended to wear white clothing, which was thought odd, and scarcely left her bedroom in her later years. She was, however, a keen gardener and botanist and made a large collection of pressed flowers. She said she had 'found my Savior' during a religious revival in Amherst when she was fifteen, but her poems suggest a sceptical intelligence. Emily Brontë's 'No Coward Soul Is Mine', one of her favourite poems, was read at her funeral.

She transcribed her poems (there are about 1,800) into hand-written books, which were discovered only after her death. A selection, edited and altered, was put together by her family in 1890. Her complete poems were not published until 1955.

Many of them are about death, sometimes imagining her own, as in the macabre and ironic:

Because I could not stop for Death –
He kindly stopped for me –

She and Death ride together in a 'Carriage' (actually, we realise, a hearse) until they come to a 'House', which seems just 'a Swelling of the Ground':

Since then – 'tis Centuries – and yet
Feels shorter than the Day
I first surmised the Horses' Heads
Were toward Eternity –

More chillingly specific is 'I heard a Fly buzz – when I died –', where she imagines herself surrounded by mourners, waiting:

For that last onset – when the King
Be witnessed – in the Room –

I willed my Keepsakes – Signed away
What portion of me be
Assignable – and then it was
There interposed a Fly –

With Blue – uncertain – stumbling Buzz –
Between the light – and me –
And then the Windows failed – and then
I could not see to see –

Sometimes the imagined death may be either hers or someone else's, we can't tell which. Nor is it always clear that the imagined death is imagined as actually happening. In this next poem, one of her best-known, some terrible shock has evidently been sustained, leaving the sufferer numbed, but still going through life's routines. It may be that we are to imagine the shock was eventually fatal – or maybe it was 'outlived'.

After great pain, a formal feeling comes –
The Nerves sit ceremonious, like Tombs –
The stiff Heart questions was it He, that bore,
And Yesterday, or Centuries before?

The feet mechanical, go round –
A wooden way
Of Ground, or Air, or Ought –
Regardless grown,
A Quartz contentment, like a stone –

This is the Hour of Lead –
Remembered, if outlived,
As Freezing persons, recollect the Snow –
First – Chill – then Stupor – then the letting go –

Sometimes the last moment of someone else's consciousness, imagined or real, is watched and questioned:

I've seen a Dying Eye
Run round and round a Room –
In search of Something – as it seemed –
Then Cloudier become –
And then – obscure with Fog –
And then – be soldered down
Without disclosing what it be
'Twere blessed to have seen –

What would it have been 'blessed' for the dying eye to have seen?
We can only guess. Doubt is built into her poems.
    But there are joyful poems, too:

The Soul has moments of escape –
When bursting all the doors –
She dances like a Bomb, abroad,
And swings upon the Hours.

Even the joyful poems, though, are often touched with irony and
strangeness, as in 'I taste a liquor never brewed –', where she imag-
ines getting 'inebriate' by drinking dew with the bees and butter-
flies one 'molten Blue' summer day:

Till Seraphs swing their snowy Hats –
And Saints – to windows run –
To see the little Tippler
Leaning against the – Sun –

By which time it is no longer just a poem about a joyful summer day.
    The inner world is her subject. But she can write wonderfully
about the external, everyday world, as this poem about a train shows:

I like to see it lap the Miles –
And lick the Valleys up –
And stop to feed itself at Tanks
And then – prodigious step

Around a Pile of Mountains –
And supercilious peer
In Shanties – by the sides of Roads
And then a Quarry pare

To fit its sides
And crawl between
Complaining all the while
In horrid – hooting stanza –
Then chase itself down Hill –

And neigh like Boanerges –
Then – prompter than a Star
Stop – docile and omnipotent
At its own stable door –

CHAPTER 25

Shaking the Foundations
BAUDELAIRE, MALLARMÉ, VERLAINE, RIMBAUD, VALÉRY, DYLAN THOMAS, EDWARD LEAR, CHARLES DODGSON, SWINBURNE, KATHARINE HARRIS BRADLEY, EDITH EMMA COOPER, CHARLOTTE MEW, OSCAR WILDE

In the closing decades of the nineteenth century European culture began to fragment. There were various reasons. In 1871 the shattering defeat of France in the Franco-Prussian War ominously redrew the power-map of Europe. Throughout the century, industry and commerce had transformed life in cities, and it seemed to many that the arts were being side-lined. Europe's population more than doubled, and people began to complain of crowds and their power. Another development was the spread of education. By 1900, state-sponsored elementary education created mass literacy, which brought with it mass-circulation newspapers and magazines. Writers' reactions varied. Some welcomed the new market for their work. Others despised it.

An early despiser was the French poet Charles Baudelaire (1821–1867). His poems were inspired, to an unusual degree, by hatred of other people. 'The rabble', he complained, 'have defiled the palace of my heart'. He had personal reasons for feeling resentful. He loved opulence and luxury, and considered them his due, regarding democracy as 'absurd'. But his mother and stepfather kept him on a tight budget. As if in revenge, he fashioned himself into a *poète maudit* on a heroic scale – drank, smoked hashish and opium, attempted suicide, and chose as his mistress an illiterate mulatto dancer, Jeanne Duval, his 'black Venus', who treated him with open contempt. In 'The Beatrice' he imagines her laughing and flirting with the 'obscene mob' who mock him and his poems.

His self-pity can pall. In 'Abel and Cain' he likens himself to the race of Cain, crawling in mud and filth. In 'The Denial of Saint Peter', God is a self-satisfied, powerful bourgeois, like Baudelaire's stepfather, pleased with the sobs of the martyrs that float up to him in heaven, and laughing while the executioners drive nails into his son's hands and feet. Yet the same self-pity can produce a poem like 'The Albatross' which tells how sailors, for fun, capture an albatross – 'the prince of the clouds' – and put him on the deck where he hobbles around comically, because 'His giant's wings keep him from walking'.

His love poems revel in sensuality. In 'The Jewels', Jeanne, naked except for her 'sonorous jewellery', reminds him of 'Moorish slave-women in their days of happiness'. He remembers how he watched her try out 'this pose and that', while the light from the log-fire 'flowed like blood over that amber skin'. In 'The Poison' he tells her that neither wine nor opium can rival 'the fearsome marvel of your acid saliva'. Writing to another woman in 'To Her Who is Too Gay', he confesses that he would like, one night, to 'chastise' and 'bruise' her:

And open in your astonished side
A wide, deep wound.

And – O blinding rapture –
Through those new lips,

More vivid and more beautiful,
Infuse my poison into you, my sister.

As its title suggests, his 1857 collection, *Les Fleurs du mal* ('The Flowers of Evil') was meant to cause a rumpus – and did. Poet, publisher and printer were found guilty of offending public decency, and fined. Six poems (including 'The Jewels' and 'To Her Who is Too Gay') were suppressed.

The 'Symbolist' poets saw themselves as followers of Baudelaire, but they are very unlike him and unlike each other. The best known are Stéphane Mallarmé (1842–1898), Paul Verlaine (1844–1896) and Arthur Rimbaud (1854–1891). 'Symbolist' is a misleading label for them. All poets use symbols – Baudelaire's albatross symbolising a poet, for example – but that kind of match-up is not the Symbolists' aim. Their single common purpose was to break away from all previous poetry.

The most astonishing was Rimbaud, who wrote all his poetry by the age of nineteen. The son of an army captain, he was a star pupil at school but ran away to Paris where he met Verlaine, who fell madly in love with him. Deserting his pregnant, seventeen-year-old wife, Verlaine fled with him in 1871 from war-torn Paris to Belgium and eventually London. Their vagabond life together, fuelled by absinthe and hashish, ended when, back in Brussels, Verlaine bought a revolver and shot Rimbaud, wounding him slightly. For this he went to prison for eighteen months. When he came out, he converted to Catholicism, but by this time Rimbaud had given up poetry and gone to Africa where he traded in coffee and guns. He died young from bone cancer.

He explains in his teenage letters that his aim in poetry is to reach a new kind of truth. 'The idea is to reach the unknown by the derangement of all the senses.' Combining different senses (known as 'synaesthesia') produces arresting moments in his poetry, as in a phrase like 'the flowery sweetness of the stars' (from 'Mystique'). But he also abandoned coherent meaning, so that his poems can read like the result of free association – which Freud was developing in Vienna, around the same time, for psychoanalytic purposes.

An example is *Le Bateau ivre* ('The Drunken Boat'), written when he was sixteen. It is spoken by a boat that breaks free when its crew are killed. The poem gets some of its images from Jules Verne's *Twenty-thousand Leagues Under the Sea* (1870), but Rimbaud's boat's visions are worlds away from Verne's popular adventure story:

> I have dreamed of the green night of the dazzled snows, the kiss rising slowly to the eyes of the seas, the circulation of undreamed-of saps, and the yellow-blue awakening of singing phosphorous.

The poet Paul Valéry (1871–1945), author of two profound and searching philosophical poems, *Le Cimetière marin* ('The Graveyard by the Sea') and *La Jeune Parque* ('The Young Fate'), once remarked that 'all known literature is written in the language of common sense – except Rimbaud's'.

Illuminations, generally considered Rimbaud's masterpiece, was written partly while he was with Verlaine in London. Like 'The Drunken Boat', its forty-two prose poems, plus two in free verse, elude rational explanation, and can sometimes seem like nonsense poetry. 'After the Deluge', for example, starts:

> As soon as the idea of the Deluge had subsided,
> A hare stopped in the clover and the swaying flower-bells, and
>   said a prayer to the rainbow through the spider's web.

In his poem *Ars Poetica* ('The Art of Poetry'), often read as a Symbolist manifesto, Verlaine advises incoherence as a poetic principle – 'Let your verse be aimless chance.' He insists, too, that the musical quality of words is more important than their meaning: 'Music first and foremost.' Symbolist poetry often illustrates this, which is maybe why it attracts musicians. Mallarmé's reverie, *L'après-midi d'un faune,* dauntingly difficult and seldom read, inspired Debussy's haunting *Prelude*, which gives pleasure to millions.

Mallarmé's poetic obscurity was deliberate, and he achieved it by tangled grammar and bewildering changes of tense. It provided a barrier against the kind of people who, he said, were fit to read only newspapers. In his poem 'The Windows', he imagines himself, close to death, as an 'angel', wearing his 'dream' as a 'crown', and scornfully rejects 'the man of vulgar spirit', 'wallowing' in happiness, who seeks 'ordure' to feed his wife and children.

Symbolism did not catch on in England or America at the time. T.S. Eliot said later that if he had not read a book about the Symbolists by the English poet Arthur Symons (1865–1945) in 1908 he would never have heard of them. But the great Welsh poet Dylan Thomas (1914–1953) acknowledged Symbolism's influence, dubbing himself 'the Rimbaud of Cwmdonkin Drive'. His bafflingly obscure poems, like 'I see the boys of summer in their ruin' or the 'Altarwise by Owl-light' sonnets, are as near as English-language poetry ever gets to French Symbolism. By contrast, the poems that have won him worldwide acclaim are universally intelligible – among them, 'The Hand that Signed the Paper', 'In My Craft or Sullen Art', 'The Force that through the Green Fuse Drives the Flower', and, most famously, the poem in which he thinks of his father's death:

Do not go gentle into that good night,
Old age should burn and rave at close of day;
Rage, rage against the dying of the light . . .

Thomas said that the poems that most influenced him were the Mother Goose rhymes his parents taught him as a child. The primitive power of nonsense poetry, preserved in nursery rhymes, was harnessed, in the closing decades of the nineteenth century, by two other British writers of genius, Edward Lear (1812–1888) and Charles Dodgson (1832–1898), better known as 'Lewis Carroll'. Both were outsiders. Lear was gay and an epileptic; Dodgson had a weakness for scantily clad little girls. Unlike the Symbolists, they did not use nonsense to baffle but to subvert accepted norms. Lear's wistful 'The Owl and the Pussy Cat' gently mocks happy-ever-after love stories, and Dodgson's 'Jabberwocky' ridicules heroic poetry:

And, as in uffish thought he stood,
The Jabberwock, with eyes of flame,

Came whiffling through the tulgey wood,
  And burbled as it came!

One, two! One, two! And through and through
  The vorpal blade went snicker-snack!
He left it dead, and with its head
  He went galumphing back.

The term used in the British press for advanced foreign writers like the Symbolists was 'decadent'. But in 1880s France decadence was thought of by some as a separate artistic movement, traceable to Baudelaire and Théophile Gautier (1811–1872), the pioneer of 'art for art's sake'. Among the Symbolists, Verlaine embraced the decadence of the late Roman Empire in his poem 'Langueur':

I am the Empire at the end of the decadence,
Watching the great blond barbarians pass,
As I compose indolent acrostics
In a golden style where the languor of the sun dances.

In Britain the *Poems and Ballads* of Algernon Charles Swinburne (1837–1909) were wildly popular, or scandalous, according to your viewpoint. His 'decadent' themes included paganism, in 'Hymn to Proserpine' ('Thou hast conquered, O pale Galilean; the world has grown gray with thy breath'), masochism in 'Dolores, Our Lady of Pain', lesbianism in his poems honouring Sappho, and flagellation in his novel *Lesbia Brandon* (not published till 1952).

Notable among British lesbians were Katharine Harris Bradley (1846–1914) and her niece Edith Emma Cooper (1862–1913). They published under the pseudonym 'Michael Field', and lived together for nearly forty years writing passionate love poems to each other. But as poets they were far outclassed by Charlotte Mew (1869–1928), one of the greatest English women poets, admired by Hardy, Virginia Woolf and Ezra Pound. She always dressed as a man and wore her hair short, but whether she had any sexual experience is unknown. Several of her siblings became insane, and she and her sister renounced marriage for fear of passing on insanity to their children. Depressed after her sister's death she killed herself by drinking Lysol.

Her poems are advanced and original in technique, and profound in feeling. Among the finest are 'Madeleine in Church' and 'The Trees Are Down'. But arguably her masterpiece is 'The Farmer's Bride', spoken by a man about his young wife who is terrified of sex:

> She sleeps up in the attic there
>   Alone, poor maid. 'Tis but a stair
> Betwixt us. Oh! my God! the down,
>   The soft young down of her, the brown,
> The brown of her – her eyes, her hair, her hair!

The foremost British 'decadent', Oscar Wilde (1854–1900), owed his early fame to the D'Oyly Carte comic opera *Patience*, with its brilliant libretto by W.S. Gilbert (1836–1911), which ridiculed decadence. The shock of Wilde's trial and imprisonment sent fear and anger through the gay community. His best-known poem, 'The Ballad of Reading Gaol', was written after his release. During his imprisonment a trooper in the Royal Horse Guards, Charles Wooldridge, was hanged for cutting his common-law wife's throat. This is what the poem refers to in the famous lines:

> Yet each man kills the thing he loves
>   By each let this be heard.
> Some do it with a bitter look,
>   Some with a flattering word.
> The coward does it with a kiss,
>   The brave man with a sword.

CHAPTER 26

New Voices at the End of an Era
HARDY, HOUSMAN, KIPLING, HOPKINS

In the closing years of Victoria's reign – she died in 1901 – four new poets emerged. The oldest, Thomas Hardy (1840–1928), the son of a Dorset stonemason, is best known as a novelist. But he wrote poetry throughout his life, and his first collection (the first of eight) was *Wessex Poems*, published in 1898.

As a poet he is deliberately unconventional. He seems to have realised, earlier than T.S. Eliot or Ezra Pound, that something drastic was needed to renovate English poetry. So he excludes everything pretty and decorous, and his language is a rag-bag of strange words, some from dialect, some his own invention – 'chasmal', 'beneaped', 'fulth', 'stillicide', 'tristfulness' – plus modernisms like 'hydrosphere' and 'wagonette'.

He updates subject-matter too. Many of his poems read like plot-summaries of unwritten Hardy novels – 'A Trampwoman's Tragedy', for example, or the satirical 'The Ruined Maid' (about a 'ruined' woman who is doing very nicely, thank you). The tone of these brief dramatic snatches often reflects Hardy's habitual pessi-mism, and can be desolating, as in 'Neutral Tones':

The smile on your mouth was the deadest thing
Alive enough to have strength to die . . .

They can unfold a whole lifetime in a few words. 'In the Study', for instance, is a little masterpiece of social observation. Ezra Pound said that it showed the benefit of having written twenty novels first.

'The Convergence of the Twain', about the sinking of the *Titanic*, is famous for its fatalism. But some of Hardy's greatest poems voice sorrow at his loss of religious faith. In 'The Darkling Thrush', the bird's song seems to resonate with:

Some blessed Hope, whereof he knew,
    And I was unaware.

In 'The Oxen', the poet recalls a countryside belief that cattle kneel on Christmas Eve to honour Christ's birth, and admits that, if someone invited him to come and see:

I should go with him in the gloom,
Hoping it might be so.

Hardy's marriage to Emma Gifford was not happy, but her death in 1912 shattered him. In 'The Going', he reproaches her for dying without warning:

Never to bid goodbye
Or lip me the softest call . . .

He remembers her, in poems such as 'The Voice', 'Beeny Cliff' and 'At Castle Boterel', as she was when he first loved her, wearing her 'air-blue gown', and with her hair loose in the wind as she rode beside 'the opal and the sapphire of the wandering western sea'. Now he is lonely and haunted:

Thus I; faltering forward.
Leaves around me falling.
Wind oozing thin through the thorn from norward,
    And the woman calling.

Heavy British losses in the Boer War (1880–81) aroused public anger. What Hardy thought of, though, was the common soldiers. In 'Drummer Hodge' he mourns a boy killed, far from his 'Wessex home', in a pointless conflict. In 'The Man He Killed' a soldier thinks how odd war is – he has shot a man dead, yet if they had met in a pub he would have bought him a drink.

But it was Rudyard Kipling (1865–1936) who gave the ordinary soldier a voice. He published *Barrack-room Ballads* in 1892 when, just married, he was living in Vermont with his American wife, Carrie. In the England of his day, soldiers were regarded as the lowest form of life – until they were needed:

I went into a public-'ouse to get a pint o' beer,
The publican 'e up an' sez, 'We serve no red-coats here.'
The girls be'ind the bar they laughed an' giggled fit to die,
I outs into the street again an' to myself sez I:
    O it's Tommy this, an' Tommy that, an' 'Tommy, go away';
    But it's 'Thank you, Mister Atkins', when the band begins to play.

That is from 'Tommy', and the same voice is heard, trenchant and critical, throughout *Barrack-room Ballads*. In 'Danny Deever', the bewildered other-ranks are lined up – '"What are the bugles blowin' for?" said Files-on-Parade' – only to discover it is to see a comrade hanged.

Kipling's Tommy has wisdom, experience, respect for the enemy, a feeling for beauty and romance, and other qualities a private soldier who drops his aitches was not supposed to have:

By the old Moulmein Pagoda, lookin' lazy at the sea,
There's a Burma girl a-settin', and I know she thinks o' me.
For the wind is in the palm-trees, and the temple-bells they say:

'Come you back, you British soldier, come you back to Mandalay!'
    Come you back to Mandalay,
    Where the old Flotilla lay,
    Can't you 'ear their paddles chunkin' from Rangoon to Mandalay?
    On the road to Mandalay
    Where the flyin'-fishes play
    An' the dawn comes up like thunder outer China 'crost the Bay!

That marvellous last line does not make sense except as poetry, and it would not be so good in standard English. In Tommy-speak, 'like thunder' comes across as a wonderful throwaway, not a deliberate poeticism.

For the poet Alison Brackenbury, Kipling is 'poetry's Dickens – an outsider and journalist with an unrivalled ear for sound and speech'. Many of his lines and phrases have entered everyday talk: 'what should they know of England who only England know?'; 'East is East, and West is West, and never the twain shall meet'; 'the female of the species is more deadly than the male'; 'You're a better man than I am, Gunga Din' (that last one is from a poem celebrating a lowly Indian water-bearer who saves a British soldier's life at the cost of his own).

Kipling was an imperialist. But he saw, in 'Recessional', the transience of all empires:

Far-called, our navies melt away;
    On dune and headland sinks the fire;
Lo, all our pomp of yesterday
    Is one with Nineveh and Tyre!
Judge of the Nations, spare us yet,
Lest we forget – lest we forget!

That was written in 1887 for Victoria's Golden Jubilee. A.E. Housman (1859–1936) wrote a poem on the same topic and used it as the preface to his collection, *A Shropshire Lad* (1896). Like Kipling, Housman is on the soldiers' side. To shouts of 'God save the Queen', he replies that men who died fighting for the Queen saved her, not God. His later poem, 'Epitaph on an Army of Mercenaries', is a tribute to the professional soldiers of the British Expeditionary Force, killed stemming the German advance in 1914:

> Their shoulders held the sky suspended;
>   They stood, and earth's foundations stay;
> What God abandoned, these defended,
>   And saved the sum of things for pay.

As a young man Housman suffered two terrible blows. He fell in love at Oxford with a heterosexual oarsman, Moses Jackson, who rebuffed him. At about the same time the examiners in his final exam failed him, though he was the most brilliant classicist of his generation, because he had skipped parts of the syllabus that bored him.

This double injustice seems to have embittered him for life. He loved nature:

> Tell me not here, it needs not saying,
>   What tune the enchantress plays
> In aftermaths of soft September
>   Or under blanching mays,
> For she and I were long acquainted
>   And I knew all her ways.

But he knew that 'heartless, witless nature' cared nothing for him. He expected no favours from God, or 'Whatever brute and black-guard made the world'. Young men ('lads') whose lives and hopes are blighted crowd his poems. In 'To an Athlete Dying Young', the shades in the underworld gather round to gaze at the dead boy's 'early-laurelled head':

> And find unwithered on its curls
> The garland briefer than a girl's.

His poem about Oscar Wilde – 'Oh who is that young sinner with the handcuffs on his wrists?' – bitterly ridicules a society that condemns a man for something that is part of his nature – 'Oh they're taking him to prison for the colour of his hair.'

A professor of classics, he was famed for his rigorous scholarship and savage reviews of colleagues' work. He admired the elegance and economy of Horace, and his own poems use mostly words of one or two syllables. In the whole of *A Shropshire Lad* there are only seven four-syllable words.

He believed that 'Meaning is of the intellect, poetry is not', and that 'Poetry is not the thing said but a way of saying it.' In his own poems, though, the way of saying it often seems inseparable from the meaning. For example, Poem VII in *More Poems*:

Stars, I have seen them fall,
   But when they drop and die
No star is lost at all
   From all the star-sown sky.
The toil of all that be
   Helps not the primal fault;
It rains into the sea,
   And still the sea is salt.

Or Poem XI in *A Shropshire Lad*:

Into my heart an air that kills
   From yon far country blows:
What are those blue remembered hills,
   What spires, what farms are those?

That is the land of lost content,
   I see it shining plain,
The happy highways where I went
   And cannot come again.

The fourth poet who belongs here is Gerard Manley Hopkins (1844–1889). He, too, wrote a new kind of poetry in the 1870s and 1880s, though it was not published until after his death.

He studied classics at Oxford, converted to Roman Catholicism, and joined the Jesuit order. In 1875 he wrote *The Wreck of the Deutschland*, often considered his masterpiece, about a shipwreck in which five Franciscan nuns, fleeing Germany's anti-Catholic laws, drowned. It displayed his revolutionary poetic style, but did not find a publisher. This damaged his confidence. Besides, he equated publishing poetry with the sin of pride. So he died unknown, though now recognised as a great poetic innovator.

His new style included what he called 'sprung rhythm', and was partly a return to the verse-form of *Beowulf*, and partly a reversion, he said, to 'the rhythm of common speech'. By varying the positions of stresses in each line and the number of syllables, he aimed to avoid what he called the 'same and tame' rhythmic effect of normal metre. Disturbed word-order, coinages, archaic words, compound adjectives and chiming vowels and consonants, imitating Welsh *cynghanned* (sound-arrangement), add to the style's strenuous richness. The opening of 'The Windhover' shows its possibilities:

I caught this morning morning's minion, king-
   dom of daylight's dauphin, dapple-dawn-drawn Falcon, in his
     riding
   Of the rolling level underneath him steady air, and striding
High there, how he rung upon the rein of a wimpling wing
In his ecstasy!

The aim of this intensity was religious. He wanted, he explained, to capture the essence (or 'inscape' – a term he took from the medieval theologian, Duns Scotus) of each of God's creatures, and to 'instress' the inscape. So ordinary things become marvels at his touch. A blacksmith with a piece of metal will 'fettle for the great grey drayhorse his bright and battering sandal'. Or:

   A lush-kept, plush-capped sloe
   Will, mouthed to flesh-burst,
   Gush!

The city of Oxford becomes 'Cuckoo-echoing, bell-swarmed, lark-charmed, rook-racked, river-rounded', and:

> A windpuff-bonnet of fawn-froth
> Turns and twindles over the broth
> Of a pool.

Hopkins suffered from depression, and is now thought to have been perhaps bipolar. The poems swerve between rapture, as in 'Glory be to God for Dappled Things', and the terror of 'I wake and feel the fell of dark, not day.' For a time he was deeply in love with a male cousin of his friend Robert Bridges, and guilt about his homosexuality may have added to his torments.

The aim of his style is dynamism – to break open the unseen wonders within everything. But his religion has quieter moments, as in 'Heaven Haven', subtitled 'A Nun Takes the Veil':

> I have desired to go
>   Where springs not fail,
> To fields where flies no sharp and sided hail
>   And a few lilies blow.

> And I have asked to be
>   Where no storms come,
> Where the green swell is in the havens dumb,
>   And out of the swing of the sea.

CHAPTER 27

The Georgian Poets

EDWARD THOMAS AND ROBERT FROST,
RUPERT BROOKE, WALTER DE LA MARE,
W.H. DAVIES, G.K. CHESTERTON, HILAIRE BELLOC,
W.W. GIBSON, ROBERT GRAVES, D.H. LAWRENCE

The Georgian poets were so-called because they emerged as a group around the start of George V's reign in 1910. Some of them used to meet in the Poetry Book Shop in London's Devonshire Street. Other poets who stopped by there included T.S. Eliot. Between 1912 and 1922, five *Georgian Poetry* collections were published.

The Georgians used to be thought of as rather a tepid bunch, sandwiched between Victorianism and modernism. What changed that was the soaring reputation of one of them, Edward Thomas (1878–1917). He almost failed to become a poet at all. 'Me? I couldn't write a poem to save my life,' he told a friend in October 1913. His salvation was meeting a visiting American later that month.

The American was Robert Frost (1874–1963), now known worldwide for poems like 'The Road Not Taken', 'Mending Wall' (a modern riddle poem to which the answer is 'Frost'), and 'Stopping by Woods on a Snowy Evening':

> The woods are lovely, dark and deep,
> But I have promises to keep,
> And miles to go before I sleep,
> And miles to go before I sleep.

After three years in Britain Frost returned to America, settling in New Hampshire, where he worked as a farmer, writing poetry in the early mornings. Influenced by Thomas Hardy, he drew on colloquial speech and rural life, as in 'After Apple-picking', where his instep 'keeps the pressure of a ladder-round', long after work has finished. He was undervalued in America until an English critic, Edward Garnett, hailed him, in the *Atlantic Monthly*, as the most distinctive American poet since Whitman.

One of his greatest poems, 'Out, Out – ', is about a sixteen-year-old boy he knew in New Hampshire who bled to death when his hand was accidentally cut off by a buzz-saw. The title quotation from Shakespeare's *Macbeth* ('Out, out, brief candle') implies (as Joyce's *Ulysses* was to do later) that ordinary people deserve to be commemorated in great literature as much as legendary heroes.

The Edward Thomas that Frost met in October 1913 was desperately unhappy. He had married young and, refusing to get a job, vowed to live by his pen. Drudgery and poverty followed. He churned out potboilers about the English countryside, and bemoaned his existence as a 'doomed hack'. Frost, his neighbour in a Gloucestershire village, urged him to change direction and write poetry ('The Road Not Taken' grew out of these talks). They both wanted poetry to be less 'poetical', and to follow the cadence of ordinary speech. Frost suggested the best place to hear it was behind a door where you could not distinguish the words but only the stresses and intonations.

Thomas's best-loved poem, 'Adlestrop', arose from some jottings he made on a train to Malvern with his wife, Helen, in June 1914 – 'Then we stopped at Adlestrop, thro the willows cd be heard a chain of blackbirds songs at 12.45 & one thrush & no man seen.' In the poem, this becomes:

> And for that minute a blackbird sang
> Close by, and round him, mistier,
> Farther and farther, all the birds
> Of Oxfordshire and Gloucestershire.

Once he had started, poems poured from him. He wrote fifteen in December 1914; sixteen in twenty days in January 1915. Enlisting, he was commissioned in the Royal Artillery in November 1916, volunteered for service in France, and was killed at Arras on Easter Monday 1917. Half a century later, Ted Hughes wrote, 'He is the father of us all.'

As a poet he has a distinctive voice, gentle and regretful. In one poem he compares himself to an aspen tree that, shaken by the wind:

> ceaselessly, unreasonably grieves,
> Or so men think who like a different tree.

That second line – concessive, unconcerned – is typical. He is a quiet poet, but his resigned cadences are unforgettable. Though he writes about the countryside, he is drawn to rain and weeds rather than pastoral landscapes. The noise of a storm – 'This roaring peace', he calls it – seems to have helped him forget himself. Weeds, particularly nettles, had the attraction of not being showy or hopeful:

> As well as any bloom upon a flower
> I like the dust on the nettles, never lost
> Except to prove the sweetness of a shower.

Uncertainty and darkness draw him, and take various shapes in his poems. In 'Old Man' it is the scent of a plant that eludes certainty ('Old Man' is a shrub with grey-green leaves, and a smell like camphor):

    I sniff the spray
And think of nothing; I see and I hear nothing;
Yet seem, too, to be listening, lying in wait
For what I should, yet never can, remember . . .

Or the uncertainty may be about himself. Writing to his wife in 'And You, Helen', he lists the things he would like to give her, ending:

    And myself, too, if I could find
    Where it lay hidden and it proved kind.

He is intrigued by dark spaces, like the crannies in walls, or the setts of badgers ('The most ancient Briton of English beasts'). In 'Swedes' the dark space is a swede-pile. (Swedes are large turnips, and country people used to cover them with earth to save them for winter eating.) In the poem he watches the swedes uncovered:

    They have let in the sun
To the white and gold and purple of curled fronds
Unsunned.

and compares it to the moment when:

    in the Valley of the Tombs of Kings,
A boy crawls down into a Pharaoh's tomb
And, first of Christian men, beholds the mummy,
God and monkey, chariot and throne and vase,
Blue pottery, alabaster and gold.

In 'Lights Out', the lure of the dark outweighs everything else:

There is not any book
Or face of dearest look
That I would not turn from now
To go into the unknown.

In 'Out in the Dark', he says that 'All the universe of sight' is 'weak and little':

Before the might,
If you love it not, of night.

The last line seems to say that if you do love the night, as he does, the universe of sight will be transformed. But that is uncertain too.

Other Georgians, even if not as great as Thomas, wrote memorable poems. Rupert Brooke (1887–1915), the golden boy of the Bloomsbury Group, who once bathed naked with Virginia Woolf (or so she boasted), wrote 'The Old Vicarage, Grantchester' – the house he lived in while at Cambridge:

... Stands the church clock at ten to three,
And is there honey still for tea?

Brooke's 'The Soldier' (1914) solaced many who had lost loved ones during the First World War, and still has power to move:

If I should die, think only this of me,
That there's some corner of a foreign field,
    That is for ever England . . .

He joined the navy and died, on the way to the Gallipoli landings, of blood-poisoning following an insect bite. His grave is in an olive grove on the Greek island of Skyros.

Walter de la Mare (1873–1956) wrote the dreamy 'Nod' and the ghostly 'The Listeners':

'Is there anybody there?' said the Traveller,
Knocking on the moonlit door . . .

Ralph Hodgson (1871–1962) wrote the proto-ecological 'Stupidity Street'. W.H. Davies (1871–1940), poet and tramp, wrote 'Leisure':

What is this life if full of care,
We have no time to stand and stare? . . .

Less famous, but haunting, is Davies's 'The Inquest', where he recalls being on the jury at the inquest into the death of a four-month-old girl:

One eye, that had a yellow lid,
    Was shut – so was the mouth, that smiled;
The left eye open, shining bright –
    It seemed a knowing little child.
For as I looked at that one eye
    It seemed to laugh, and say with glee:
'What caused me death you'll never know,
    Perhaps my mother murdered me' . . .

G.K. Chesterton (1874–1936) wrote 'The Donkey', spoken by the donkey that carried Christ on Palm Sunday, and the gloriously sonorous battle-poem, 'Lepanto'. His friend Hilaire Belloc (1870–1953), another prolific author, wrote 'On a General Election':

The accursed power which stands in Privilege
(And goes with Women, and Champagne and Bridge)
Broke – and Democracy resumed her reign:
(Which goes with Bridge, and Women and Champagne).

W.W. Gibson (1878–1962) wrote 'Flannan Isle' (1912), based on a real-life mystery – the disappearance of three lighthouse keepers.

John Masefield (1878–1967), later Poet Laureate, wrote a notable long poem, 'Dauber' (1913), about an artist working as a sailor (as Masefield did) who is persecuted by brutal shipmates. Despite his famous expression of yearning in 'Sea Fever' – 'I must go down to the sea again, to the lonely sea and the sky', Masefield hated the sea. He hated philistinism too. His poem, 'Cargoes', contrasts the modern world's – and especially the British – contempt for art and beauty with an imagined aesthetic past. The 'Quinquireme of

Nineveh from distant Ophir', and the 'Stately Spanish galleon' of long ago, carried peacocks, gems, spices and other exotica. But the 'Dirty British coaster with a salt-caked smoke-stack' is loaded with pig-lead, ironware and cheap tin trays.

Robert Graves (1895–1985) started as a Georgian, writing his first poems in the summer of 1914, but moved into far other fields. He joined up at the start of the war and was so badly wounded at the Battle of the Somme that he was given up for dead. He omitted his war poems from his later collections because he did not want to be a part of 'the war poetry boom'.

He is famous for his wartime memoir, *Goodbye to All That* (1929), his controversial *The White Goddess* (1948), which traces 'true' poetry to the ancient cult of the Mother Goddess, his historical novel, *I, Claudius* (1934) and later novels, and much else. His poetic reputation now seems less assured. But (though immensely proud of his regiment, the Royal Welch Fusiliers) he wrote a very funny poem about the Welsh, 'Welsh Incident', and a poem about the impossibility of writing poetry, 'The Cool Web', which is arguably his masterpiece.

> Children are dumb to say how hot the day is,
> How hot the scent is of the summer rose,
> How dreadful the black wastes of evening sky,
> How dreadful the tall soldiers drumming by.
>
> But we have speech to chill the angry day,
> And speech to dull the rose's cruel scent,
> We spell away the overhanging night,
> We spell away the soldiers and the fright.
>
> There's a cool web of language winds us in,
> Retreat from too much joy or too much fear . . .

But if, Graves adds, we throw off language's clasp:

> Before our death, instead of when death comes,
> Facing the wide glare of the children's day,

Facing the rose, the dark sky, and the drums,
We shall go mad no doubt and die that way.

The most surprising Georgian poet is D.H. Lawrence (1885–1930), whose poem 'Snake' appears in the fifth collection of *Georgian Poetry*, and outshines everything else. It recalls how, when in Sicily, he saw a snake, 'earth-golden', drinking from the overflow of his water trough. He knew he should kill it. But he felt 'so honoured', watching him sip 'with his straight mouth', and then look around, 'like a god', that he hesitated. When it started to slide back into a hole in the wall, he plucked up courage and threw a log at it. It disappeared like lightning:

> And immediately I regretted it.
> I thought how paltry, how vulgar, what a mean act!
> I despised myself and the voices of my accursed human education.

> And I thought of the albatross,
> And I wished he would come back, my snake.

> For he seemed to me again like a king,
> Like a king in exile, uncrowned in the underworld,
> Now due to be crowned again.

> And so, I missed my chance with one of the lords
> Of life.
> And I have something to expiate:
> A pettiness.

CHAPTER 28

Poetry of the First World War
STADLER, TOLLER, GRENFELL, SASSOON, OWEN, ROSENBERG, GURNEY, COLE, CANNAN, SINCLAIR, McCRAE

Many people, young and old, English and German – including poets – rejoiced at the outbreak of war. 'How the hearts of all poets were on fire when war came,' wrote the German novelist Thomas Mann in 1914, 'It was a cleansing.' In his poem, 'The Awakening', the German poet, Ernst Stadler (1883–1914), imagined that 'bullets raining down' would be 'earth's most glorious sound'. He was killed in October 1914. 'We live in an ecstasy of feeling,' declared another German poet, Ernst Toller (1893–1939). 'I adore war,' the English poet Julian Grenfell (1888–1915) wrote home from France. His poem, 'Into Battle', anticipates the 'joy' of combat. He was killed in May 1915.

Two English poets, Siegfried Sassoon (1886–1967) and Wilfred Owen (1893–1918), challenged this perception of war as glorious and patriotic. Sassoon was from a wealthy Jewish family and spent much of his time pre-war hunting and playing cricket. Owen, the son of a railway worker, scraped a living tutoring. They were both sent back from the trenches suffering from shellshock, and met at Craiglockhart Military Hospital, near Edinburgh. Owen idolised Sassoon and learned from him. The manuscripts of some of his poems, including 'Anthem for Doomed Youth' ('What passing bells for these who die as cattle?') and 'Dulce et Decorum Est' (the ironic title is from an ode by Horace and translates, 'It is sweet and fitting to die for your country'), are annotated in Sassoon's hand.

Sassoon was an embarrassment to the authorities. An outstandingly brave officer, dubbed 'Mad Jack' by his men, and awarded the Military Cross, he wrote an open letter to his Commanding Officer refusing to return to France. The war, he said, had become a war of 'aggression and conquest' not 'defence and liberation'. Sending him to Craiglockhart avoided having to court martial him. In 1918 both men did return to France, and Owen was killed a week before the Armistice.

Sassoon's war poetry is often bitter and satirical. He thinks resentfully of the people back home – the happy theatre-audiences ('I'd like to see a tank come down the stalls'), the 'smug-faced crowds' who cheer when soldiers march past, and the tabloid journalists who glorify war. In 'Fight to a Finish' he imagines his 'grim fusiliers' fixing bayonets and charging a mob of journalists, who 'grunt and squeal'. He resents, too, the incompetence of military high-ups. In 'The General', two Tommies agree that their Commanding Officer is a 'cheery old card' – 'But he did for them both by his plan of attack'.

The horrors of trench warfare are captured in his poems with sickening vividness – how corpses, 'face-downward in the stinking mud, / Wallowed like trodden sand-bags loosely filled', or what it was like to kill German soldiers 'screaming for mercy' and 'green-faced' with terror – 'Our chaps were sticking 'em like pigs'. The folks back home have to be shielded from such truths. In one poem a colonel writes to a mother of the heroic death of her son, when in fact he was a 'cold-footed, useless swine'.

Owen's pre-war poetry was romantic, and his war poetry is less savage than Sassoon's. In the Preface to his poems, which he did not live to see published, he wrote, 'My subject is War, and the pity of

War. / The Poetry is in the pity.' In 'Disabled', he tries to put himself into the mind of a young, crippled soldier in a wheelchair:

Tonight he noticed how the women's eyes
Passed from him to the strong men that were whole.

In 'Futility' ('Move him into the sun'), a soldier has been killed. Trying to get the 'kind old sun' to revive him is hopeless. Pity suffuses both poems.

There is horror, too. The gassed soldier in 'Dulce et Decorum Est', with blood 'gargling from the froth-corrupted lungs', or the terrified, blinded man in 'Sentry', are as searing as anything in Sassoon. They are poems you have to steel yourself to read. 'I try not to remember these things now,' Owen wrote.

The unreason of war, where strangers, who might be friends, kill each other, inspires Owen's great visionary poem 'Strange Meeting'. Movingly, the bayoneted German is made to sound almost apologetic for getting killed: 'I parried, but my hands were loath and cold.' Owen, like Sassoon, was an officer, and in 'Inspection' he writes a poem against himself. On parade he reprimands a soldier for having a spot of dirt on his uniform:

He told me afterwards, the damned spot
Was blood, his own, 'Well, blood is dirt', I said.

The soldier laughs at the absurdity. A technical device Owen uses to convey the war world as absurd or distorted is the use of half-rhymes – rhyming 'knive us' with 'nervous' and 'silent' with 'salient', for example, in the first stanza of 'Exposure'.

Two soldier-poets who served in the ranks were Isaac Rosenberg (1890–1918) and Ivor Gurney (1890–1937). Rosenberg's parents were poor Lithuanian Jewish immigrants, living in London's East End. A gifted artist, he studied at the Slade School of Fine Art. A self-portrait hangs in the National Portrait Gallery. He believed 'Nothing can justify war', but joined up nevertheless because 'I suppose we must get the trouble over'.

He records scenes an officer might not care to – naked soldiers 'yelling in lurid glee' by firelight as they rid themselves of vermin in 'Louse Hunting', for example. In his most famous poem, 'Break of Day in the Trenches', darkness 'crumbles away', and everything looks the same:

> Only a live thing leaps my hand,
> A queer, sardonic rat,
> As I pull the parapet's poppy
> To stick behind my ear.
> Droll rat, they would shoot you if they knew
> Your cosmopolitan sympathies.
> Now you have touched this English hand
> You will do the same to a German
> Soon, no doubt, if it be your pleasure
> To cross the sleeping green between.

The musician and composer Ivor Gurney enlisted as a private and began writing poetry at the front. He hated the 'blither' about war 'written by knaves for fools' in the popular press, and noticed the 'small trifles' of trench life, like Fray Bentos corned beef tins and 'café-au-lait in dugouts on Tommies' cookers' (in 'Laventie'). But these domestic moments only intensify the realities of destruction. His poem 'To His Love' is addressed to the fiancé of his childhood friend Will Harvey. He remembers how the three of them used to walk together in the Gloucestershire countryside, among quietly browsing sheep:

> His body that was so quick
> Is not as you
> Knew it on Severn river
> Under the blue,
> Driving our small boat through.

> You would not know him now,
> But still he died

Nobly, so cover him over
With violets of pride
Purple from Severn side.

Cover him, cover him soon!
And with thick-set
Masses of memoried flowers –
Hide that red wet
Thing I must somehow forget.

Unlike Rosenberg, who was killed in April 1918, Gurney survived the war, but he was wounded and caught in a gas attack, and spent his last fifteen years in psychiatric hospitals.

Until quite recently it was not realised that the war prompted women to write poetry on an unprecedented scale. The librarian Catherine Reilly, whose research revealed this, gathered eighty women poets in her anthology *Scars Upon My Heart*. They came from every kind of social and educational background. Some later became famous, such as Vera Brittain (1893–1970), Eleanor Farjeon (1881–1965), Rose Macaulay (1881–1958), Alice Meynell (1847–1922) and Marie Stopes (1880–1958), the pioneer of birth control, but the majority are little remembered now.

There are American poets as well as English, such as Amy Lowell (1874–1925), Sara Teasdale (1884–1933) and her friend Harriet Monroe (1860–1936), founder of *Poetry*, the first American magazine devoted exclusively to verse.

Grief at the loss of loved ones is their commonest theme, as in 'Afterwards' by Margaret Postgate Cole (1893–1980), which remembers special treats, such as luxurious iced cakes, that they will never share again. Educated at Girton College, Cambridge, Cole was a pacifist and anti-conscription campaigner. Her brother, a conscientious objector, was imprisoned. Active in socialist politics after the war, she married the political theorist G.D.H. Cole. Her most famous war poem, 'The Falling Leaves', is about war's casualties, as is 'The Veteran':

We came upon him sitting in the sun,
Blinded by war, and left. And past the fence
There came young soldiers from the Hand and Flower,
Asking advice of his experience.

And he said this and that, and told them tales,
And all the nightmares of each empty head
Blew into air; then, hearing us beside,
'Poor chaps, how'd they know what it's like?' he said.

And we stood there, and watched him as he sat,
Turning his sockets where they went away,
Until it came to one of us to ask,
'And you're – how old?', 'Nineteen, the third of May.'

Women poets also wrote denunciations of women who tried to
shame non-combatant men by handing them white feathers. Some
record how the war has released women from conventional roles,
making them munitions workers, bus conductors and, of course,
nurses. Several poets, among them the suffragist Cicely Hamilton
(1872–1952), the playwright Winifred Letts (1882–1972) and the
historian Carola Oman (1897–1978), joined the Voluntary Aid
Detachment or the Red Cross.

The society hostess, Millicent, Duchess of Sutherland (1867–1955),
organised an ambulance unit at the siege of Namur, and was trapped
behind enemy lines, but escaped. Volunteers from less grand back-
grounds were M. Winifred Wedgwood (1873–1963), whose poems
include 'The VAD Scullery Maid's Song' and 'Christmas 1916,
Thoughts in a VAD Hospital Kitchen', and Eva Dobell (1867–1963),
whose poems 'Night Duty' and 'Gramophone Tunes' are set in a
hospital ward full of wounded and dying men.

In her poem 'Rouen', May Wedderburn Cannan (1893–1973)
recalls her time in France during the First World War, when she
volunteered for four weeks in a railway canteen for soldiers. She
remembers how trains full of wounded men would arrive daily,

with their 'Woodbines' and their 'gay, heart-breaking mirth'. From an older generation, the suffragette May Sinclair (1865–1946) was already a published novelist when, at the start of the war, she joined an ambulance unit in Belgium. The Germans had taken Antwerp, and the British were retreating, as her poem 'Field Ambulance in Retreat' remembers:

> The straight flagged road breaks into dust, into a thin white cloud,
> About the feet of a regiment driven back league by league,
> Rifles at trail, and standards wrapped in black funeral cloths.
> Unhasting, proud in retreat,
> They smile as the Red Cross Ambulance rushes by.
> (You know nothing of beauty and of desolation who have not seen
> That smile of an army in retreat.)

There is little mention of religion in these poets, though 'Christ in Flanders', by Lucy Whitmell (1869–1917), was read from pulpits and widely anthologised, and sold thousands in pamphlet form.

Poppies, like the one Rosenberg tucks behind his ear, flourished on the battlefields because the artillery tore up the ground, bringing the seeds to light. It was a poem by John McCrae (1872–1918) that led to the poppy being adopted as a symbol for the war and its dead. McCrae was a Canadian and studied medicine at the University of Toronto, then trained as an artilleryman. He served in the Canadian Field Artillery in the Second Boer War (1899–1902) and, as Medical Officer of the 1st Brigade, treated the wounded at the Second Battle of Ypres in 1915. His friend Lt. Alexis Helmer was killed in the battle, and his burial inspired the poem 'In Flanders Fields', first published in the magazine *Punch* in 1915. It is spoken by the dead:

> In Flanders fields the poppies blow
> Between the crosses, row on row,
>   That mark our place, and in the sky

The larks, still bravely singing, fly
Scarce heard amid the guns below.

McCrae died of pneumonia shortly before the end of the war while commanding No. 3 Canadian General Hospital, Boulogne.

CHAPTER 29

The Great Escapist
W.B. YEATS

In the introduction to his *Oxford Book of Modern Verse* (1936) the Irish poet William Butler Yeats (1865–1939) explains that he has entirely omitted the war poets from his selection on the grounds that 'passive suffering is not a theme for poetry. In all the great tragedies, tragedy is a joy to the man who dies; in Greece the tragic chorus danced.' It is hard to imagine a more foolish comment. But for Yeats the war poets were simply too real. His whole life as a poet was an attempt to escape from reality into a world of art, myth and magic.

He spent his early years in Sligo with his mother's family. They belonged to the Protestant Ascendancy (that is, people of English descent who kept apart from the native Irish Catholics). His father was a noted painter, and the family moved to London where Yeats went to school, returning to Dublin to attend art college. Back in London in 1887 he joined the Hermetic Order of the Golden Dawn, a secret society with ceremonial costumes, rituals and a temple to 'Isis-Urania'. The Order studied magic, mysticism, spiritualism, astrology, alchemy and other aspects of the paranormal, and held seances.

A new breakthrough on the paranormal front came later in Yeats's life when, in 1917, at the age of fifty-two, he married twenty-five-year-old Georgie Hyde-Lees. She discovered, after their marriage, that she could contact spirit-guides while in a trance, and could record what they told her in 'automatic' (unconscious) writing. The spirits gave Georgie a complex account of history and human life, based on the twenty-eight phases of the moon, in which intersecting 'gyres' (or cones) represent historical periods of 2,000 years, and humans undergo successive reincarnations. Much of Yeats's later poetry is based on this system, and he published an account of it as *A Vision* in 1925.

Some critics, among them W.H. Auden, have deplored Yeats's belief in magic, judging it unworthy of an intelligent adult. But for Yeats it was indispensable. Magic, he said, was his 'constant study'. 'The mystical life is the Centre of all that I do.'

His marriage to Georgie was a success. They had two children, and she was tolerant of his infidelities. But the great passion of his life lay far in the past. In 1889 when he was twenty-four he fell madly in love with an English heiress, Maud Gonne. It is usual to consider Yeats's later poetry his greatest. But the exuberance of the poems he wrote in his first flush of love for Maud is matchless. In 'The Rose of the World' (published in 1893) he identifies her with Helen of Troy. It was for Maud's 'red lips' that 'Troy passed away in one high funeral gleam'. By the last stanza she has become divine:

Bow down, archangels, in your dim abode,
Before you were, or any hearts to beat,
Weary and kind one lingered by His seat;
He made the world to be a grassy road
Before her wandering feet.

The early poems get some of their magic from the Irish legends and folktales Yeats learned about during his Sligo boyhood. In 'The Song of Wandering Aengus', the poet takes a hazel wand (a symbol of Aengus, the mythical Irish love god), hooks a berry to a fishing line and catches 'a little silver trout'. But when he lays it on the floor it becomes:

> . . . a glimmering girl
> With apple blossom in her hair
> Who called me by my name and ran
> And faded through the brightening air.

So he vows to find her and kiss her and take her hands:

> And walk among long dappled grass,
> And pluck till time and times are done
> The silver apples of the moon,
> The golden apples of the sun.

Critics who complain about his belief in magic fail to see that it gives his imagination this boundless, surreal freedom. Magic frees him from 'time and times', so in 'When You Are Old', Maud, actually twenty-seven, is imagined 'old and grey and full of sleep'. 'Nodding by the fire', she will:

> Murmur, a little sadly, how love fled,
> And paced among the mountains overhead
> And hid his face amid a crowd of stars.

The triumphant escapism of the last two lines is typical of Yeats's early poetry, and they find no match in the French sonnet by Pierre de Ronsard (1524–1585) that Yeats is loosely translating. In Yeats, as not in Ronsard, mythical beings are always ready to take over from the time-bound humans. The natural world is also abundant in these early poems – in luxurious lines like 'When summer gluts the golden bees' (in 'The Madness of King Goll'), or in 'The Lake Isle of Innisfree', with its 'bee-loud glade' and 'evening full of linnet's wings'. But the natural is always on the verge of becoming supernatural, as in 'The Secret Rose', where a woman's hair is of such 'shining loveliness':

That men threshed corn at midnight by a tress,
A little stolen tress.

Without his adoration of Maud Gonne, none of these early poems would have been written. However, she was an ardent Irish Nationalist (that is, she wanted Ireland to be a separate nation, no longer part of Britain), whereas Yeats hated violence and tended to think of the Nationalists as lower class. Though he proposed to Maud several times, she repeatedly turned him down, and in 1903 she married a prominent Nationalist, Major John MacBride. When the marriage broke down he proposed to Maud again, but was again rejected.

Then, in 1916, came the Easter Rising, when armed Nationalists seized buildings in Dublin and proclaimed a republic. The British brutally suppressed the Rising, using overwhelming military might, and executed fifteen 'ringleaders', including MacBride, by firing squad. Yeats wrote 'Easter, 1916' to honour them and Ireland's cause:

I write it out in a verse –
MacDonagh and MacBride,
And Connolly and Pearse
Now and in time to be,
Wherever green is worn,
Are changed, changed utterly,
A terrible beauty is born.

Earlier in the poem Yeats admits that he had thought MacBride 'A drunken vainglorious lout', and had dismissed the other Nationalist leaders with 'a mocking tale or a gibe'. But now they are 'changed utterly'. The poem gives them the grandeur of myth, just as he had given mythical grandeur to Maud Gonne by imagining her Helen of Troy.

Did he really admire the Nationalists? He seems to have been divided. Writing of Maud's Nationalism later, he said that she taught 'ignorant men most violent ways', like 'an old bellows full of angry wind'. He was critical, too, of the leading Nationalist,

Constance Markievicz (née Gore-Booth), a highborn young woman who married a Pole, fought in the Rising, and was sentenced to death, but reprieved and imprisoned. In 'On a Political Prisoner' Yeats accuses her of 'conspiring among the ignorant', and allowing her mind to become:

> . . . a bitter, an abstract thing
> Her thought some popular enmity:
> Blind and leader of the blind
> Drinking the foul ditch where they lie.

Yet these are the heroes that he glorifies in 'Easter, 1916'.

'We make out of the quarrel with others, rhetoric, out of the quarrel with ourselves, poetry,' Yeats wrote. The contrast between his respect for Irish nationhood (he later served as a Senator in the Irish Parliament) and contempt for the Irish populace is part of the quarrel between him and what he called his 'anti-self'. He was proud of his upper-class ancestors, who had (he boasted) provided him with blood that 'has not passed through any huckster's loin' (a 'huckster' was a shop-keeper). He loved the old, ancestral Irish houses, like Coole Park, the home of Lady Gregory, with whom he founded Dublin's Abbey Theatre. He believed, rather fancifully, that the horsey upper-class Anglo-Irish families were comparable to the great aristocratic patrons of Italian Renaissance art. Meanwhile the common people of Dublin earned his contempt because he thought they hated art and culture.

His views became more right-wing as he aged. He saw the European Fascist movements in the 1930s as the triumph of political order over the ignorant mob. He believed Ireland should have a caste system, like India, and that it was 'the caste system that has saved Indian intellect'. These opinions have understandably dismayed many of his admirers. But they could produce powerful poems. 'The Second Coming', one of his greatest, written after the Bolshevik revolution in Russia, is a lament for the collapse of European civilisation:

Turning and turning in the widening gyre
The falcon cannot hear the falconer;
Things fall apart; the centre cannot hold;
Mere anarchy is loosed upon the world,
The blood-dimmed tide is loosed, and everywhere
The ceremony of innocence is drowned;
The best lack all conviction, while the worst
Are full of passionate intensity.

The 'gyre' represents one of the phases of history from *A Vision*. The 'rough beast' in the poem that 'Slouches towards Bethlehem to be born', with its 'lion body and the head of a man', and its gaze 'blank and pitiless as the sun', marks the end of the 2,000-year Christian era in the historical scheme the spirits dictated to Georgie Yeats. But the poem reaches beyond these scholarly details and expresses something universal.

'The Second Coming' shows Yeats making political reality into a myth. He can also take a myth and make it real. Hundreds of poets and artists have alluded to the myth of Leda being raped by Zeus disguised as a swan. But Yeats's 'Leda and the Swan' gives it sensory and psychological realism. He imagines Leda's 'terrified vague fingers' trying to push the 'feathered glory' away – imagines her 'loosening thighs' as she yields, and how she feels the creature's 'strange heart beating' against her. He imagines how Zeus feels, too, and how his 'indifferent beak' lets her drop once he is satisfied.

Raped Leda gave birth to Helen of Troy, which is why, in the poem, 'A shudder in the loins engenders' the fall of Troy and the death of Agamemnon. In Yeats's cyclical version of history the rape of Leda was 'the annunciation that founded Greece', as Mary's annunciation (and Christ's birth – 'The uncontrollable mystery on the bestial floor', as he calls it in 'The Magi') founded the Christian era.

In *A Vision* Yeats selects as his ideal historical place and time Byzantium, around 500 CE, when the emperor Justinian was building the church of St Sophia. There, mosaic-workers and gold-smiths were, he believes, close to the world of spirits. In his poem

'Sailing to Byzantium', they make a bird of 'hammered gold and gold enamelling', and set it on a golden bough to sing. The poem contrasts nature with art. Nature is:

> The young
> In one another's arms, birds in the trees.

Art is the golden bird, and the reader feels the attraction of both. But Yeats declares that, 'once out of nature' (that is, dead), he wants to be the golden bird, not 'any natural thing'.

In the related poem, 'Byzantium', where spirits 'flit' like flames, waiting for reincarnation, nature is disparaged as 'The fury and the mire of human veins', whereas the golden bird of art can:

> scorn aloud
> In glory of changeless metal
> Common bird or petal
> And all complexities of mire or blood.

But nature, in the form of physical love, continued to lure Yeats. He hated growing old, and underwent, at sixty-nine, a surgical operation to restore his sexual potency. In 'Among School Children' he imagines how he must seem an 'old scarecrow', and he dreams of Maud Gonne when she was young and one of the 'daughters of the Swan', like Helen.

When, in one of his last poems, 'The Circus Animals' Desertion', he realises that imagination has failed him, he concludes that art has its source in nature after all, physical and imperfect though nature is:

> I must lie down where all the ladders start
> In the foul rag and bone shop of the heart.

CHAPTER 30

Inventing Modernism
ELIOT, POUND

Thomas Stearns Eliot (1888–1965) was born into a wealthy family related to America's cultural elite. He grew up in St Louis where his father was chief executive of a brick company. A shy, nervous child, he suffered from a congenital double inguinal hernia, wore a truss, and missed out on sports and physical exercise. As a boy he read Wild West stories and wrote poetry influenced by Edward FitzGerald's popular *Rubaiyat of Omar Khayyam*. He seemed an unlikely person to change poetry worldwide.

Financed by his father, he pursued postgraduate study, after Harvard, in Paris, Germany and Italy, returned to Harvard to work on Indian philosophy and Sanskrit, then moved to Oxford in 1914 to write a philosophical thesis about appearance and reality.

In London he met Ezra Pound, Virginia Woolf and other Bloomsbury Group members, and, in 1915, married Vivienne Haigh-Wood, partly to give himself an excuse for not returning to America. It was a disaster. She suffered from various physical and mental problems, and they lived increasingly apart. He later told his friend John Hayward that he had never known sexual pleasure with a woman. They separated in 1933 and she was admitted to a mental hospital in 1938. Eliot never visited her and she died in 1947.

Meanwhile in 1917 he became a British citizen (there was, he told a friend, 'not much worth preserving' in America), and secured a post in Lloyds Bank, working on foreign accounts. In 1925 he became a director of publishers Faber and Gwyer (later Faber and Faber), and in 1927 he converted to the Church of England (he had been brought up among Unitarians, that is Christians who believe that Jesus was a man, not God incarnate). His secretary at Faber and Faber after the war was Valerie Fletcher and they married in 1957.

Of Eliot's longer poems two, *The Love Song of J. Alfred Prufrock* and *Portrait of a Lady* were written before he came to England. He sent the typescript of *The Waste Land* to Pound, who made several alterations before it was published in 1922. *The Hollow Men* appeared in 1925, and *Ash Wednesday*, the first poem written after his conversion, in 1930. *Four Quartets*, also religious in theme, are meditations on time and timelessness. *Burnt Norton* came out in 1936, *East Coker* in 1940, *The Dry Salvages* in 1941 and *Little Gidding*, which refers to Eliot's service as an Air Raid Warden in the London Blitz, in 1942.

Back in 1908 Eliot had read *The Symbolist Movement in Literature* by the English poet Arthur Symons (1865–1945), which has a chapter on the little-known poet Jules Laforgue (1860–1887). It was Laforgue, Eliot said, who taught him that his own experience as an adolescent in an industrial city in America could be material for poetry. Poetic props such as paper roses and geraniums tend to occur in Eliot because they occur in Laforgue.

That is typical of Eliot's poetry. He was a kleptomaniac of other poets' phrases and admits as much at the end of *The Waste Land*: 'These fragments I have shored against my ruins'. In his critical essays the best bits are often the quotations. His poem *Journey of the Magi* (written, he said, after church one Sunday morning 'with the assistance of' half a bottle of gin), builds on a chance phrase he had noticed in a sermon by a seventeenth-century preacher, Lancelot Andrewes.

Eliot is known as a 'difficult' poet. In fact he is not. His ear for linguistic resonance and genius for evocative phrases give immediate pleasure. The 'meaning' of his poems matters less. Asking who Prufrock is visiting, or who the Lady is in *Portrait*, is pointless, because Eliot has withheld this information. Instead he depicts states of feeling, ranging from rapture ('The awful daring of a moment's surrender') to awkwardness and embarrassment, as when the speaker in *Portrait* is so rattled by the Lady's woeful reproaches that he wants to stop having human feelings – 'cry like a parrot, chatter like an ape'. You can read these poems as novellas with most of the humdrum stuff left out but with feelings left in. *The Waste Land* is different only because of its abrupt changes of speaker, location and time.

Eliot wrote of John Donne, 'A thought to Donne was an experience. It modified his sensibility.' Ordinary people, he explained, might be in love, smell cooking, and hear a typewriter, and the three things would not connect. But 'in the mind of the poet those experiences are always forming new wholes'. 'New wholes' are what Eliot writes. Thought combines with emotion and sensation – touch, sight, hearing – to create lines like 'I will show you fear in a handful of dust', or 'I have measured out my life with coffee spoons', or 'Weave, weave the sunlight in your hair', or 'April is the cruellest month', or 'White light folded, sheathed about her, folded', or 'Not with a bang but a whimper'.

He is a master of succinct scene-setting – 'sawdust restaurants with oyster-shells', for example, or 'They are rattling breakfast plates in basement kitchens', or 'Scent of pine and the woodthrush singing through the fog', or 'the torchlight red on sweaty faces', or 'the silken girls bringing sherbet', or 'Whisper of running streams, and winter lightning', or 'Out at sea the dawn wind / Wrinkles and slides.'

In *The Waste Land* even the briefest phrase can mirror the themes of the whole poem. 'Trams and dusty trees', for example, combines aridity and the contrast between mechanised life (the typist with her 'automatic hand') and nature.

For Eliot the poem had more personal origins. Speaking of his first marriage, he said it brought no happiness to Vivienne, and to him 'it brought the state of mind out of which came *The Waste Land*'. It is partly a poem about sexual failure, from the girls deserted by 'the loitering heirs of city directors', to Lill and Albert and the pills Lill took 'to bring it off'.

It can also be read as a meditation on humanity's need for beliefs – from the vegetation myths, referred to in Eliot's notes, to the Buddha's *Fire Sermon* and the Christian mystery:

> where the walls
> Of Magnus Martyr hold
> Inexplicable splendour of Ionian white and gold.

Ezra Pound (1885–1972) came from a humbler background than Eliot. Born in provincial Idaho (he never lost his Idaho accent), he studied Provençal, Old English and Dante at Hamilton College, New York, and resolved that at thirty he would know more about poetry than any man living. He signed on for a PhD at the University of Pennsylvania, but left without finishing. Sacked from an Indiana teaching job, he sailed for Europe in 1908, settling in London.

His early poetry imitated the fake medievalism of Pre-Raphaelites like Dante Gabriel Rossetti (1828–1882). So despite his eagerness to be modern, and his watchword, 'Make it new', he seemed out of date. The inaccuracy of his translations (*The Wanderer* and *The Seafarer* from Old English; the Latin of Propertius in *Homage to Sextus Propertius*) also attracted criticism. But he made many friends in London, including Eliot, and in 1914 married Dorothy Shakespear, the daughter of Yeats's lover Olivia.

Hugh Selwyn Mauberley (1920), a semi-autobiographical poem in eighteen short parts, marked a turning point in his life. It records his struggle to wring 'lilies from the acorn' in a 'half-savage country', and to revive the 'dead art' of poetry. 'Out of key with his time', he feels sterile and meaningless, and denounces commercialism and materialism, personified by the successful novelist Arnold Bennett ('Mr Nixon') in 'the cream-gilded cabin of his steam-yacht'.

The poem also laments the carnage of the First World War, in which several of Pound's friends died, including the sculptor Henri Gaudier-Brzeska. By comparison, the culture he has lived for seems worthless:

There died a myriad,
And of the best, among them,
For an old bitch gone in the teeth,
For a botched civilisation.

Charm, smiling at the good mouth,
Quick eyes gone under earth's lid,

For two gross of broken statues,
For a few thousand battered books.

The poem was Pound's farewell to London. In 1921 he moved with Dorothy to Paris where he made friends among Dadaists and Surrealists and with the Northumbrian poet Basil Bunting (1900–1985), author of the long autobiographical poem, *Briggflatts* (1966). He also began an affair with the concert violinist Olga Rudge. Their child, Mary, was given to a peasant woman to bring up. In 1924 the Pounds moved to Rapallo, in Italy, where their son Omar was born. He, too, was given away to be reared by Dorothy's mother.

In Italy Pound began work on his long, formless, unfinished poem, the *Cantos*, in which he expounded his ideas about economics. He wanted a fairer distribution of wealth, and hated capitalism because it was not truly productive. It just made money out of money, and he wanted to replace money with a currency that could not be hoarded, such as vegetables or natural fabrics. He favoured a system called Social Credit devised by a Scot, Major C.H. Douglas. It would have to be imposed by the state, he realised, and this led him to Fascism.

He met Mussolini in 1933 (recorded in Canto 41) and admired him because he believed he would get things done. He hoped, too, that Hitler's Third Reich would be the natural civiliser of Russia. Blaming the First World War on usury and international capitalism, he became virulently anti-Semitic in the 1930s. During the Second World War he was paid by the Italian government to make hundreds of broadcasts on Rome Radio criticising America and Jews.

Arrested by American forces in 1945, he spent three months in a military camp in Pisa and for some weeks was in an outdoor, 6 foot by 6 foot steel cage, floodlit at night. He suffered a breakdown, recorded in Canto 80. The start of Canto 84 was written on toilet paper while in the cage. The 'Pisan Cantos', 74–84, recall his years in London and Paris and the writers he met, including Yeats.

After his arrest he continued to insist that Hitler was a saint, comparing him to Joan of Arc. Charged with treason, he was judged unfit to stand trial and taken to St Elizabeth's mental hospital, Washington DC, where he wrote Cantos 85–95 ('Section: Rock Drill') and Cantos 96–109 ('Thrones'). Eliot, among others, visited him there. Released in 1958 as incurably insane, he gave the Nazi salute as he left.

By and large the *Cantos* become less poetic as they go on. An early high-spot, in Canto 2, adapts a story from Ovid about Bacchus rescuing a boy from pirates and turning their ship into a magical vine-grove where leopards and panthers roam. Cantos 14 and 15 present a vision of hell populated by bankers, newspaper editors and other villains, from which Pound is liberated by William Blake. Canto 21 explains Social Credit, and Canto 45 – a key canto, Pound said – is a litany against usury ('Usura'), claiming that it destroys art, people and the produce of the earth.

Less immediately appealing are Cantos 52–61, which are based on a twelve-volume history of China by an eighteenth-century French Jesuit. Pound favoured China because he believed it had not allowed usury. Confucius is one of his heroes because Pound regarded him as the figurehead of an orderly, well-governed state, like Mussolini. Cantos 62–71 ('The Adams Cantos') have frequent citations from the writings of John Adams, the Enlightenment lawyer and American president, another hero. Anti-Semitism is mostly limited to Cantos 35, 50 and 52, the last of which contains a virulent attack on the Rothschild family. Cantos 72–3 are in Italian, imitating Dante, and were originally published in Fascist magazines as wartime propaganda.

Some critics, among them Robert Graves, have dismissed the *Cantos* with contempt. But they have proved important for the Beat Generation poets, especially Gary Snyder (b.1930) and Allen Ginsberg (1926–1997).

CHAPTER 31

West Meets East
WALEY, POUND, THE IMAGISTS

The poetry of China and Japan was scarcely known in the English-speaking world until Arthur Waley (1889–1966) published *A Hundred and Seventy Chinese Poems* (1918) and *Japanese Poetry: The Uta* (1919). Waley taught himself to read classical Chinese and Japanese while he was Assistant Keeper of Oriental Prints and Manuscripts at the British Museum. (The Keeper was another poet, Laurence Binyon [1869–1943], whose poem 'For the Fallen' is often read on Remembrance Sundays.)

In addition to his poetry translations, he translated Japanese Noh plays and the eleventh-century *Tale of Genji*, written by Murasaki Shikibu, a lady-in-waiting at the Japanese court, which is famed as the world's first novel. In his introduction to the *Chinese Poems* he observes that, by contrast with Western poets, Chinese poets write about friendship rather than love, and express not passion but tranquillity, reflection and self-analysis. Figures of speech such as metaphors and similes are relatively rare. The need for sex is taken for granted but not considered a reason for emotion. Poems about deserted wives or concubines are common.

All this sounds rather downbeat. But for Western readers with no previous knowledge of Chinese poetry, the variety, subtlety and sophistication – and, of course, the antiquity – of the poems Waley translates are astonishing, and their glimpses of ordinary life communicate instantly across the centuries. On a freezing winter morning, for example, the smell of hot cakes from a baker's shop sets the mouths of passers-by watering (this casual scrap of social observation occurs in a poem written around AD 281 – that is, five centuries before English literature lumbered into being with *Beowulf*).

Reactions to common human ills such as bereavement are vividly recognisable, too. Writing poetry was regarded as a civilised accomplishment that all should possess, so a (to us) surprising number of Chinese poets, both men and women, were powerful and aristocratic. But we can share their feelings, whatever their rank. The Emperor Wu-Ti (157 to 87 BC) writes on the death of his mistress:

The sound of her silk skirt has stopped.
On the marble pavement dust grows.
Her empty room is cold and still.
Fallen leaves are piled against the doors.
    Longing for that lovely lady,
How can I bring my aching heart to rest?

Many Chinese poets were government officials, like the prolific Po Chu-I (AD 772–846), whose poems – about planting flowers, or his dreams, or his baldness – often read like diary entries. Another bureaucrat, and evidently rather browned off, was Su Tung-p'o (AD 1036–1101) who wrote 'On the Birth of a Son':

Families when a child is born
Want it to be intelligent.
I, through intelligence,
Having wrecked my whole life
Only hope the baby will prove

Ignorant and stupid.
Then he will crown a tranquil life
By becoming a Cabinet Minister.

Chinese poems about the natural world tend to be more focused than Western nature poetry. Wang Yi (AD 89–158) venerates a lychee tree, its soft fragrances, its sweet juice, its fruit 'lustrous as a pearl'. His son Wang Yanshou (AD 112–133) records every detail of a small, tail-less ape – how it sniffs and snorts and cocks its 'knowing little ears'. Ouyang Xiu (1007–1072) examines a cicada with similar dedication. A poem every Chinese child is said to know is 'Ode to a Goose' by Luo Binwang (AD 640–684), a child prodigy, who wrote it when he was seven:

Goose, goose, goose,
You bend your neck towards the sky and sing,
Your white feathers float on the emerald water,
Your red feet push the clear waves.

Integration with nature at death is powerfully expressed by Zhang Heng (AD 78–139), an astronomer, mathematician and scientist as well as a poet, who imagines the bones of the Taoist philosopher Chuang Tzu speaking:

I am a wave
In the river of darkness and light,
The maker of all things is my father and mother,
Heaven is my bed and earth my cushion,
The thunder and lightning are my drum and fan,
The sun and moon my candle and my torch,
The Milky Way my moat, the stars my jewels.

Centuries before European Romanticism dawned, Chinese poets were idealising a life spent with nature. Li Po (AD 701–763) envies the hermit Tan Ch'iu his outdoor existence:

My friend is lodging high in the Eastern Range,
Dearly loving the beauty of valleys and hills.
At green Spring he lies in the empty woods,
And is still asleep when the sun shines on high.
A pine-tree wind dusts his sleeves and coat;
A pebbly stream cleans his heart and ears.
I envy you who, far from strife and talk,
Are high-propped on a pillow of blue cloud.

The Tang dynasty (AD 618–907) is reckoned the golden age of Chinese poetry and Li Po, with his friend Du Fu (AD 712–770), was one of its leading lights. But Chinese women excelled as poets too. The most famous was Li Qingzhao (1084–1156) whose renown now reaches out across the solar system. The International Astronomical Union has named two impact craters on the planet Mercury after her.

The *uta* in Waley's translations from Japanese are poems of five lines (also known as *tanka*, meaning short poem, or *waka*) in which the first and third lines contain five sound-units or *on* (loosely translated as 'syllables') and the rest seven. Almost all classical Japanese poetry is written in this form, which contrasts with the range and technical freedom of Chinese poetry.

Japanese *uta* are often about transience and the passing seasons, emphasising the appreciation of fleeting moments of beauty that Buddhism encouraged. But love is treated with more emotion and sensuality than in Chinese:

My morning-sleep hair
I will not comb;
For it has been in contact with
The pillowing hand of my beautiful
Lord.

That is by Hitomaro, one of the greatest Japanese poets, who died around AD 710. An anonymous poem from a tenth-century anthology is equally outspoken:

When dawn comes
With the flicker, flicker
Of sunrise,
How sad the helping each other to
Put on our clothes!

Another anonymous poem from the same anthology makes higher claims:

Can even the God of Thunder
Whose foot-fall resounds
In the plains of the sky
Put asunder
Those whom love joins?

The *uta* form, though brief, is capable of great tenderness, as in the poem on the death of his son by the soldier-poet Otomo no Tabito (665–731):

Because he is young,
And will not know the way to go,
Would I could bribe
The messenger of the Underworld,
That on his shoulders he might carry him!

In time the five-line *uta* contracted to three, and the *haiku* became the standard metre of the seventeenth and eighteenth centuries. Like much oriental poetry it is, Waley points out, almost impossible to translate into Western languages, not only because of fundamental linguistic differences, but also because calligraphy – the beauty of the pen-strokes or brushwork – was historically an important part of the Japanese poem and cannot be reproduced in Western print-culture. In the *Tale of Genji*, it is only when Genji has taught his future bride calligraphy that he marries her.

A typical *haiku* is a three-line observation of a moment in nature, in which the first and last lines have five sound-units and the

middle line seven. It is elusive and elliptical, avoiding abstract state-
ments and direct expressions of personal emotion, and implying
everything by images and the order of images. The most famous
haiku poet was Matsuo Basho (1644–1694). A bare, literal transla-
tion of his best-known poem (often used by Japanese when they try
to explain the niceties of *haiku* to Westerners) might read:

> Old pond,
> Frog jumps in,
> Water's sound.

Apart from Waley, the best-known English-language poet who
translated Chinese and Japanese poetry was Ezra Pound. In fact he
knew no Chinese when he published translations of fifteen Chinese
poems in *Cathay* (1915). But he worked from papers given him by
the American orientalist Ernest Fenollosa's widow. Some critics
familiar with Chinese praise *Cathay*. Others regard it as a kind of
colonial project, imposing Western meaning on Asian culture.
Typical of its indirectness is Li Po's 'The Jewel Stairs' Grievance',
which Pound renders:

> The jewelled steps are already quite white with dew.
> It is so late that the dew soaks my gauze stockings,
> And I let down the crystal curtain
> And watch the moon through the clear autumn.

Though it is not stated, we can deduce that the woman is a court
lady, and waiting for a faithless lover, who has no excuse for not
coming since it is a clear autumn night. Pound says in a note that the
poem was especially prized because she utters no direct reproach.

Pound did not know any Japanese either, but his attempt at an
English *haiku*, 'In a Station of the Metro', published in 1913, has
been hailed as the first Imagist poem:

> The apparition of these faces in the crowd
> Petals on a wet, black bough.

The idea for it came to him, he said, when he got out of the Paris underground at Concorde and saw, in the jostle, beautiful faces. He worked at it for a year, gradually reducing it from thirty lines to ten then to two.

The aims behind Imagism were brevity, the exclusion of superfluous words and abstractions, and concentration on 'the thing', whether subjective or objective. According to one story, Pound, the American Hilda Doolittle (1886–1961), who had come to London from Philadelphia in 1911, and the English poet Richard Aldington (1892–1962), whom Doolittle married in 1913, thought up Imagism one afternoon in 1912 in the British Museum tea room.

In reality, though, the inventor of Imagism was Thomas Ernest Hulme (1883–1917) who had the distinction of being thrown out of Cambridge University twice, once for rowdy behaviour on Boat Race night and the second time for having an affair with a girl at the exclusive boarding school, Roedean. After that he travelled, learned languages, became interested in philosophy, and published the first Imagist poems in an anthology in 1909. 'Autumn' was one of them:

A touch of cold in the Autumn night –
I walked abroad,
And saw the ruddy moon lean over a hedge
Like a red-faced farmer.
I did not stop to speak, but nodded,
And round about were the wistful stars
With white faces like town children.

As a poet he recommended 'dry hardness' and rejected Romanticism as 'spilt religion'. He joined up in 1914, served as an artillery officer and was killed in 1917.

Pound's anthology, *Des Imagistes* (1914), does not include Hulme, nor, despite its title, any French writers. But it has poems by Pound himself, Aldington and Doolittle (who published under the name H.D.), a poem by James Joyce ('I Hear an Army'), which seems unrelated to Imagism, and a poem by the wealthy American Amy

Lowell (1874–1925) who tried unsuccessfully to keep Imagism alive after Pound had broken ranks and joined Wyndham Lewis's (equally short-lived) Vorticist movement.

An outstanding poet in *Des Imagistes*, now almost unknown, is Frank Stuart Flint (1885–1960). Born in Islington, the son of a commercial traveller, he left school at thirteen but made himself into an authority on modern French poetry. He has five poems in *Des Imagistes*, among them 'The Swan':

Under the lily shadow
And the gold
And the blue and mauve
That the whin and the lilac
Pour down on the water,
The fishes quiver.

Over the green cold leaves
And the rippled silver
And the tarnished copper
Of its neck and beak,
Toward the deep black water
Beneath the arches,
The swan floats slowly.

Into the dark of the arch the swan floats
And into the black depth of my sorrow
It bears a white rose of flame.

Flint abandoned poetry in the 1930s, and had a distinguished career in the Statistics Division of the Ministry of Labour. The year 1929 saw the beginning of the Great Depression and Flint remarked, wryly, that the proper study of mankind was, for the time being, economics.

CHAPTER 32

American Modernists
WALLACE STEVENS, HART CRANE, WILLIAM CARLOS WILLIAMS, ESTHER POPEL, HELENE JOHNSON, ALICE DUNBAR-NELSON, JESSIE REDMON FAUSET, ANGELINA WELD GRIMKÉ, CLAUDE MCKAY, LANGSTON HUGHES

Eliot's greatness was a problem for American poets. He had renounced America and opted to become a European. Should they follow suit? Different American modernists responded differently, but none followed Eliot's example.

Wallace Stevens (1879–1955) was the son of a prosperous lawyer and spent most of his life working as an executive for an insurance company. He did not publish his first poetry collection, *Harmonium*, until 1923, the year after Eliot's *The Waste Land*. It included 'Bantams in Pinewoods', which has been read as a declaration of independence for American poetry, directed against Eliot (the 'Damned universal cock'). Whereas *The Waste Land* values life's spiritual dimension, Stevens' poetry rejects spirituality. In 'Sunday Morning' (which the critic Yvor Winters called 'the greatest American poem of the twentieth century', and Stevens described as 'simply an expression of paganism'), a woman sits at home, with coffee and oranges, dreaming in the sun instead of going to church – or, as the poem puts it, instead of going to:

> silent Palestine,
> Dominion of the blood and sepulchre.

Stevens dismissed belief in God, and believed that poetry could take its place as a redemptive force.

His great theme is the imagination, which, for him, makes the world, and makes it a marvel not a waste land. He hymns:

> The magnificent cause of being,
> The imagination, the one reality
> In this imagined world.

As he sees it, the 'soul' is composed of 'the external world', and the external world is created by the imagination. He came to realise that:

> I was the world in which I walked, and what I saw
> Or heard or felt came not but from myself,
> And there I found myself more truly and more strange.

The imagination creates a different world for each individual. Twenty men crossing a bridge into a village:

> Are twenty men crossing twenty bridges
> Into twenty villages.

In the poem 'To a High-toned Old Christian Woman' he argues that religion and morality come from the imagination like everything else. The imagination also allows the poet to find beauty in ordinary or repulsive things:

The hair of my blonde
Is dazzling
As the spittle of cows
Threading the wind.

Many of Stevens' poems are baffling. You cannot tell who is speaking or to whom or what about. The titles, too, often seem meaningless, and some critics think them jokes at the expense of modernism's pretentiousness. His poetry's obscurity seems to result from his fidelity to the imagination. For, given that the imagination does not need to be intelligible, it follows that poetry does not need to be either (except, of course, that poetry uses words, each of which has an intelligible meaning). This may be what Stevens meant when he wrote in 'Man Carrying Thing', 'The poem must resist the intelligence / Almost successfully'.

So, for example, 'The only emperor is the emperor of ice-cream' (probably Stevens' most famous line) is unintelligible, though composed of intelligible words. Its gain is that it puts 'emperor' and 'ice-cream' together as no one has before, and so opens a new vista for the imagination. Stevens writes many poems that are, in this way, wild new jaunts for the imagination. 'Exposition of the Contents of a Cab', for instance, imagines a 'negress' in a golden sedan, 'Thridding the squawkiest jungle', wearing a 'breech-cloth' of 'topaz and ruby' and accompanied by 'seven white dogs'.

Another poet who felt himself caught in Eliot's backwash was Hart Crane (1899–1932). Born in Ohio, the son of a man who made a fortune out of candy bars, he dropped out of high school when his parents' marriage crashed. Moving to New York, he fell in love, in 1923, with Emil Opffer, a Danish merchant marine. For a while he found a home with the Opffer family in Brooklyn Heights. From his room he could see Brooklyn Bridge and it was this view that inspired him to write his 'epic', The Bridge (actually fifteen lyric poems of various lengths and subjects). Begun in 1923 and published in 1930, it was meant as 'a mystical synthesis of America', looking back to Whitman's Leaves of Grass, and countering the despair of The Waste Land.

He moved to Paris in 1929 and, on a visit to Marseilles, looking for sex, he got drunk, was arrested, and badly beaten by the police. The poor reviews of *The Bridge* added to his sense of failure, and he began to drink heavily. In Mexico from 1931 to 1932 he had an affair with Peggy Cowley, wife of the writer Malcolm Cowley, his only recorded heterosexual relationship. On the voyage back to New York from Mexico, he was beaten up after making sexual advances to a crew member, and jumped overboard. His body was never found.

He says in his letters that the principle behind his poetry is 'the logic of metaphor', which seems to mean that the metaphoric meanings of a word matter more than its literal meaning. There is a simple example in his poem 'Carrier Letter':

My hands have not touched water since your hands,
No: nor my lips freed laughter since 'farewell',
And with the day distance again expands
Between us, voiceless as an uncoiled shell.

Yet – much follows, much endures . . . Trust birds alone:
A dove's wings clung about my heart last night
With surging gentleness, and the blue stone
Set in the tryst-ring has but worn more bright.

The dove in the second stanza is not literally a dove, but stands for the associations of the word 'dove' – softness, hope, peace and so on. In the love poem 'Voyages', written for Emil, and regarded as one of his greatest poems, and also in *The Bridge*, this non-literal use of words is persistent, and can seem, at first sight, like nonsense. The way to read it, it seems, is to pay attention only to the meta-phorical or associational meanings of words while ignoring their literal meanings. This is difficult, but easier if you read very quickly, and aloud.

William Carlos Williams (1883–1963) was born in Rutherford, New Jersey. His father was English, his mother a Puerto Rican painter who passed her love of visual art on to her son. Graduating from the University of Pennsylvania medical school (where he met

Ezra Pound), he became head of paediatrics at a hospital in Passaic, New Jersey.

Through Pound he met the Imagists, and his poem 'The Red Wheelbarrow', published in his collection *Spring and All* (1922), shows their influence:

> so much depends
> upon
>
> a red wheel
> barrow
>
> glazed with rain
> water
>
> beside the white
> chickens

Equally well known is 'This Is Just to Say':

> I have eaten
> the plums
> that were in
> the icebox
>
> and which
> you were probably
> saving
> for breakfast
>
> Forgive me
> they were delicious
> so sweet
> and so cold

It was possibly based on a note his wife Florence left for him on the breakfast table one morning.

The 1922 publication of *The Waste Land* was a shock. But he rebelled against Eliot's erudite allusions and European elitism, preferring colloquial American idiom and poetry that was rooted in the place that had brought it into being. This was his aim in *Paterson*, published in five volumes from 1946 to 1958. It centres on the city of Paterson, New Jersey, and was inspired by James Joyce's *Ulysses* with its multi-faceted depiction of Dublin.

Paterson is part poem, part 'collage', meaning pieces of other works stuck together (from the French *coller*, to stick). It contains, for example, sections from Allen Ginsberg's letters (in 1956 Williams wrote the introduction to Ginsberg's manifesto of the Beat Generation, *Howl and Other Poems*). Williams dismissed Hart Crane's *The Bridge* as a regression to the poetry of the French Symbolists, which he deplored, and which, he thought, reached its regrettable climax in T.S. Eliot. He distrusted abstraction, and believed that ideas must be rooted in concrete realities. To gather material for *Paterson*, he said, he had walked around the streets and gone to the park on Sundays in summer and watched what people did and made it part of the poem.

Williams was a social critic, not just an observer. The mindlessness of a happy American crowd, which can quickly turn to racism, is his target in 'At the Ball Game'. In 'The Yachts', it is the mega-wealth of magnates like J.P. Morgan and the Vanderbilts, whose graceful craft compete in the America's Cup yacht races, but, in the poem, ruthlessly careen over human bodies. More cheerfully, 'To a Poor Old Woman' shares the relish of a woman on the sidewalk munching plums from a paper bag.

The contrast between these three white American modernists and their contemporaries, the black poets of the Harlem Renaissance, is extreme. After the First World War many black Americans emigrated to Harlem, a northern suburb of New York, to escape the institutionalised racism of the south. Others came from the Caribbean. The cultural movement they created was unprecedented in American history. It embraced – besides poetry – drama, fiction, music, fashion in clothes and a mix of religious beliefs: Judaism, Christianity and Islam in various forms, as well as voodoo from Jamaica and Haiti, as studied by the black woman anthropologist Zora Neale Hurston (1891–1960).

The Renaissance was ahead of mainstream American culture in promoting feminism and other forms of sexual liberation. The number of black women writers involved was remarkable. Not all were poets, but they included Esther Popel (1896–1958), whose poem 'Flag Salute' was a bitter response to a 1933 lynching:

> . . . They dragged him naked
> Through the muddy streets,
> A feeble-minded black boy!
> And the charge? Supposed assault
> Upon an aged woman . . .

Also famous was 'Bottled' by Helene Johnson (1906–1995), which is about how Western dress diminishes the majesty of the African-American male. The poet watches a black man dancing for joy in the street, and imagines him:

> . . . dancin' black and naked and gleaming.
> And he'd have rings in his ears and on his nose,
> And bracelets and necklaces of elephants' teeth . . .

The political activist Alice Dunbar-Nelson (1875–1935), daughter of an ex-slave and a white seaman, wrote essays exploring the mixed-race dilemma and the role of black women in the workforce and education. The novelist Jessie Redmon Fauset (1882–1961) became literary editor of the magazine *The Crisis*, and promoted work that gave a realistic representation of the African-American community. The dramatist Angelina Weld Grimké (1880–1958), wrote an anti-lynching play *Rachel* (1920), for the National Association for the Advancement of Colored People, which was praised (by the NAACP) as 'the first attempt to use the stage for race propaganda'.

A pioneer among male Harlem Renaissance poets was the Jamaican Claude McKay (1889–1948) whose 1919 poem, 'If We

Must Die', challenged white oppression (and used the sonnet form, regarded by white modernists as old hat). The modish side of modernism cut no ice with the Harlem poets. Unlike Wallace Stevens, they did not regard the world as imaginary, but knew it to be real and unjust. Nor did they pursue obscurity, but wrote to be understood.

The greatest male poet of the movement, Langston Hughes (1902–1967), identified with exploited black people, defending their right to express 'our individual dark-skinned selves without fear or shame'. His first published poem, 'The Negro Speaks of Rivers' (1920), glorifies the black past:

> . . . I bathed in the Euphrates when dawns were young.
> I built my hut near the Congo and it lulled me to sleep.
> I looked upon the Nile and raised the pyramids above it . . .

> I've known rivers:
> Ancient, dusky rivers.

> My soul has grown deep like the rivers.

Hughes writes in several voices, including 'Negro dialect', or Ebonics, and 'jazz-poetry'. In 'I, Too', for some his greatest poem, the speaker has the power of prophecy:

> I, too, sing America.

> I am the darker brother.
> They send me to eat in the kitchen
> When company comes,
> But I laugh,
> And eat well,
> And grow strong.

> Tomorrow,
> I'll be at the table

When company comes.
Nobody'll dare
Say to me,
'Eat in the kitchen,'
Then.

Besides,
They'll see how beautiful I am
And be ashamed –

I, too, am America.

CHAPTER 33

Getting Over Modernism
Marianne Moore and Elizabeth Bishop

Marianne Moore and Elizabeth Bishop were highly individual poets and they steered modernism in new directions. Both wrote poems that, though unmistakably modern, have left the obscurities of modernism behind.

The older of the two, Marianne Moore (1887–1972), was strongly influenced by her maternal grandfather, a Presbyterian pastor, and grew up believing that it was not possible to live without a religious faith. She and her brother, who became a naval chaplain, were brought up by their mother (her father, an engineer, was admitted to a mental hospital before her birth). After graduating from Bryn Mawr, she devoted herself to caring for her mother. They were hard up, and lived in cramped apartments, often sharing a bed.

Apart from a brief infatuation at college with a niece of Henry James, there is no record of Moore being sexually attracted to anyone. Her satirical poem 'Marriage' is addressed to a man who had taken an unwanted romantic interest in her, and remarks:

> . . . Men are monopolists
> of 'stars, garters, buttons
> and other shining baubles' –
> unfit to be the guardians
> of another person's happiness.

In 1918 she and her mother moved from Carlisle, Pennsylvania, to New York's Greenwich Village, where she edited the literary journal *The Dial* and met avant-garde writers, including Ezra Pound, William Carlos Williams and Wallace Stevens. Continuing to care for her ailing mother, she moved to Brooklyn in 1929, where their basement flat was so small they had to eat meals perched on the bath.

Her mother's death in 1947 left her grief-stricken. After a long period of mourning she moved back to Manhattan in 1965, and became a much-loved Greenwich Village eccentric, conspicuous in her cloak and tricorn hat, a keen admirer of Muhammad Ali, and a fan of the Brooklyn Dodgers – later of the New York Yankees. Over her lifetime her poetry won virtually all of America's literary prizes.

Caring for her mother made her feel confined and resentful, and this is voiced indirectly in her poems, some of which subtly mock her mother's pieties. Entrapment is a persistent theme. In 'A Grave' the sea is a deadly trap in which:

> things are bound to sink –
> in which if they turn and twist, it is neither with volition nor
> consciousness.

Her poems often feature small creatures in cramped or menacing surroundings. A pangolin, for example, is a kind of anteater. It is covered in scales, and when threatened it curls in a ball, resembling (in Moore's poem 'The Pangolin') an 'ant- and stone-swallowing uninjurable / artichoke'.

Moore's wonder at nature's power to survive embraces plants as well as animals. Her poem 'Nevertheless' features a prickly-pear leaf, caught on barbed wire that sends down a shoot to take root in the earth 'two feet below'. She applauds its courage – a moral quality she recognises in other plants:

What is there

like fortitude! What sap
went through that little thread
to make the cherry red!

'An Octopus', her longest and most magnificent poem, is entirely free of modernist obscurity and centres on Mount Rainier, an extinct volcano in Washington's Cascade Range. Moore sees the mountain, surrounded by glaciers, as resembling an octopus and its tentacles. The poem celebrates the trees – fir, larch and spruce – and the diversity of animals – bears, elks, deer, wolves, goats, marmots, wild ponies, 'thoughtful beavers', 'the exacting porcupine' – that survive in this world of ice. The mountain's rocks and ice-fields seem alive too. The poem includes quotations from National Parks Service publications and other factual documents, and this kind of collage was common with Moore. Her poems pluck quotations from many real-life sources, perhaps illustrating her famous advice that poets should create 'imaginary gardens with real toads in them'.

That advice is given in her poem 'Poetry', which also includes 'the bat holding on upside down', and other examples of animal survival. At its start, 'Poetry' seems dismissive of poetry altogether:

I, too, dislike it: there are things that are important beyond all this
    fiddle.
    Reading it, however, with a perfect contempt for it, one
        discovers in
    it, after all, a place for the genuine.

The poem distrusts 'high sounding interpretations', and declares that:

we
do not admire what
we cannot understand . . .

All the same, Moore's poems, including this one, can be very hard to understand, and she seems to have wanted to simplify them. As time went on she ruthlessly cut and discarded. By 1967 she had reduced 'Poetry' to just three lines, and other poems were similarly shortened.

Disguise, admired in the pangolin, was something she practised herself. Some of her poems are based on an exact syllable-count in every line, repeated in every stanza. 'Poetry', for example, has lines of 19, 19, 11, 5, 9 and 17 syllables in each stanza. Keeping to the exact syllable-count means that she has sometimes to divide words in the middle – one part of the word at the end of one line, the rest at the start of the next. Syllabic verse was not her invention. It had been used by English-language poets before. But readers generally do not count syllables, so they do not notice what Moore is doing, which means that her disguise has worked.

One of her most loved poems, 'The Steeple Jack', describes a peaceful New England seaside town, where you can see a 'twenty-five pound lobster' and fishing nets hung out to dry. The trees and flowers are covered in fog so they seem like a tropical forest. There are snapdragons and foxgloves, morning glories trained on fishing twine by the back doors, sunflowers, daisies, petunias, poppies and black sweet peas. A 'diffident' little newt, spotted with white 'pin-dots' on his black stripes, also appears. It all seems – and is – far away from the usual conundrums of modernist poetry.

But there is also something oblique about the poem that marks it as modern. The only human characters are a mysterious college student named Ambrose, who sits on a hillside reading, and a steeplejack, with a sign giving his name – C.J. Poole – and a red and white sign saying 'Danger'. He is at work on the church spire, letting down a rope 'as a spider spins a thread', and gilding the star on the top of the steeple, which 'stands for hope'. Critics have offered many 'high sounding interpretations' of 'The Steeple

Jack'. But it succeeds because it remains subtly elusive, as well as beautiful.

Elizabeth Bishop (1911–1979) was a protégée of Marianne Moore's but a very different kind of person. Because of her father's early death and her mother's mental illness, she lived as a child with her grandparents in rural Nova Scotia. An inheritance from her father allowed her to travel widely, and after graduating at Vassar she spent half her life outside the USA, first in France with Louise Crane and then in Brazil, where she bought a house and lived for fifteen years with another lover, Lota Soares.

Friends described Bishop as 'very soignée', 'always going to the hairdresser'. She 'loved clothes' and had a kind of 'English' elegance and wit, a love of laughter and of domestic pleasure. She was a singer of hymns, played the harpsichord, and counted among her favourite poets George Herbert and Gerard Manley Hopkins. 'I think we are still barbarians, barbarians who commit a hundred indecencies and cruelties every day of our lives', she wrote, but she believed we should be joyful, 'even giddy', in spite of it, to make life 'endurable'. She confessed to hating 'the oh-the-pain-of-it-all poems' of Emily Dickinson.

For a major American poet she had a small output, barely a hundred poems. But she has a wider range of tone and feeling than any other modernist, even Eliot. In 'First Death in Nova Scotia' and 'In the Waiting Room' she writes witty, engaging poems about the irreverence and incomprehension with which children view the adult world, based on incidents in her own childhood. Wit is prominent, too, in 'The Man-moth', a kind of nonsense poem, but darker than Victorian nonsense poetry and inspired, she explained, by a newspaper misprint for 'mammoth'. Her man-moth is a lonely, bewildered, nocturnal creature, who thinks the moon is a hole in the sky he can climb through, and who weeps one tear, 'his only possession, like the bee's sting'.

Feeling for the non-human runs deep in her poetry. In 'The Fish' she examines a caught fish in exacting detail – its barnacled skin, five pieces of old fish-line, with their big hooks, 'grown firmly in his mouth'. She imagines its 'coarse white flesh / packed in like feathers'. All the while, she keeps us aware, it is breathing in 'the terrible oxygen' through its 'frightening gills'. So when she lets it go at the end you feel real relief. 'The Armadillo', written in Brazil, is about the fire balloons that float up into the night sky at carnival time, and about the panic and terror they cause creatures in the wild.

Her greatest animal poem is 'The Moose', which took her twenty years to finish and is set in the Nova Scotia of her childhood. It starts with a lyrical, almost dreamy, evocation of life on the Nova Scotia coast with its maples and birches and clapboard farmhouses and humdrum diet, 'fish and bread and tea'. It lingers on details – the flowers in the gardens, cabbage roses, lupins, sweet peas, foxgloves. Then we are on a rural bus, 'its windshield flashing pink', going west through the 'hairy, scratchy, splintery' woods of New Brunswick. Outside there is darkness, but inside it is cosy and safe. Some passengers nod off; others engage in quiet, desultory talk about ordinary things. Grandparents remember 'deaths and sick-nesses', childbirths, a son lost at sea.

> Suddenly the bus driver
> stops with a jolt,
> turns off his lights

> A moose has come out of
> the impenetrable wood
> and stands there, looms, rather,
> in the middle of the road.
> It approaches; it sniffs at
> the bus's hot hood

> Someone says it's 'Perfectly harmless':

> Some of the passengers
> exclaim in whispers,
> childishly, softly,
> 'Sure are big creatures.'

'It's awful plain.'
'Look! It's a she!'

Taking her time,
she looks the bus over,
grand, otherworldly.

Then the driver says, 'Curious creatures', puts the bus into gear, and drives on leaving the moose 'on the moonlit macadam'. The poem asks:

Why, why do we feel
(we all feel) this sweet
sensation of joy?

Bishop avoided publishing poems about her personal life, though her most popular poem, 'One Art', is clearly personal and appeared in 1977. Its form is that of a villanelle: five stanzas rhyming aba and a sixth rhyming abaa. The first line of the first stanza ('The art of losing isn't hard to master') reappears as the last line of the second, the last line of the fourth and, modified, as the third line of the sixth:

– Even losing you (the joking voice, a gesture
I love) I shan't have lied. It's evident
the art of losing's not too hard to master
though it may look like (*Write* it!) like disaster.

In a volume of uncollected poems, drafts and fragments, published after her death and never intended for publication, she writes about her drink problem, her mother's breakdown, the suicide of her lover, Soares, and her own sexuality. In 'Vague Poem (Vaguely Love Poem)' the central image is a rose-rock, a crystalline formation found in deserts:

. . . Just now, when I saw you naked again,
I thought the same words: rose-rock; rock-rose . . .

Rose-rock, unformed, flesh beginning, crystal by crystal
clear pink breasts, and darker, crystalline nipples,
rose-rock, rose-quartz, roses, roses, roses,
exacting roses from the body,
and the even darker, accurate, rose of sex.

'Breakfast Song' is addressed to a younger lover:

My love, my saving grace,
Your eyes are awfully blue,
I kiss your funny face,
Your coffee-flavored mouth.
Last night I slept with you,
Today I love you so,
(how can I bear to go,
as soon I must, I know),
to bed with ugly death
in that cold, filthy place,
to sleep there without you.

CHAPTER 34

The Thirties Poets
Auden, Spender, MacNeice

The Wall Street Crash of 1929 was the start of a decade of unemployment and poverty throughout the West, known as the Great Depression. In Britain, the National Hunger March of September 1932 drew a crowd of 100,000 to Hyde Park, clashing with 70,000 police. Elsewhere, civil unrest and fear of anarchy led to the rise of right-wing regimes. Hitler came to power in Germany in 1933, and imposed the Nuremberg Laws, victimising Jews and other ethnic minorities. In Spain there was civil war between General Franco's Fascists and the elected Republican government. The Republicans were aided by an 'International Brigade' of foreign volunteers; Franco, by Hitler and Mussolini. There were atrocities on both sides, and in 1939 the Fascists were victorious. On 1 September 1939 Hitler's invasion of Poland led to the outbreak of the Second World War.

In response to these developments large numbers of young Western intellectuals turned to Marxism, among them the most gifted of Britain's 'Thirties poets', W.H. Auden. Many critics regard him as the greatest English-language poet since Wordsworth, and he powerfully influenced later poets. Philip Larkin said that reading him was like being on a telephone line to God.

Christened Wystan Hugh Auden (1907–1973) – but always referred to as 'W.H. Auden' – he was born in York, a doctor's son. After public school he went to Christ Church, Oxford, where he met Cecil Day-Lewis, Louis MacNeice and Stephen Spender (the 'Auden set'). He also read T.S. Eliot's poetry, and told his tutor he had torn up his own poems because he now knew the way he wanted to write. His early poems are often baffling, and were sometimes constructed by putting together odd lines salvaged from rejected poems. Leaving Oxford with a third-class degree in English, he spent five years school-teaching and travelling to Berlin, Iceland and China.

Between 1935 and 1938 he collaborated with Christopher Isherwood, who was intermittently his lover, on three plays written in the manner of the German Marxist Bertolt Brecht. In 1937 he visited war-torn Spain and broadcast propaganda for the Republicans. He had lost his religious faith at school, but in 1940, after a mystical experience, he returned to the Anglican communion, renouncing Marxism. In 1939 he moved to New York, where he fell in love with the poet Chester Kallman (1921–1975). They lived together in a 'marriage' (Auden's word) from 1947 till his death, collaborating on opera libretti such as *The Rake's Progress* with music by Igor Stravinsky.

Auden's 'desertion' of his native country just before the outbreak of war attracted criticism, and some dubbed him a 'traitor'. (In 1946 he was to become an American citizen.) But surveying world events from America brought cosmopolitan authority to his poetry, evident in 'September 1, 1939':

> I sit in one of the dives
> On Fifty-Second Street
> Uncertain and afraid
> As the clever hopes expire
> Of a low, dishonest decade.
> Waves of anger and fear

Circulate over the bright
And darkened lands of the earth,
Obsessing our private lives;
The unmentionable odour of death
Offends the September night.

That God's-eye view of the earth's bright and darkened lands helps
to explain Larkin's telephone-line joke. Auden's great poetic gift is
his authoritative tone. He combines clarity, certainty and profound
insight into the human condition, with wit and intelligence.

The commanding tone and the lofty viewpoint had featured
previously in 'On This Island'. Written in 1935, the poem is already
apprehensive that its peaceful seaside scene will not last:

Look, stranger, on this island now
The leaping light for your delight discovers,
Stand stable here
And silent be,
That through the channels of the ear
May wander like a river
The swaying sound of the sea.

Here at the small field's ending pause
Where the chalk wall falls to the foam and its tall ledges
Oppose the pluck
And knock of the tide,
And the shingle scrambles after the suck-
-ing surf,
And the gull lodges
A moment on its sheer side . . .

Written later, when war was imminent, 'In Memory of W.B.
Yeats' has a more wide-angle scope:

In the nightmare of the dark
All the dogs of Europe bark,

And the living nations wait,
Each sequestered in its hate;

Intellectual disgrace
Stares from every human face,
And the seas of pity lie
Locked and frozen in each eye.

Auden famously declares, in this poem, that 'poetry makes nothing happen'. But its final stanzas clearly state that the poet's role is to bring peace and joy:

Follow, poet, follow right
To the bottom of the night,
With your unconstraining voice
Still persuade us to rejoice;

With the farming of a verse
Make a vineyard of the curse,
Sing of human unsuccess
In a rapture of distress;

In the deserts of the heart
Let the healing fountain start,
In the prison of his days
Teach the free man how to praise.

'A rapture of distress' could describe 'Stop all the clocks' – now, thanks to the film *Four Weddings and a Funeral*, Auden's most famous poem. It is a distraught (or mock-distraught) lament for a dead lover:

The stars are not wanted now: put out every one;
Pack up the moon and dismantle the sun;
Pour away the ocean and sweep up the wood,
For nothing now can ever come to any good.

These are the illusory – yet heartfelt – extravagances of grief. By contrast Auden's greatest love poem, 'Lullaby', is free from illusion:

> Lay your sleeping head, my love,
> Human on my faithless arm;
> Time and fevers burn away
> Individual beauty from
> Thoughtful children, and the grave
> Proves the child ephemeral:
> But in my arms till break of day
> Let the living creature lie,
> Mortal, guilty, but to me
> The entirely beautiful . . .

'Faithless', 'ephemeral', 'guilty', are words that contradict the usual love-poem platitudes, yet they add depth and poignancy. In real life, Kallman's infidelities would reduce Auden to tears.

Similar realism about people, and how they truly behave, distinguishes another of his greatest poems, 'Musée des Beaux Arts'. Half-joking, but deadly serious, it is a comment on Brueghel's famous painting, 'The Fall of Icarus'. In the painting Icarus, dropping out of the sky to his death, is almost invisible compared to the coastal scene with peasants ploughing and tending their sheep. For Auden this becomes a lesson in how personal tragedies happen, 'While someone else is eating or opening a window or just walking dully along', or while a horse 'Scratches its innocent behind on a tree'.

The 'healing fountain' that Auden refers to in 'In Memory of W.B. Yeats' could be taken as a reference to the healing power of Freudian psychology, which replaced Auden's faith in Marxism. Freud had died in the month war broke out and Auden's poem 'In Memory of Sigmund Freud' praises him as a bringer of peace who was hated by 'avengers' and by those who believe things can be 'cured by killing'.

Freud taught us, the poem says, to trust love, which is the true civiliser: 'Eros' is the 'builder of cities'. 'Most of all', he taught us 'to be enthusiastic over the night', not only for 'the sense of wonder' it has to offer, but because 'it needs our love':

> ... With large sad eyes
> its delectable creatures look up and beg
>   us dumbly to ask them to follow ...

That the inner life is what matters, not mere biographical data, is the point of Auden's sonnet, 'A shilling life will give you all the facts'. People who repress their emotions are depicted in 'Miss Gee' and 'Victor', and in Auden's poem about A.E. Housman, who would have been ashamed to be seen weeping (or, as the poem puts it, 'Kept tears like dirty postcards in a drawer').

But the real criminals are dictators like Hitler and Mussolini and those who pander to them, as 'Epitaph on a Tyrant', written in 1939, spells out:

> When he laughed, respectable senators burst with laughter,
> And when he cried the little children died in the streets.

Auden did not improve with time. At his greatest in the 1930s, he could be facile, flippant and saunteringly expansive in his later poetry. Yet his God's-eye view still works occasionally, as in 'The Fall of Rome':

> Altogether elsewhere, vast
> Herds of reindeer move across
> Miles and miles of golden moss,
> Silently and very fast ...

Or in 'Ode to Gaea':

> ... leaves by the mile hide tons of
> Pied pebbles that will soon be birds.

The reputations of the other Thirties poets, once thought his equals, have now seriously declined. Stephen Spender (1909–1995), was a literary mover and shaker, knighted in 1983. His wealthy, artistic parents sent him to various private schools and

Oxford, but he left without taking a degree. (He boasted he had never passed an exam in his life.) A convert to fashionable Marxism, he joined the Communist Party and was sent to observe the war in Spain by the *Daily Worker*, a Communist newspaper.

He was bisexual, and said that he found males much more attractive than females. He married twice, had a daughter by his second wife, and was a founding member of the Homosexual Reform Society which sought the repeal of the persecutory laws against gays.

His most famous poem is the rhapsodic and wistful, 'I think continually of those who were truly great'. But his finest poetic moment is the first stanza of 'The Landscape Near an Aerodrome':

More beautiful and soft than any moth
With burring furred antennae feeling its huge path
Through dusk, the air-liner with shut-off engines
Glides over suburbs and the sleeves set trailing tall
To point the wind. Gently, broadly, she falls,
Scarcely disturbing charted currents of air . . .

At the poem's end this evident delight in a new toy for the wealthy gives way to a dutiful Marxist moan about a church 'blocking the sun'.

Louis MacNeice (1907–1963) was Irish, born in Belfast, the son of a minister (later bishop) in the Protestant Church of Ireland. Educated at Marlborough College and Oxford, he got a first-class degree in classical literature and became a Lecturer in Classics at Birmingham University, moving to a London lectureship in 1936. He married in 1930, but in 1935 his wife left him and their infant son for another man.

Unlike other Thirties poets he was not drawn to Communism, but in 1937 he visited Barcelona, shortly before it fell to Franco. He spent a year in America, lecturing at Cornell, before returning to London in 1940 where he worked for the BBC writing scripts and radio plays.

Autumn Journal (1939), generally considered his masterpiece, records his feelings about the Spanish Civil War, his personal life, and the impending war with Germany. Though he thinks the

254 A LITTLE HISTORY OF POETRY

current social system 'utterly lost and daft', he does not pretend to
feel common cause with the masses:

> It is so hard to imagine
> A world where the many would have their chance without
> A fall in the standard of intellectual living.

He seems to be thinking of 'the many' and their low aspirations in
'Bagpipe Music' (1937): 'All we want is a bank balance and a bit of
skirt in a taxi.'

As a historical document, 'Bagpipe Music', like *Autumn Journal*,
records the 1930s feeling of being dragged helplessly towards
disaster:

> The glass is falling hour by hour, the glass will fall for ever,
> But if you break the bloody glass you won't hold up the weather.

Another 1937 poem voices the sense of doom more lyrically:

> The sunlight on the garden
> Hardens and grows cold,
> We cannot cage the minute
> Within its nets of gold,
> When all is told,
> We cannot beg for pardon.

MacNeice was not an optimist. 'Prayer before Birth' (1944) foresees
little improvement post-war:

> I am not yet born, console me.
> I fear that the human race may with tall walls wall me,
> With strong drugs dope me, with wise lies lure me,
> On black racks rack me, in blood-baths roll me.

CHAPTER 35

Poetry of the Second World War

DOUGLAS, LEWIS, KEYES, FULLER, ROSS, CAUSLEY, REED,
SIMPSON, SHAPIRO, WILBUR, JARRELL, PUDNEY, EWART,
SITWELL, FEINSTEIN, STANLEY-WRENCH, CLARK

The poetry of the Second World War was quite different from that of the First, reflecting radical differences between the two conflicts. The First World War was comparatively local, remembered for trench warfare on the Western Front. The Second World War was vast. Its battlefields spanned the globe, from Africa to the Pacific. In the great bombing raids civilians were killed on an unprecedented scale. An estimated 20 million people died in the First World War; an estimated 80 million in the second, 55 million of them civilians. Two events in the Second World War permanently changed the way we think about humans and their future. The first was the Holocaust, the systematic murder of 6 million Jews by the Nazis. The second was the dropping of atomic bombs on the Japanese cities of Hiroshima and Nagasaki.

Compared to these cataclysms, the poetry of the war has understandably received little attention, and it is often said there was none. But that is untrue. Poets who served in the armed forces wrote about their experiences, both while serving and, if they survived, later. The two most remembered British war poets were Keith Douglas (1920–1944) and Alun Lewis (1915–1944).

Douglas wrote poetry as a student at Oxford, where his tutor was the poet Edmund Blunden (1896–1974). He enlisted in 1940, and was posted to Cairo where, disobeying orders, he got hold of a truck and joined his cavalry unit in time to take command of a tank in the battle of El Alamein, which he describes in his memoir, *Alamein to Zem-Zem*, a masterpiece of war writing. Though he survived the North African campaign, he was killed in Normandy three days after the Allied landings. In a poem written before he went out to the Middle East he had asked: 'Remember me when I am dead / and simplify me when I'm dead.'

Among his most famous poems is '*Vergissmeinnicht*' ('Forget-me-not'), in which he finds the body of a dead German soldier, with a photo of his girl inscribed, 'Steffi. *Vergissmeinnicht*':

But she would weep to see today
how on his skin the swart flies move;
the dust upon the paper eye
and the burst stomach like a cave.

His harshness has attracted criticism. In 'How to Kill', he looks calmly through his telescopic sight at his victim: 'Now in my dial of glass appears / the soldier who is going to die.' But, he wrote, 'I see no reason to be either musical or sonorous about things at present.' In 'Sportsmen', he admires the courage of the aristocratic cavalry officers he finds himself among. He is not of their class, sees that they are an 'obsolescent breed', and compares them to unicorns. But he wonders at their sang-froid. In the middle of a tank battle, he watches one of them crawling in the sand, fatally wounded, and remarking, 'It's most unfair, they've shot my foot off.'

The Welsh poet Alun Lewis was a pacifist at heart, but enlisted and was commissioned in the South Wales Borderers. On 5 March 1944, in the course of a campaign against the Japanese, he was found shot in the head, with his revolver in his hand. Suicide was suspected, but an army court of enquiry ruled his death accidental. His poems, such as 'All Day It Has Rained' (which evokes the tedium of life under canvas in wartime England), and the farewells to his wife, 'Postscript: For Gweno' and 'So We Must Say Goodbye, My Darling', are reflective and moving, and show the influence of Edward Thomas. He can be resonantly simple, as in 'Raiders' Dawn':

Blue necklace left
On a charred chair
Tells that Beauty
Was startled there.

His poem 'The Peasants', like much Second World War poetry, is less about war than the exotic landscapes the poet finds himself in, and the rhythms of existence that will continue long after he has gone. He watches a barefoot man driving oxen, 'Stepping lightly and lazily among the thorntrees'. He watches women breaking stones on a highway, or walking erect with bundles on their heads:

Across scorched hills and trampled crops
The soldiers straggle by.
History staggers in their wake,
The peasants watch them die.

The majority of those who fought in the war were not professional soldiers but civilians in uniform. Many were 'browned off' (a term invented during the war). They felt uneasy about the roles they were forced into, and their poems find different ways of escaping them. Sidney Keyes (1922–1943) knew Keith Douglas at Oxford, was commissioned, sailed for North Africa, and was killed after only a fortnight. His poetry, written before he left England, is highly literary, largely ignoring the reality of service life, and drawing on Rilke, Yeats and Eliot.

Roy Fuller (1912–1991) joined the Fleet Air Arm and was sent to East Africa (Kenya). He did not see combat, and back in England was commissioned and posted to the Admiralty. His poem, 'Soliloquy in an Air Raid', written in March 1941, foresees the destruction to come – 'A billion tons of broken glass and rubble' – and despairs of finding adequate language:

> Who can observe this save as a frightened child
> Or careful diarist? And who can speak
> And still retain the tones of civilization?

In 'Royal Naval Air Station' he records the tawdriness of barrack-room life, and his love poems to his wife express the pain of absence. In Africa the animals – 'These creatures walking without pain or love', in 'The Giraffes', for example – seem lucky by comparison.

The war at sea is evoked in the poetry of Alan Ross (1922–2001) and Charles Causley (1917–2003). Ross joined the navy and was almost killed in the Battle of the Barents Sea when his destroyer, HMS *Onslow*, escorting a convoy, engaged a German flotilla. His poem 'JW51B. A Convoy' describes the engagement, and its aftermath:

> Beneath the ice-floes sleeping,
> Embalmed in salt
> The sewn-up bodies slipping
> Into silent vaults.

Causley, unlike Fuller or Ross, was working class, and started writing poetry in the navy – on the day, as he recalled, that he joined the destroyer *Eclipse* at Scapa Flow in August 1940. He uses the rhythms of ballads and popular songs, transforming war into something mythical, dreamlike and richly coloured, as in 'Song of the Dying Gunner A.A.1':

> Oh mother my mouth is full of stars
> As cartridges in a tray
> My blood is a twin-branched scarlet tree
> And it runs all away.

Singularly, Henry Reed (1914–1986) found escape in comedy. In 'Naming of Parts' the poet's dreamy imaginings interrupt the NCO who is explaining how the standard British Lee-Enfield rifle works:

And this you can see is the bolt. The purpose of this
Is to open the breech, as you see. We can slide it
Rapidly backwards and forwards: we call this
Easing the spring. And rapidly backwards and forwards
The early bees are assaulting and fumbling the flowers;
    They call it easing the Spring.

Among the many American poets caught up in the war, the Jamaican-born Louis Simpson (1923–2012) stands out. He served with the elite 101st Airborne Division, and his masterpiece is 'Carentan O Carentan', a ballad-style poem based on his experience of a bloody engagement in the Cherbourg peninsula in June 1944. The poem, with its sinister half-rhymes, conveys the bewilderment of troops, fresh to battle, coming under fire, with their officer and sergeant killed.

Karl Shapiro (1913–2000) served in the South Pacific and his poem 'Sunday: New Guinea' is an account of Church Parade, where the familiar prayers and hymns bring back memories of home: 'Books and thin plates and flowers and shining spoons'. 'V-letter', addressed to his fiancée, is an avowal of love, compared to which his death, if he should be killed, will be 'matter-of-fact and simple'. His longest war poem, 'Elegy for a Soldier', mourns a friend, killed in action and hurriedly buried – 'A white sheet on the tail-gate of a truck / Becomes an altar'.

Richard Wilbur (1921–2017) fought in France and Germany with the 36th Infantry, but chose to preserve only two of his war poems. Both are powerful. In 'First Snow in Alsace', he recalls how snow excited him as a child, but here it 'fills the eyes / Of soldiers dead a little while'. 'Mined Country' is about death lurking beneath innocent-looking fields, where 'Cows in mid-munch go splattered over the sky'.

Randall Jarrell (1914–1965) served in the United States Army Air Force as an instructor in celestial navigation (navigation using the stars) – a job-description he considered the most poetic in the Air Force. He had studied at Vanderbilt under the academic poets Allan Tate (1899–1979), Robert Penn Warren (1905–1989) and John Crowe Ransom (1888–1974), and he uses words with precision and economy. His poem 'Mail Call' ('The letters always just evade the hand') is about soldiers lining up for news from home, and it shows, in a terse, understated way, the human being inside every uniform. 'Absent With Official Leave' comments ironically on the unnaturalness of making killing into a job. A soldier covers his ears with his pillow, and lets his mind drift:

> To the ignorant countries where civilians die
> Inefficiently, in their spare time, for nothing . . .

Many consider Jarrell's 'The Death of the Ball Turret Gunner' the greatest English-language poem of the Second World War:

> From my mother's sleep I fell into the State,
> And I hunched in its belly till my wet fur froze.
> Six miles from earth, loosed from its dream of life,
> I woke to black flak and the nightmare fighters.
> When I died they washed me out of the turret with a hose.

Air power was a new feature of the war, and 'For Johnny', written during an air raid by RAF officer John Pudney (1909–1977), became one of its most popular poems in England:

> Do not despair
> For Johnny-head-in-air,
> He sleeps as sound
> As Johnny underground . . .

A sharper poem is 'When a Beau Goes In' by Gavin Ewart (1916–1995), who served in the Royal Artillery. It satirises the flip, heartless jargon that war bred. A 'Beau' was a Bristol Beaufighter, and 'goes in' means 'crashes into the sea'. When it happens, Ewart writes, nobody 'goes about looking sad / Because, you see, it's war, / It's the unalterable law.'

Londoners, and those in Britain's other major cities, experienced air power in the form of the bombing raids which, together with separation and bereavement, were the most common subjects among Second World War women poets. The best-known was Edith Sitwell (1887–1964) whose poem 'Still Falls the Rain' curiously views the Blitz as a religious event. Less eccentrically, Elaine Feinstein (1930–2019) remembers her uncomfortable old air raid shelter in 'A Quiet War in Leicester'. For the young, the air war was exciting, as well as deadly, and Margaret Stanley-Wrench (1916–1974), who knew Keith Douglas at Oxford, conveys this in 'The New Swallows':

Suddenly tumbling over the wadded clouds,
Like puppies playing, like mating butterflies,
Tossing brittle and white in the cloudless midday pause,
The Spitfires come. Sunlight dashes on their wings
Like the sea breaking, splintered sharply on rocks.
They trail their shadows that clumsily lob over roofs
And clamber on hedges, and sprawl like a swallow's shadow
Angular over hills, and straddle streams . . .

One of the most memorable Second World War poems is by Lois Clark, of whom almost nothing is known except that she drove a stretcher-party car during the Blitz on Brixton. It is called 'Picture from the Blitz' and is printed in Catherine Reilly's *Chaos of the Night* anthology. Clark remembers finding a woman, sitting in a big armchair, with the ruins of her house around her. She is stiff with shock, and covered in dust, but alive, and still holding steel knitting needles in her 'work-rough hands':

They lift her gently
Out of her great armchair,
Tenderly,
Under the open sky,
A shock-frozen woman trailing khaki wool.

CHAPTER 36

American Confessional Poets, and Others

LOWELL, BERRYMAN, SNODGRASS, SEXTON, ROETHKE

Confessional poetry is poetry that reveals personal confidences, especially relating to mental illness and hospitalisation. It reflects a change in attitude towards mental illness in post-war America – and, later, Britain. Whereas it had been regarded as something shameful, to be hidden, it became a matter of public debate and, among the literati, almost a mark of cultural status. The first poetry collection to be labelled 'confessional' was *Life Studies* (1959) by Robert Lowell, who became America's unofficial poet laureate after the death of Robert Frost in 1963.

Lowell (1917–1977) was born into a family belonging to the east-coast elite, known as 'Boston Brahmins'. On his mother's side he could trace his ancestry to immigrants aboard the *Mayflower*. His father was a naval officer who, nagged by his snobbish wife, resigned from the navy in 1927 but never found a civilian career. Lowell's attitude to his ancestry was two-sided. He lived partly on the proceeds of a family trust fund, but his poems vilify his fore-bears for their money-worship and their participation in the massacre of Native Americans. His poem 'At the Indian Killer's Grave' is about a seventeenth-century ancestor, Josiah Winslow, who warred against the Pequot.

As a child Lowell was 'thuggish' (his own term) and bullied other children, earning the nickname 'Cal', apparently short for 'Caliban' or 'Caligula'. He was once banned from a public park for assaulting playmates. He was unhappy at Harvard and went, on his psychia-trist's advice, to study with the poet-professor Allen Tate, moving with Tate and the poet John Crowe Ransom to Kenyon College, Ohio.

In rebellion against his parents, who were Unitarians, he became a Catholic in 1941, but renounced Catholicism towards the end of the 1940s. He was a conscientious objector in the Second World War and served five months in prison (recalled in the poem 'Memories of West Street and Lepke'). In the 1960s he was promi-nent in anti-Vietnam War protests. He taught at various universi-ties. At Boston his students included Sylvia Plath and Anne Sexton.

Lowell was bipolar and subject to violent manic episodes which required hospitalisation. The first occurred in 1949, and after that they were frequent. (His poems 'Waking in the Blue' and 'Home after Three Months Away' recall respectively a spell in and a weekend release from McLean mental hospital near Boston.)

In 1940 he married Jean Stafford, later a well-known novelist. She had been permanently scarred in a car crash while he was driving – he emerged unscathed. Their alcohol-fuelled marriage ended in 1948. The next year he married the writer Elizabeth Hardwick and their daughter was born in 1957. Lowell's woman-ising and drink problem added to the strains on the marriage, which is depicted in his poetry collection *For Lizzie and Harriet*.

In 1970 he left Hardwick and, on a visit to England, began a liaison with Lady Caroline Blackwood. She was the eldest child of the 4th Marquess of Dufferin and Ava and his wife, the brewery heiress Maureen Guinness. Blackwood had already been married twice, to the artist Lucian Freud and to the composer Israel

Citkowitz, and had three children. She and Lowell married in 1972, and had a son Sheridan. *The Dolphin* (1973) told the story of their relationship ('Dolphin' was his nickname for her).

The *Dolphin* poems incorporate (and alter) private letters and phone calls from Hardwick. This went against the advice of Elizabeth Bishop, a close friend of Lowell's, and was severely criticised at the time. The radical feminist poet Adrienne Rich (1929–2012) called it 'a cruel and shallow book'. Love poetry was not Lowell's medium, and *The Dolphin*'s love poems are often sentimental. He died in the back of a New York taxi, clutching one of Lucian Freud's portraits of Blackwood, while on his way back to Elizabeth Hardwick.

Seemingly random images and memories are common in Lowell's poems, making them hard to follow. They also strive to enhance their significance by strained allusions to religion, mythology and literature. 'Skunk Hour', for example, contains the line, 'I myself am hell', echoing Satan in *Paradise Lost* ('Which way I fly is hell, myself am hell') – though Lowell seems an absurdly inadequate stand-in for Milton's Arch-fiend. 'The Quaker Graveyard in Nantucket', about the death by drowning of Lowell's cousin, clutches at grandeur by alluding to Herman Melville's novel *Moby Dick*.

For many readers Lowell is at his best and most approachable in the personal poems about his immediate family in Part 4 of *Life Studies*. They include 'My Last Afternoon with Uncle Devereux Winslow', 'Dunbarton', 'Commander Lowell', 'Terminal Days at Beverly Farms' and 'Father's Bedroom'. Written in free verse, several of them recall his childhood and have a simplicity and tenderness unusual in Lowell. There is no reaching for grandeur. Of his father's death he remembers:

> After a morning of anxious repetitive smiling,
> his last words to Mother were:
> 'I feel awful.'

In 'To Speak of the Woe that is in Marriage' (a title taken from Chaucer's Wife of Bath), he sees things, for once, from his wife Hardwick's point of view. She 'speaks' the poem, as she thinks of him out on the street, cruising for prostitutes, or remembers his violent love-making: 'Gored by the climacteric of his want / He stalls above me like an elephant.'

The childhood memories evoked in *Life Studies* are drawn on again at the start of one of Lowell's most famous poems, 'For the Union Dead'. Its subject is the memorial on the Boston Common honouring Colonel Shaw's all-black infantry that fought in the American Civil War. But it starts with Lowell remembering how as a boy, with his nose pressed to the glass, he would watch fish in the old South Boston Aquarium.

Lowell's translations in *Imitations* (1990) have been criticised for inaccuracy. His version of 'The Infinite' by the great Italian poet and philosopher Giacomo Leopardi (1798–1837), for example, has been faulted for a negativism not in Leopardi. But the collection, spanning from Homer to Rilke, testifies to his deep knowledge and love of European poetry.

It also contains ten translations of poems by Eugenio Montale (1896–1981), whom Lowell met in Venice in the 1950s. A Nobel laureate, Montale is regarded as the greatest Italian poet since Leopardi, but his poems are notoriously difficult. The Russian-born American poet Joseph Brodsky (1940–1996) likened them to a man muttering to himself. Montale has been classed with the self-styled 'Hermeticists', Giuseppe Ungaretti (1888–1970) and Salvatore Quasimodo (1901–1968), who attempted an Italian version of French Symbolism. But Montale rejected this classification. Dante and T.S. Eliot strongly influenced him, and his 'Arsenio' has been called an Italian version of *The Waste Land*.

The reputations of the other confessional poets have been rather eclipsed by Lowell's. John Berryman (1914–1972) was brought up in Oklahoma, then Florida, and went to college at Columbia. He married in 1942, and taught at Harvard and other universities. He had started an affair with a married woman in 1947, and wrote 'confessional' sonnets about it, but did not publish them until 1967 because they would have revealed the relationship to his wife. She ended the marriage anyway in 1953, tired of his affairs, break-downs and alcohol abuse.

His father, a banker, had shot himself when Berryman was eleven, a disaster that, he said, 'wiped out my childhood'. His poetry constantly returns to it:

he only, very early in the morning,
rose with his gun, and went outdoors by my window
and did what was needed.

I cannot read that wretched mind, so strong
& so undone.

The Dream Songs (1964, and, in an enlarged edition, 1968) are his best-known work (the above is from 'Dream Song 145'). They centre on a figure called Henry who, Berryman insisted, was not him, though he conceded that Henry resembled him and he resembled Henry. Henry seems to be a device for distancing pain and despair. He can sound deranged, but he is also jokey. *The Dream Songs* often read like someone being funny about a tragedy, and trying to look beyond it. In 'Dream Song 14' he admits to being bored with life, literature, art – and Henry. Yet: 'After all, the sky flashes, the great sea yearns'. His poetry is sometimes unintelligible, but Berryman wrote in 'Dream Song 366', 'These Songs are not meant to be understood, you understand, / They are only meant to terrify & comfort'. He experienced a religious conversion in 1970, but continued to struggle with depression, and on 7 January 1972 killed himself by jumping from the Washington Avenue Bridge in Minneapolis.

W.D. Snodgrass (1926–2009) was among Berryman's students at Brown University. He is often said to have inaugurated confessional poetry with his ten-poem sequence *Heart's Needle* (1959), but he rejected the label. After serving in the US Navy in the Second World War, he became an academic, teaching in various universities. He married four times, and *Heart's Needle* is about the pain of being separated from his daughter by his first marriage, Cynthia, who stayed with her mother after the divorce. It is a moving poem, wider and more immediate in its appeal than most confessional poetry. Addressed to the child, it remembers her birth and growing-up, the toys and good-night stories they shared, and the rare visits her mother now allows. It sets the poet's loss and hurt in wider contexts: the passage of the seasons, American soldiers freezing in their trenches during the Korean War at the time of Cynthia's birth, and the animal world as exhibited in a museum of natural history.

Anne Sexton (1928–1974) was poorly educated, a school drop-out with an alcoholic and abusive father. She scandalised the literary world by writing openly about menstruation, abortion, incest, masturbation, drug addiction and other taboo subjects, but her poems captured a huge readership among women who did not normally read poetry. Nearly half a million of her books sold in America, and *Transformations* (1971), her hip versions of Grimm's fairy tales, were published in *Cosmopolitan* and *Playboy*.

She writes about the brutality of men in a way that can seem to border on madness, as in 'After Auschwitz':

Anger
as black as a hook
overtakes me.
Each day
each Nazi
took, at 8:00 A.M., a baby
and sautéed him for breakfast
in his frying pan.

After many breakdowns and suicide attempts, she killed herself by running the car in a closed garage. Her psychiatrist released tapes of sessions with her after her death, and her elder daughter accused her of incestuous abuse.

Theodore Roethke (1908–1963) was not one of the confessional poets, though he was, like them, mentally unstable. The poet and novelist James Dickey (1923–1997) rated him the greatest poet America had yet produced, and for Sylvia Plath he was 'one of my most particularly favourite poets'. His father, Otto, was a market gardener, with 25 acres of greenhouses in Saginaw, Michigan, and the greenhouse became, for Roethke, 'my symbol for the whole of life, a womb, a heaven-on-earth' – words that are now inscribed on his memorial at Saginaw. His short poem, 'Child on Top of a Greenhouse', is based on a childhood escapade and illustrates his vividness and economy. It is composed of snatches of memory – the wind 'billowing out the seat of my britches', his feet 'crackling splinters of glass and dried putty', 'half-grown chrysanthemums staring up like accusers', and:

> A line of elms plunging and tossing like horses,
> And everyone, everyone pointing up and shouting!

His mood is often one of sorrowful introspection. In 'Elegy for Jane' he mourns one of his students killed in a fall from a horse. She is evoked in natural images – a wren, a sparrow, her 'neck curls limp and damp as tendrils'. That he had no special bond with her makes the poem, in the end, more desolate:

> If only I could nudge you from this sleep,
> My maimed darling, my skittery pigeon.
> Over this damp grave I speak the words of my love:
> I, with no rights in the matter,
> Neither father nor lover.

CHAPTER 37

The Movement Poets and Associates
LARKIN, ENRIGHT, JENNINGS, GUNN,
BETJEMAN, STEVIE SMITH

The 'Movement' poets were not a group, but they had common aims. They believed poetry should make sense, and should communicate with ordinary people, not just highbrows. It was an English movement. Nothing like it happened in America. The poets involved did not choose to be called the Movement. It was a journalist's label first used in the *Spectator* in 1954. The most celebrated of them nowadays is Philip Larkin (1922–1985). A 2003 survey voted him Britain's best-loved poet.

He was born in Coventry. His father, the city treasurer, was an enthusiastic Nazi who attended Nuremberg rallies, but also an avid reader who introduced Larkin to modern literature, above all D.H. Lawrence, whom both father and son idolised. Larkin went to King Henry VIII School, Coventry, and St John's College, Oxford, where he read English and got a first. Typically, he used to tell people he had got a second, which played up to his reputation for glumness. He once said that deprivation for him was what daffodils were for

Wordsworth. On the night of 14 November 1940 the Luftwaffe blitzed Coventry, killing over 500 people. When Larkin hitchhiked from Oxford the next day he found much of his hometown reduced to rubble. His lifelong xenophobia may date from this.

He wanted to be a novelist, published two sensitive, discriminating novels, *Jill* (1946) and *A Girl in Winter* (1947), and supplied his friend Kingsley Amis with ideas for *Lucky Jim* (1954). After Oxford he drifted into librarianship as a career (poor eyesight exempted him from military service) and proved very good at it, while grumbling about it endlessly (see, for example, his poem 'Toads'). As a librarian he worked in Wellington (Shropshire), Leicester, Belfast, and eventually Hull, where he became University Librarian in 1955.

He seems to have regarded marriage and children ('selfish, noisy, cruel, vulgar little brutes') as a threat to his art, so he remained single. However, despite his claim (in 'Annus Mirabilis') that 'Sexual intercourse began / In nineteen sixty-three', which was 'rather late for me', he led, from 1945 on, an active sex-life with several women, among them Monica Jones, an English lecturer at Leicester University, who became his wife in all but name.

But his true 'muse', some critics have concluded, was his mother, Eva. From 1948, when his father died, until her death in 1977, aged ninety-one, he took responsibility for her, writing many hundreds of letters. Several of his poems are associated with her. He wrote 'The Old Fools', his tirade against the humiliations of old age, while she was slipping into dementia. He completed 'Aubade', his poem about the terror of death, a few days after her life ended.

His first collection, *The North Ship* (1945), was strongly influenced by Yeats. He explained that he wrote it while he was 'isolated in Shropshire with a complete Yeats stolen from the local girls' school' (actually it was stolen for him by a girl at the school, Ruth Bowman, then aged sixteen, with whom he had an affair). A permanent reaction against Yeats followed. His new model was Hardy, whose poems he took to reading every morning before work. When he edited *The Oxford Book of Twentieth-century*

English Verse (1973) he included twenty-seven poems by Hardy (as against nine by T.S. Eliot).

It was Hardy's attention to the commonplace, contrasting with Yeats's Byzantine grandeurs, that attracted Larkin. 'I love the commonplace,' he wrote, 'Everyday things are lovely to me.' In his poems he chooses symbols that show how the commonplace is bound up with our deepest feelings. 'Mr Bleaney', a howl of rage at fate's unfairness, is about a tacky bedsit (actually one Larkin lived in when he first moved to Hull). 'Sunny Prestatyn', relating time's rape of beauty, is about a seaside poster. 'An April Sunday brings the snow', which mourns his father's death, is about some pots of jam.

The poems express two different personalities. One is abrasive ('They fuck you up, your mum and dad'; 'in a pig's arse, friend'). The other reacts tenderly to nature and to people. 'Water' and 'Solar' are virtually expressions of nature-worship. Trees (in 'Trees') come into leaf 'like something almost being said'. The imagined thoughts of the stricken rabbit in 'Myxomatosis' – 'Perhaps you thought things would come right again / If only you could keep quite still and wait' – are piercingly human. But this sensitivity combines with a vision of reality that is brutally bleak. Life, in 'An April Sunday brings the snow', is 'sweet / And meaningless, and not to come again'. Both these ways of reacting to the world display an unsparing accuracy – intellectual, but also an accuracy about what is seen and felt, noticing, for example, how the snow makes plum blossom seem 'green / Not white'.

Accuracy debars sentimentality. So in 'An Arundel Tomb' the sentimental outburst, 'What will survive of us is love', has already been identified in the previous line as only 'almost true'. Similarly, in 'Talking in Bed', the aim of finding 'words at once true and kind', is modified, realistically, to 'not untrue and not unkind'. In 'Afternoons' the young mothers, happily watching their children play, are, Larkin reminds us, being replaced by their children even as they watch: 'Something is pushing them / To the side of their own lives.'

Movement poetry is capable of argument because it employs reason, whereas for some theorists and practitioners of modernism reason and logic are inherently unpoetic. Larkin's 'Church Going', for example, develops into a profound and imaginative argument about the future, or non-future, of religion that makes it one of the great religious poems in the language.

A theme Larkin often reverts to, as in 'Wants', for example, is 'the wish to be alone'. But by the end 'Wants' desires not solitude but oblivion. 'Beneath it all, the desire of oblivion runs.' This wish for nothingness contrasts with 'Aubade' where nothingness, 'Not to be anywhere', is terrifying. Here it is desired. Several of Larkin's poems end with an upward sweep into emptiness, which surmounts argument and seems transcendent rather than threatening. 'Here' ends with 'unfenced existence'; 'High Windows', with 'deep blue air, that shows / Nothing, and is nowhere, and is endless'; 'Cut Grass', with a 'high-builded cloud / moving at summer's pace'; 'The Explosion', with a religious vision. The effect is of a poem opening itself to the unknown, rather than ending.

The other notable Movement poets are unlike each other and unlike Larkin, apart from their rejection of modernism. Whereas Larkin left Britain's shores rarely and reluctantly (he once said he wouldn't mind going to China if he could be there and back in a day), D.J. Enright (1920–2002) was widely travelled, working for the British Council in Egypt, Japan, Thailand and Singapore. He witnessed poverty on a scale unknown to other Movementeers. His poem 'The Short Life of Kazuo Yamamoto' tells of a thirteen-year-old Japanese bootblack who killed himself with rat poison. His last recorded words were. 'I wanted to die / Because of a headache.' He was, Enright adds, 'Quite alone, and had no personal belongings, / Other than a headache.'

Besides such knowledge, Enright also had a distinctive sense of humour. He was born on a Leamington council estate, the son of an Irish postman, and when he won a scholarship to Cambridge the wife of one of his teachers, 'genuinely enraged', stopped him in the street to tell him Cambridge was not for the likes of him (that was, Enright wryly adds, precisely the opinion of the working class too).

His verse autobiography 'The Terrible Shears' is witty and sardonic about the lot of the poor. His father had fought at the Somme and saved the life of an officer called Crawford, heir to the biscuit empire. One Christmas his father wrote to Crawford for help. 'In return / There came a free packet of assorted biscuits.'

Apart from being associated with the Movement, Elizabeth Jennings (1926–2001) could not have been less like Enright. A devout Roman Catholic, she came from a well-off Oxford family and read English at St Anne's. She wrote poems that are seemingly simple but often disquieting, with turns of phrase that can shake a poem out of one dimension into an uncertain elsewhere. Some are about varieties of religious experience, such as 'Friday', 'A Chorus' and 'Answers', some about personal reminiscence, such as 'One Flesh', where she thinks about her parents in bed:

Lying apart now, each in a separate bed,
He with a book, keeping the light on late,
She like a girl, dreaming of childhood,
All men elsewhere – it is as if they wait
Some new event: the book he holds unread,
Her eyes fixed on the shadows overhead.

Thom Gunn (1929–2004) had two careers. He began as a Movement poet. His first collection, *Fighting Terms*, was published in 1954. Soon after, he moved to California with his partner, Mike Kitay, and lived the rest of his life in San Francisco, becoming a prominent figure in the gay counterculture. He wrote tender, intimate love poems such as 'Touch' and 'The Hug', and lost many friends in the 1980s AIDS epidemic, writing elegies for them in *The Man with Night Sweats* (1992).

Hostile critics called Larkin's *Oxford Book* a 'triumph of philistinism', partly because it included twelve poems by John Betjeman (1906–1984), a best-selling poet and TV personality, sneered at by highbrows. But Larkin knew and admired Betjeman, rightly seeing that beneath the posturing there was a sharp critical brain. Besides, he shared some of his prejudices about the vulgarity of modern life (as voiced in Betjeman's notorious, 'Come, friendly bombs, and fall on Slough').

Wistful evocation of past times, places and lifestyles are a Betjeman stand-by, as in 'Middlesex', which remembers when Perivale was a 'parish of enormous hayfields', or 'A Subaltern's Love Song', probably Betjeman's most popular poem, which is a young officer's jokily masochistic account of playing tennis with the doughty Miss Joan Hunter Dunn. 'The Metropolitan Railway', another poem Larkin includes, poignantly relates the story of a young couple who made their home in Ruislip while it was still semi-rural. Now 'an Odeon flashes fire' where their villa once stood. 'How much more interesting and worth writing about Betjeman's subjects are than most other modern poets', Larkin remarked to Monica.

The most original poet in the *Oxford Book* is Stevie Smith (1902–1971). She wrote nursery rhymes, cautionary tales, hymns and nonsense verse in a style that mixes naïveté, flippancy and acerbity. She accompanied her poems with skittish drawings, and gave public readings in a high, quavering well-bred voice. A blow from which she never recovered was her father's desertion of the family when she was three – recounted in her autobiographical *Novel on Yellow Paper* (1936). She lived all her life in the London suburb of Palmers Green with her sister and a staunch feminist aunt, becoming a semi-recluse. Life, she said, was like being in enemy territory.

She is best known for 'Not Waving but Drowning':

> Nobody heard him, the dead man,
> But still he lay moaning:
> I was much further out than you thought
> And not waving but drowning.

But he is only one of the sick minds and unhappy animals that populate her work. Her favourite painting was Tintoretto's *Creation*, which shows the animals streaming out from the hand of God, all except one that has turned back. 'That's me,' she said. She gathered unexpected admirers. Sylvia Plath wrote to her, out of the blue, three months before killing herself, to say that she was 'a desperate Smith addict'.

She had a complicated attitude to religion, describing herself as a lapsed atheist. But she hated cruelty, and her nonsense poem 'Our Bog is Dood', arguably her masterpiece (though that seems a heavy word to use about a poet so wary of grandeur), satirises militant religionists who repeat meaningless mumbo-jumbo and become lethal when it is questioned.

> We know because we wish it so
> That is enough, they cried,
> And straight within each infant eye
> Stood up the flame of pride,
> And if you do not think it so
> You shall be crucified.

CHAPTER 38

Fatal Attractions

HUGHES, PLATH

Ted Hughes (1930–1998) and Sylvia Plath (1932–1963) are famous as tragic lovers as well as poets, and for many Plath is a feminist martyr.

Hughes was born in a small rural community in the Calder valley in Yorkshire. His parents ran a newspaper and tobacconists shop. His elder brother was a gamekeeper and used to take him up on the moors shooting, where Hughes fell in love with the wild. Returning to the valley was, he recalled, like 'a descent into the pit . . . This was when the division of body and soul for me began.' The idea of animal life as truer and more real than human, and the association of animal life with killing and masculinity, are constants in his poetry. His father had served in the First World War and was one of only seventeen men from an entire regiment to return from the doomed Gallipoli campaign. This, too, filled young Hughes's imagination with images of bloodshed.

From grammar school he won a place at Pembroke College, Cambridge, to read English Literature. But he felt that academic study betrayed his poetic self. He had a dream in which a creature with a fox's head came into his room, put bloody pawmarks on an unfinished essay he had written, and said, 'You are killing us.' So in his third year he changed from English to Anthropology – the beginning of his lifelong interest in magic and shamanism. He graduated in 1954, and on 25 February 1956 met Sylvia Plath at a party when, famously, she bit his cheek, drawing blood. They married four months later.

Plath was brilliant and rightly ambitious, though unstable. Both her parents were first-generation German immigrants living in a suburb of Boston, Massachusetts. Her father Otto was a university professor, specialising in bumblebees. Plath's later interest in beekeeping, and her linking of her father with Nazi Germany in the poem 'Daddy', derive from this family history (though Otto had left Germany at sixteen, before the Nazi era, and was a pacifist).

When Plath was four her father's health deteriorated. Fearing he had cancer, he refused to see a doctor. Actually he had diabetes and could have been saved. But he stubbed his toe, gangrene set in, his leg was amputated (hence Plath's reference to his single 'black shoe' in 'Daddy') and he died when Plath was eight. She told her mother 'I'll never speak to God again', and in her *Journals* she seems to blame her father for dying and deserting her.

She won a place at prestigious Smith College, where she worked hard to get A grades. A high-flier, she could not, she admitted, stand the idea of being mediocre, and she was conscious, too, of the need to feel physically desirable. With other top achievers she gained a brief internship on *Mademoiselle* magazine in New York, but found it unnerving. In August 1953 she attempted suicide, taking her mother's sleeping pills and locking herself in a cellar. She was rescued by chance and received psychiatric treatment at McLean hospital, Massachusetts, later recalled in her acclaimed novel *The Bell Jar*. Recovering, she won a Fulbright scholarship to Newnham College, Cambridge, which is how she came to meet Hughes.

Her *Journals* record her reaction to their first meeting: 'Oh, he is here, my black marauder, oh, hungry, hungry.' To her mother she wrote: 'I have fallen terribly in love which can only lead to great hurt. I met the strongest man in the world ... a large, hulking, healthy Adam ... with a voice like the thunder of God.' At first they were supremely happy. When her Cambridge course finished they sailed to New York on the *Queen Elizabeth* and she taught for a year at her old college, Smith. In the summer of 1959 they travelled across Canada and the United States, sometimes camping out in the wild. Their first child, Frieda, was born in April 1960.

By that time they were back in England, living in a flat near London's Primrose Hill, and a second child, Nicholas, was born in January 1962. Deciding to move to the country, they bought an old thatched house in Devon, and let the London flat to a Canadian poet, David Wevill, and his beautiful wife, Assia. Within months Hughes had fallen passionately in love with Assia and walked out of his marriage to Plath. Distraught, she committed suicide in February 1963 by putting her head in a gas oven. Six years later Assia, whom Hughes refused to marry, killed herself and her daughter by Hughes, Shura.

Plath's belief in Hughes as a great poet never wavered, even after his betrayal, and she had worked hard while they were together to promote his career, taking on secretarial work to help pay for his keep and sending his poems to magazines and publishers. Her efforts paid off when he won a big poetry prize she had entered him for (the judges were Auden, Spender and Marianne Moore). That led to the publication of his first collection, *The Hawk in the Rain*, in 1957.

The poems in it, such as 'Wind' and 'Egg-head', take up a persistent Hughes theme – the fragility and misplaced pride of the human intellect that tries to shut out the anarchic, man-slaughtering world of nature. Another kind of violence, his father's war experiences, gets into 'Griefs for Dead Soldiers'. Hughes is interested in violence because (like the Pennine moors he went up to with his brother) it opens the way to an elemental, non-human level where primal energies flow and drive. 'Any form of violence,' he wrote, 'any form of vehement activity, invokes the bigger energy, the elemental power circuit of the universe.'

This theme continues in his second collection, *Lupercal* (1960). Plath's favourite poem in it was 'Fire-Eater', which seems baffling at first reading. Why are the stars 'the fleshed forebears' of the hills, and of Hughes's blood? Why is the death of a gnat 'a star's mouth'? Hughes had a keen interest in modern science and what he is referring to is the theory, then new, that the atoms in our bodies, excluding only the primordial hydrogen atoms, were originally fashioned in stars that formed, grew old and exploded countless aeons ago, scattering the elements as a fine dust through space, and allowing planets like the earth to form. So the earth and our bodies are made of star-dust, which is why the stars are 'forebears' of the hills and of Hughes's blood. According to the same theory, the universe is constantly recycling matter and energy, re-grouping molecules, so what feeds the universe is the death of anything in it. Even a gnat's death feeds the stars.

When Hughes looks at nature he sees relentless predators – the hawk in 'Hawk Roosting' ('My manners are tearing off heads'); the thrushes in 'Thrushes' ('Nothing but bounce and stab'); the pike in 'Pike' ('Killers from the egg'). His pliant use of language is Shakespearean, inventing new words, making nouns into verbs. The thrushes are 'attent', a punchier word than 'attentive'; the pike's colour is variegated, 'green tigering the gold' – where the noun 'tiger' becomes a verb. Hughes's aim is to reinvigorate language. 'Words', he warned, 'are continually trying to displace our experience. And in so far as they are stronger than the raw life of our experience, and full of themselves, and all the dictionaries they have digested, they do replace it.' But not if he can help it.

In the two months after Plath's death he wrote 'The Howling of Wolves' and 'Song of a Rat'. Both were published in *Wodwo* (1967) and both, as if in self-excuse, are about the inescapable cruelty and pain throughout the whole of nature. Then there was a gap. He started writing again in 1966, and *Crow*, subtitled *From the Life and Songs of the Crow*, appeared in 1970 (dedicated 'In Memory of Assia and Shura'). Hughes considered it his masterpiece and many critics agree. Others shrank from its violence and negativity. The Crow of the title cannot be equated with any single concept. He changes from poem to poem – sometimes victim, sometimes tyrant, sometimes hero, sometimes fool. He is mythic in stature, but he demolishes myths – Christianity, humanism, the Genesis creation story and all hopeful and positive takes on life – reducing them to farce and slapstick. Crow's anarchic refusal to conform to any existing stereotype was deliberate. 'My main concern', Hughes wrote, 'was to produce something with the minimum cultural accretions of the museum sort.'

Paradoxically, the inventiveness of Crow can be matched, in Hughes's later work, only by his translations from Ovid's Metamorphoses. Titled Tales from Ovid (1997), they are not remotely like conventional translations. Hughes freely adds new passages to the original, and charges Ovid's passionate, disturbing stories with a sensuousness that makes them unmistakably his own.

Plath published only one volume of poetry, The Colossus (1960), before her death. Her voice in it is often daring and sardonic, as it is in her later work. But the Colossus poems are less original, imitating Dylan Thomas, Yeats, Marianne Moore and Roethke. She owes her lasting fame to the poems she wrote in the months after Hughes had left her, which were published by him in 1965, titled Ariel.

Her letters to her mother tell how she is writing 'the best poems of my life', at the rate of a poem a day, getting up at 4.00 in the morning while it is still dark ('like writing in a train tunnel or God's intestine'), and breaking off only when the children wake. The winter of 1962–3 was one of the coldest on record, and the cold is felt in the poems (for example, 'Nick and the Candlestick' with its 'panes of ice', or the bee-poem 'Wintering'). In Devon she had joined the village beekeepers, but the poems are about her rage and resentment, not beekeeping. The 'terrible' queen bee in 'Stings', with her 'lion-red body', is a female avenger, like the speaker in 'Lady Lazarus':

> I rise with my red hair
> And I eat men like air.

'Stings', like many of these late poems, incorporates bits of recent autobiography. Plath's letters record how Hughes had put a handkerchief on his head (a 'square of white linen' in the poem), hoping to keep the bees off, and had been badly stung. Bees die when they sting, but her bees 'thought death was worth it' so long as they could take their revenge.

In her letters to her American psychotherapist, Dr Ruth Beuscher, Plath describes Hughes as mocking, threatening and triumphant in his adultery, asking why she has not killed herself, and saying Assia and he thought she would. She claims too that in February 1961 he 'beat me up physically', causing a miscarriage. The fury in the late poems should be read in this context. Adverse critics, however, accuse Plath of exorbitant self-dramatisation. They object to her appropriating, in 'Daddy', the fate of the victims of the Holocaust, as if it were her own:

Chuffing me off like a Jew,
A Jew to Dachau, Auschwitz, Belsen . . .

This criticism is serious, and the debate continues.

On 5 February 1963 she wrote her last poem, 'Edge'. It describes a woman who has killed herself and also her two infant children, who now lie, one at each of her breasts. The dead woman is smiling 'the smile of accomplishment'. Critics have accused the poem of glorifying suicide and idealising infanticide. For them it is 'sick' and complacent. This seems questionable. The woman in the poem is said to illustrate 'The illusion of a Greek necessity', and the word 'illusion' prohibits any simple approval of her action. It is a poem that inspects and criticises itself. Plath did the same. When she gassed herself a week later she had first safeguarded her sleeping children by sealing the intermediate doors with tape and towels.

CHAPTER 39

Poets in Politics

TAGORE, AKHMATOVA, MANDELSTAM, MAYAKOVSKY,
BRODSKY, LORCA, NERUDA, PAZ, SEFERIS, SEIFERT,
HERBERT, MACDIARMID, R.S. THOMAS, AMICHAI

The twentieth century was the most politicised in world history. It began with the Russian Revolution of 1917, which established the first-ever Communist state. In reaction, a genocidal Fascist dictatorship, aiming at world domination, came to power in Germany, and was defeated in the 1939–45 war. The war weakened the European colonial powers, and their empires disintegrated as new nations sought independence. The number of nation states worldwide increased from about fifty to more than two hundred.

These events had poetic repercussions, and a number of poets are now chiefly remembered in relation to them. Opposition to British rule in India began long before the twentieth century, and a poet whose name has become associated with it is Rabindranath Tagore (1861–1941). He was born into a large, wealthy, cultured Calcutta family, and was enormously prolific from an early age, writing novels, short stories, dramas and thousands of songs, including the national anthems of India and Bangladesh. He also travelled widely, achieving global fame as a sage and polymath. In Britain he met W.B. Yeats and Ezra Pound, among others. His best-known poetry collection was *Gitanjali* ('Song Offerings'). His English translation of some of its poems was published in 1912, and the next year he became the first non-European to win the Nobel Prize in Literature. However, it is generally agreed that Tagore's Bengali is untranslatable, which probably accounts for his much-diminished reputation today. Even Yeats, an admirer, dismissed Tagore's English translations as 'sentimental rubbish'.

Totalitarian regimes seek to control every aspect of life, including writing. So for Russian poets the 1917 Bolshevik revolution was disastrous. In her twenties Anna Akhmatova (1889–1966) was already a celebrated poet. Her raven-black hair and aristocratic bearing gave her power over men. In Paris, Amadeo Modigliani fell for her, commemorating her in drawings and paintings including several nudes. With her husband Nicolay Gumilyov she formed the avant-garde Acmeist group, who rejected Symbolism and culti-vated simplicity and clarity, like the Imagists.

The revolution changed all that. On Lenin's orders Gumilyov, with sixty other supposed conspirators, was taken to a forest and shot. Henceforth 'bourgeois' poetry such as Akhmatova's was offi-cially censured, and in the 1930s she found herself caught up in what became known as Stalin's Great Terror, which cost an esti-mated million lives. Her son Lev was arrested and tortured, and for seventeen months she waited every day outside Leningrad prison, with other women seeking news of their loved ones. One day a woman in the crowd recognised her and, whispering through lips blue with cold, asked Akhmatova if she was capable of describing what they were going through. She replied that she was, and this was the origin of her poem-cycle, *Requiem*, composed between 1935 and 1961, which recounts her experience of this time. It was too dangerous to make written copies, so she memorised each section and then burnt it. A copy was smuggled out and published in Munich in 1963, but it could not be published in the USSR until 1987.

There were other poetic victims of Bolshevism. Osip Mandelstam (1891–1939) was a close friend of Akhmatova, and belonged to the Acmeist group. He came from a wealthy Polish-Jewish family and was educated at the Sorbonne in Paris and the University of Heidelberg. In 1933 he wrote a poem criticising Stalin, spent four years in prison, and was then sent to a correction camp in eastern Russia. Though he managed to get a note to his wife asking for warm clothes, none came, and he died of cold and hunger. Vladimir Mayakovsky (1893–1930) was of Georgian Cossack stock. A natural rebel and ardent Marxist, he designed agitprop posters for the Communists during the Russian civil war. But the Bolshevik literary establishment considered his experimental poetry too difficult for the proletariat. In 1930 he shot himself, perhaps realising, as the critic Clive James suggests, that his creative gifts had been used to cosmeticise mass murder. Joseph Brodsky (1940–1996) survived the siege of Leningrad as a child and began writing poetry at fifteen. It was denounced as 'pornographic and anti-Soviet', and he was sent to a mental institution, then sentenced to five years of hard labour in a region close to the Arctic circle. Expelled from the Soviet Union in 1972, he settled in America and in 1987 won the Nobel Prize in Literature.

The most famous poet to become a victim of twentieth-century politics was Federico García Lorca (1898–1936). Born in Fuente Vaqueros, near Granada in southern Spain, the son of a landowner, he was the most gifted Spanish poet since the great baroque poet Luis de Góngora (1561–1627), who was one of his heroes. Lorca's poetry combines the ballads and folklore of the Andalusian countryside with Symbolism and Surrealism (the Surrealist Salvador Dali was a close friend). His most famous book, *Romancero Gitano* ('Gypsy Ballads'), came out in 1928. In 1930 the Republican government appointed him director of a student drama group, and he toured poverty-stricken rural Spain bringing theatre to the people. However, the Fascists were gaining power in Spain, and were soon to unite under General Franco and defeat the democratically elected Republicans in the Spanish Civil War (1936–1939). In August 1936 Lorca was murdered by a Fascist militia group. His body was never found. He was gay, and Franco's press later described him as engaging in 'homosexual and abnormal practices'.

Another twentieth-century Spanish-language poet who gained a global reputation was Pablo Neruda (1904–1973). Born in Parral, Chile, the son of a railway employee, he had a long career in the Chilean diplomatic service. He began writing poems at fourteen. His second collection, the joyfully sensuous *Twenty Love Poems and a Song of Despair* (1924), was to become the best-selling Spanish poetry book of all time, and was translated into many languages. He was awarded the Nobel Prize in 1971.

Neruda had known Lorca personally, and after Lorca's murder he became an ardent Communist and a fervent admirer of Stalin. In 1970, when the socialist Salvador Allende was elected president of Chile, it was with Neruda's support. Three years later, at the time of General Augusto Pinochet's right-wing military coup, Neruda was in hospital suffering from cancer, but he discharged himself because he suspected a doctor had, on Pinochet's orders, given him a toxic injection. Hours after leaving hospital, he died.

A third Spanish-language Nobel Prize-winning poet was the Mexican Octavio Paz (1914–1998). He was born into Mexico's cultural elite but, drawn to the political left, he sent some early work to Neruda, who reviewed it favourably. He fought against the Fascists in the Spanish Civil War, before becoming a career diplomat. Among his best-known works is *The Labyrinth of Solitude* (1950), which sees the Mexican character as essentially defensive, taking refuge behind masks.

A philosophical poet, he can vacillate between poetry and prose as in *The Monkey Grammarian*, his anatomy of India, where he spent six years as Mexican ambassador. He was attracted to Hindu religious thought because it could embrace opposites as, he felt, Western thought cannot. The ancient Mexican concept of 'burnt water', uniting contraries, has been seen as his dominant image. He resigned from the diplomatic service in 1968 as a protest against government suppression of a student demonstration.

Prominent among poets who became national figureheads by taking a stand against a political regime is the Greek Nobel laureate

Giorgos Seferis (1900–1971). His home town, Smyrna, was captured by the Turks in 1922, and later, as a diplomat with the Greek foreign service, he travelled widely, especially during the Second World War, when Greece was occupied by the Nazis. So his poems are often about exile and wandering, and they mingle contemporary speech and politics with Homeric myth. In 1967 a right-wing military junta seized power in Greece, introducing censorship, political detention and torture. Seferis denounced the regime on the BBC World Service, and when he died (of natural causes) huge crowds thronged the streets of Athens singing Mikis Theodorakis's setting of his poem 'Denial' which the junta had banned.

The Czech poet Jaroslav Seifert (1901–1986) made his decisive political statement late in life. In 1977 he was one of the signatories of Charter 77, which criticised the human rights record of the Czechoslovak Socialist Republic (a satellite state of the Soviet Union). Born into a working-class family in Prague, he had previously been active in Communist literary circles. The Czech government denounced Charter 77 signatories as traitors and renegades. But, perhaps partly in recognition of his decisive act, he was awarded the Nobel Prize in Literature in 1984. He died two years later. There was a strong secret police presence at his funeral to discourage any political demonstration. He is an exuberantly metaphoric poet, and the Nobel citation testified that he was 'loved as dearly for the astonishing clarity, musicality and sensuality of his poems as for his unembellished but deeply felt identification with his country and its people'. One of his most moving works, *A Wreath of Sonnets* (1956), addresses the war-damaged city of Prague, expressing his undying love and loyalty.

With the Polish poet Zbigniew Herbert (1924–1998) hatred of Communism began much earlier. In 1939 Poland was overrun by Soviet and Nazi troops, and Herbert joined the Polish Resistance Movement. After the war his home town, Lwow, became a Ukrainian Soviet city and its Polish population was expelled. In the 1960s he travelled abroad, visiting various European countries and America. He was a signatory to the 1975 'Letter of 59', which opposed the Polish government's declaration of eternal loyalty to the Soviet Union. In 1981, during the Solidarity movement, he returned to Poland, and joined the editorial team of an underground journal.

Refusing to adhere to socialist realism, the only literary mode Communism permitted, he did not publish till the mid-1950s. His poetry is profoundly moral, but subdued, casual and often ironic in tone, at times experimenting with humorous fantasy, and always avoiding anything declamatory. His poems do not foresee any kind of victory. Defeat is inevitable. But that does not alter the poet's responsibility, spelt out in the poem 'The Envoy of Mr Cogito':

Go where those others went to the dark boundary
for the golden fleece of nothingness your last prize

go upright among those who are on their knees
among those with their backs turned and those toppled in the dust

Nationalist poets in Britain were more muted and less threatened. The Scottish Nationalist Hugh MacDiarmid (1892–1978) wrote *A Drunk Man Looks at the Thistle* (1926), a long, rambling, serio-comic, learnedly allusive contemplation of Scots nationhood, written in a 'synthetic Scots' that MacDiarmid invented. The Welsh clergyman poet R.S. Thomas (1913–2000) was a ferocious nationalist (he supported the fire-bombing of English-owned holiday cottages in rural Wales). But he was primarily a religious poet, tormented by a sense of God's absence, and berating his parishioners for using refrigerators, washing machines, and other modern evils.

When Zbigniew Herbert visited Israel he was befriended by Yehuda Amichai (1924–2000), who is widely regarded as the national poet of modern Israel. Amichai was born in Germany but his parents emigrated to Jerusalem when he was twelve. He fought with the British army in the Second World War, and with the Israeli army in the Israeli War of Independence, the Sinai War and the Yom Kippur War. His poems are often autobiographical, but they link the personal with general human experience, and have

reached an exceptionally wide readership. They express his diffi-
culties with religious faith, often with wry humour, as in 'And That
is Your Glory' where he imagines God as a car-mechanic, stretched
out on his back, tinkering with the engine above him, and invisible
except for the soles of his shoes.

CHAPTER 40

Poets who Cross Boundaries
HEANEY, WALCOTT, ANGELOU, OLIVER, MURRAY

This final chapter looks at five poets of our own time who show poetry's power to cross cultural boundaries.

Seamus Heaney (1939–2013) grew up on the family farm, Mossbawn, in County Londonderry, Northern Ireland. He had no intention of becoming a poet. 'I had some notion that modern poetry was far beyond the likes of me – there was Eliot, and so on.' It was reading Ted Hughes's poem, 'View of a Pig', that started him. 'In my childhood we'd killed pigs on the farm ... Suddenly the matter of contemporary poetry was the material of my own life.'

As a Catholic in Protestant Northern Ireland he was used to being a suspect. In 'The Ministry of Fear' he recalls being stopped at a road-block, and how the police crowded round the car, 'like black cattle, snuffing and pointing / The muzzle of a sten gun in my eye'. In the late 1960s the political situation deteriorated, and the Provisional IRA emerged. Heaney was pressured to write political poetry, but refused. Expecting poets to write about politics was misguided, he said. 'In the end they will only be worth listening to if they are saying something about and to themselves'. Fearing for his family's safety, he left Northern Ireland with his wife Marie and their children in 1972, moving to Wicklow in the Irish Republic.

A book that made an impact on him was P.V. Glob's *The Bog People* (1969). Its photographs of the Iron Age corpses of sacrificial victims, discovered in Danish peat bogs, prompted him to write, indirectly, about the conflict in Northern Ireland. 'Punishment', for example, is about the corpse of an Iron Age girl, executed, he imagines, for adultery, and he likens her to the young women in Northern Ireland suspected of being informers, and publicly punished. He blames himself for not speaking out against it, just as, he writes, he would have cast 'the stones of silence' while the young adulteress was being stoned to death.

Self-accusation is evident, too, in two poems about his cousin Colum McCartney, who was shot by Protestant terrorists while driving home in County Armagh. In 'The Strand at Lough Beg' he imagines finding Colum, 'with blood and roadside muck in your hair and eyes', and kneeling to wash him with 'cold handfuls of the dew'. But in the later 'Station Island', the ghost of Colum denounces him for 'evasion', because 'The Strand at Lough Beg' had 'whitewashed ugliness' and 'saccharined my death with morning dew'.

Heaney always emphasised he was Irish, not English. He was not neutral. For him, seeing British armoured cars on the roads around Mossbawn was an outrage. But he was a peacemaker, as the award of the Nobel Prize acknowledged. His poem 'From the Republic of Conscience' was written at the request of Amnesty International to celebrate United Nations day and the work of Amnesty.

Derek Walcott (1930–2017) grew up on the Caribbean island of St Lucia. His father died before he was born, leaving the family poor. His masterpiece is *Omeros* (1980), an epic poem of sixty-four chapters each of three sections. It is loosely based on Homer's *Iliad*, but is a completely different kind of work. Its main characters are not warriors but St Lucia fishermen, Achille and Hector. They quarrel because Achille borrows a rusty old bailing tin from Hector's canoe. But really the quarrel is about Helen, a servant girl of panther-like beauty. She leaves Achille for Hector, who becomes a taxi-driver and is killed in a car crash.

Other characters include Philoctete (based on Homer's Philoctetes), a fisherman whose shin has been torn by a rusty anchor and won't heal, a wise-woman, Ma Kilman, who owns the 'No Pain Café', and a blind ex-seaman, Seven Seas, roughly equated with Homer, who turns up in various locations – in Dublin as James Joyce, 'our age's Omeros' (39.3), in London as a vagrant sleeping on a park bench (38.1–3).

The speakers change and blend as the poem goes on. One is Walcott himself who says goodbye to his mother in a St Lucia care home (32.1–3), and meets the ghost of his father, who wrote poetry but never felt part 'of the foreign machinery known as Literature' (12.1). Despite the poem's Homeric allusions Walcott rejects Homer and classicism. 'There's no need to have these associations,' he insisted, 'Things have to become themselves and stand in their own light without history and without literature.' The poem says the same:

> why not see Helen

> as the sun saw her, with no Homeric shadow,
> swinging her plastic sandals on the beach alone,
> as fresh as the sea-wind?

> (54.2)

Walcott says he 'never really read' Homer's epics, or 'not all the way through'. St Lucia, wild and innocent, is his ideal, and he evokes it in luxuriant, haunting poetry – see, for example, the description of Achille diving for conches among wrecked ships and 'fanned vaults of silvery mackerel' (8.1–3). By comparison Homer is merely, 'All that Greek manure under the green bananas' (44.3).

Classicism is rejected because the Greeks were slave owners. Athens foreshadowed the brutal American South (35.1). The ancestors of St Lucia's present inhabitants were slaves brought from Africa. The poem also draws into its orbit the massacre of Native

Americans by the expanding United States. Through the eyes of the
Boston activist Catherine Weldon (1844–1921) we witness the near-
extermination of the Sioux and the Crow (34.1–3, 35.1–3, 43.1–3).

However the poem's message is reconciliation. 'We shall all heal',
is its optimistic conclusion (63.2). Ma Kilman heals Philoctete's leg-
ulcer (symbolising the chained ankles of his slave ancestors) with
ancient African wisdom, invoking Voodoo spirits (48.2), and using
an African plant, its seed brought by a migrating sea-swift (47.3).
This bird, which resembles a cross against the sky, is a recurrent
symbol. God tells Achille it is 'the sign of my crucifixion' (25.1).
When Walcott won the Nobel Prize the committee praised his
work's 'global human implication', showing how different cultures
could enrich one another.

Maya Angelou (1928–2014) was a spokesperson for black
women, and a civil rights activist alongside Martin Luther King Jr
and Malcolm X, as well as a poet. Born in St Louis, she earned her
living in early adulthood as a cook, nightclub dancer, sex worker,
singer and actress. The first of her seven autobiographies, *I Know
Why the Caged Bird Sings* (1969), takes its title from the Black
American poet Paul Dunbar (1872–1906). It reveals how, at eight,
she was abused by her mother's boyfriend; the book brought her
instant fame, though it was banned in some American schools.

Her poems remember early humiliation:

The child I works for calls me girl.
I say 'Yes, ma'am' for working's sake.

Being deserted by unreliable men is another theme:

Silence
turns the key
into my midnight bedroom
and comes to sleep upon your
pillow.

Self-critical, she realises she cannot write without resentment:

My pencil halts
and will not go
along that quiet path.
I need to write
of lovers false

and hate
and hateful wrath
quickly.

Descended from West African slaves, Angelou sees 'the auction block' and slaves' chains in the faces of old people. Her most famous lyric, 'Caged Bird', is about slavery, and 'Child Dead in Old Seas' evokes the Africa from which the slaves came. But she has a quieter voice, noticing, in a piece of amber, 'The heatless fire consuming itself', or a child's body, 'light / As winter sunshine'.

Her poem 'On the Pulse of Morning', like Whitman's 'Song of Myself', embraces all Americans, and looks forward in hope:

History, despite its wrenching pain,
Cannot be unlived, and if faced with courage,
Need not be lived again.

The boundary crossed by Mary Oliver (1935–2019) is between poetry and the book-buying public. Though sneered at by some highbrow critics as simplistic, she is, says the *New York Times*, 'far and away this country's best-selling poet'. Born in Maple Heights, Ohio, she was abused as a child (as recalled in her collection *Dream Work*), but found solace in nature, retreating into huts she built of sticks and grass, and writing poems. After studying at Ohio State University and Vassar College, she settled in Provincetown, Massachusetts, with her partner, the photographer Molly Malone Cook. Many of her poems were composed on walks in the surrounding countryside.

Inspired by the Sufi mystics, Rumi (1207–1273) and Hafez (1315–1390), she discerns the natural world as a window on the sacred, but the sacred does not include, for her, belief in an afterlife or a divine creator. She rejects, too, the religious idea that the body and its desires should be suppressed. Like Rilke, whom she admires, she believes that humans are alienated by reason and culture from the natural joy of birds and animals, and her delight in nature is not diminished by a realisation that it is a world of predators and prey.

Her best-known poem is 'The Summer Day' and her challenging, incisive reading of it can be heard on the Internet:

> Who made the world?
> Who made the swan, and the black bear?
> Who made the grasshopper?
> This grasshopper, I mean –
> the one who has flung herself out of the grass,
> the one who is eating sugar out of my hand,
> who is moving her jaws back and forth instead of up and down,
> who is gazing around with her enormous and complicated eyes.
> Now she lifts her pale forearms and thoroughly washes her face.
> Now she snaps her wings open, and floats away.
> I don't know exactly what a prayer is.
> I do know how to pay attention, how to fall down
> into the grass, how to kneel down in the grass,
> how to be idle and blessed, how to stroll through the fields,
> which is what I have been doing all day.
> Tell me, what else should I have done?
> Doesn't everything die at last, and too soon?
> Tell me what is it you plan to do
> with your one wild and precious life?

The great Australian poet Les Murray (1938–2019) grew up in poverty on his father's dairy farm in Bunyah, New South Wales. As a child his job was tending cattle, barefoot even in winter, and he remembers jumping into fresh cowpats to warm his feet. He was beaten for any fault. At school he was shunned and taunted. But he loved reading, so spent his days alone, dreaming over a book. A scholarship took him to Sydney University where he started publishing poetry in student magazines. He found he had a facility for learning European languages, ancient and modern, and got work as a translator while hitchhiking around Australia. In 1961 he married a fellow-student, Valerie Morelli, who converted him to Roman Catholicism. After that he dedicated his poetry 'to the glory of God'.

His values were down-to-earth and Australian. He detested Anglo-American modernism because it excluded ordinary readers. He was suspicious of liberals and intellectuals. He preferred rural life to corrupting, sterile, urban existence. His densely figurative, strenuous poetry is rooted in Gerard Manley Hopkins, his hero. Like Hopkins, and many of the poets we have looked at, his persistent subject is the natural world and how we relate to it.

He wonders whether the natural world can have any meaning. Or did the human invention of language invent meaning too? He imagines a cow talking in 'The Cows on Killing Day', and a bush talking in 'Cockspur Bush'. These are dazzling feats of ventriloquism, but they are make-believe. In reality, are all creatures, except humans, doomed to exist meaninglessly because they lack language? Murray seems to deny this in his poem, 'The Meaning of Existence'. But does he? Or does the poem's ending show poetry's power to unsettle beliefs and question certainties, even its own?

Everything except language
knows the meaning of existence.
Trees, planets, rivers, time
know nothing else. They express it
moment by moment, as the universe.

Even this fool of a body
lives it in part, and would
have full dignity within it
but for the ignorant freedom
of my talking mind.

Acknowledgements

We are grateful to the following for permission to reproduce copyright material:

Excerpts from 'The Waste Land'; 'Portrait of a Lady'; 'The Love Song of J. Alfred Prufrock'; 'La Figlia Che Piange'; 'Ash Wednesday'; 'The Hollow Men'; 'Morning at the Window'; 'Marina'; 'Journey of the Magi'; 'Four Quartets'; and 'East Coker' by T.S. Eliot from *The Complete Poems and Plays*, Faber & Faber Ltd, 1969, reproduced by permission of the publisher. Excerpts from *The Complete Canzoniere* by Petrarch and translated by A.S. Kline, copyright © 2002, published via Poetry in Translation, https://www.poetryintranslation.com, and reproduced by permission. Excerpts from *Faust: Part One* and *Faust: Part Two* by Goethe, translated by Philip Wayne, Penguin Classics, copyright © 1949, 1959 by the Estate of Philip Wayne; and 'The Albatross' by Charles Baudelaire from *Selected Poems*, translated by Carol Clark, Penguin Books, p. 7, copyright © 1995 by Carol Clark, reproduced by permission of Penguin Books Ltd. Excerpts from *Selected Verse of Arthur*

Rimbaud, introduced, edited and translated by Oliver Bernard, copyright © 1962, The Penguin Poets, reproduced by kind permission of the Estate of Oliver Bernard. An excerpt from 'After the Deluge' by Arthur Rimbaud, translated by Louise Varese from *Illuminations*, copyright © 1957 by New Directions Publishing Corp, reproduced by permission of New Directions Publishing Corp. An excerpt from 'Ars Poetica' by Paul Verlaine from *One Hundred and One Poems* by Paul Verlaine. A Bilingual Edition, translated by Norman R. Shapiro, University of Chicago Press, 1999, p. 129, reproduced with permission. Excerpts from 'The Windows' by Stephane Mallarmé from *Selected Poems*, translated by C.F. MacIntyre, University of California Press, 1957, reproduced with permission. An extract from 'Poetry Hero: Rudyard Kipling' by Alison Brackenbury, http://archive.poetrysociety. org.uk/content/publications/poetrynews/hero/kipling/, reproduced with permission of the author. Excerpts from 'Mending Wall'; 'Stopping by Woods on a Snowy Evening'; and 'After Apple-Picking' by Robert Frost from *The Poetry of Robert Frost*, edited by Edward Connery Lathem, copyright © 1923, 1930, 1939, 1969 by Henry Holt Company; © 1951, 1958 by Robert Frost; © 1967 by Lesley Frost Ballantine, reproduced by permission of Henry Holt Company, all rights reserved. An excerpt from 'The Listeners' by Walter de la Mare from *Collected Poems*, Faber & Faber, 1979, p. 84, reproduced by permission of The Literary Trustees of Walter de la Mare and The Society of Authors as their Representative. The poem 'On a General Election' by Hilaire Belloc from *Complete Verse*, Pimlico, 1991, p. 115, reproduced by permission of Peters Fraser & Dunlop, www.petersfraserdunlop.com, on behalf of the Estate of Hilaire Belloc. Excerpts from 'Sea Fever' and 'Cargoes' by John Masefield from *The Collected Poems of John Masefield*, Heinemann, 1925, pp. 27–56, reproduced by permission of The Society of Authors as the Literary Representative of the Estate of John Masefield. An excerpt from 'The Cool Web' by Robert Graves from *Collected Poems*, 2/e, Cassell, 1959, p. 56, reproduced by permission of Carcanet Press Limited. Excerpts from 'Fight to a Finish'; 'The General'; 'Counter-Attack'; 'Remorse'; 'The Hero';

'Blighters'; and 'Suicide in the Trenches' by Siegfried Sassoon from *Collected Poems 1908–1956*, Faber & Faber Ltd, 1968, pp. 21, 39, 68, 75, 77, 91, copyright © Siegfried Sassoon, reproduced by kind permission of the Estate of George Sassoon. An excerpt from 'Afterwards' and the poem 'The Veteran' by Margaret Postgate Cole from *Scars Upon My Heart, Women's Poetry and Verse of the First World War*, selected by Catherine Reilly, Virago, 2006, reproduced by permission of David Higham Associates Ltd. Excerpts from 'Rouen' by May Wedderburn Cannan from *Scars Upon My Heart, Women's Poetry and Verse of the First World War*, selected by Catherine Reilly, Virago, 2006, p. 17, reproduced with kind permission of Mrs Clara May Abrahams. Excerpts from 'Ash Wednesday'; 'The Hollow Man'; 'Marina'; 'Journey of the Magi'; and 'Four Quartets' from *Collected Poems 1909–1962* by T. S. Eliot, copyright © 1952 by Houghton Mifflin Harcourt Publishing Company, renewed 1980 by Esme Valerie Eliot, reproduced by permission of Houghton Mifflin Harcourt Publishing Company, all rights reserved. Excerpts from 'Hugh Selwyn Mauberley [Part I]'; and the poem 'In a Station of the Metro' by Ezra Pound from *Personae*, Faber & Faber Ltd, 1952, pp. 119, 197, 200, copyright © 1926 by Ezra Pound, reproduced by permission of the publisher and New Directions Publishing Corp. An excerpt from 'The Jewel Stairs' Grievance' by Ezra Pound from *Personae*, Faber & Faber Ltd, 1952, p. 142, and *Translations*, New Directions, 1963, copyright © 1963 by Ezra Pound, reproduced by permission of the publisher and New Directions Publishing Corp. Excerpts from 'Bantams in Pinewoods'; 'Sunday Morning'; 'Another Weeping Woman'; 'Anecdote of Men by the Thousand'; 'Tea at the Palaz of Hoon'; 'Metaphors of a Magnifico'; 'To a High-Toned Old Christian Woman' and 'The Emperor of Ice-Cream' by Wallace Stevens from *Harmonium*, Faber & Faber, 2001, pp. 22, 29, 74, 75, 77, 80, 91, reproduced by permission of the publisher. Extracts and excerpts from 'Exposition of the Contents of a Cab' by Wallace Stevens from *Opus Posthumous* by Wallace Stevens, copyright © 1957 by Elsie Stevens and Holly Stevens; and 'Man Carrying Thing' by Wallace Stevens from *The Collected Poems of Wallace Stevens* by Wallace Stevens, copyright © 1954 by Wallace Stevens and copyright renewed 1982 by Holly Stevens, reproduced by permission of the publisher and Alfred A. Knopf, an imprint of the Knopf Doubleday Publishing Group, a division of Penguin Random House LLC, all rights reserved. The poems 'The Red Wheelbarrow' and 'This Is Just to Say' by William Carlos Williams from *The Collected Poems: Volume I, 1909–1939*, Carcanet, 2000, pp. 224, 322, copyright © 1938 by Directions Publishing Corp, reproduced by permission of Carcanet Press Limited and New Directions Publishing Corp. An excerpt from 'Flag Salute' by Esther Popel, published in *The Crisis*, August 1934; the publisher wishes to thank the Crisis Publishing Co., Inc., the publisher of the magazine of the National Association for the Advancement of Colored People, for the use of this material first published in the August 1934 issue of Crisis Magazine. An excerpt from 'Bottled' by Helene Johnson, 1927, reprinted from *Waiting for Love: Helene Johnson, Poet of the Harlem Renaissance*, copyright © 2000 by the University of Massachusetts Press. Excerpts from 'I, Too,' and 'The Negro Speaks of Rivers' from *The Collected Poems of Langston Hughes* by Langston Hughes, edited by Arnold Rampersad with David Roessel, Associate Editor, copyright © 1994 by the Estate of Langston Hughes, reproduced by permission of David Higham Associates Ltd, and Alfred A. Knopf, an imprint of the Knopf Doubleday Publishing Group, a division of Penguin Random House LLC, all rights reserved. Excerpts from 'Marriage'; 'A Grave'; 'The Pangolin'; 'Nevertheless'; 'An Octopus'; and 'The Steeple Jack' by Marianne Moore from *Complete Poems Revised Edition*, Faber & Faber, 1984, pp. 50, 67, 72, 125–6, reproduced by permission of the publisher and Simon Schuster, Inc., all rights reserved. Excerpts from 'Poetry' by Marianne Moore from *The Poems of Marianne Moore*, ed. Grace Schulman, Faber & Faber, 2003, p. 135, reproduced by permission of Faber & Faber and Penguin Random House LLC, all rights reserved. Excerpts from 'The Man-Moth'; 'The Fish'; 'The Moose'; and 'One Art' by Elizabeth Bishop from *Complete Poems by Elizabeth Bishop*, published by Chatto and Windus, copyright © 2011, reproduced by permission of The Random House Group

Limited and Farrar, Straus & Giroux, LLC, all rights reserved. Excerpts from 'Vague Poem' and 'Breakfast Song' by Elizabeth Bishop from *Edgar Allan Poe & The Juke-Box. Uncollected Poems, Drafts and Fragments*, edited and annotated by Alice Quinn, Farrar, Straus and Giroux, 2007, pp. 153, 158, reproduced by permission of Farrar, Straus & Giroux, LLC, all rights reserved. Excerpts from 'On This Island' and 'Who's Who' copyright © 1937 and renewed 1965 by W.H. Auden; 'September 1, 1939'; 'In Memory of W.B. Yeats'; 'Stop All The Clocks'; 'Lullaby (1937)'; 'Musée des Beaux Arts'; 'In Memory of Sigmund Freud' and 'Epitaph on a Tyrant' copyright © 1940, renewed 1968 by W.H. Auden; 'The Fall of Rome' copyright © 1947 by W.H. Auden, renewed 1975 by The Estate of W.H. Auden; 'A.E. Housman' and 'Ode to Gaea' from *Collected Poems* by W.H. Auden, copyright © 1976 by Edward Mendelson, William Meredith and Monroe K. Spears, Executors of the Estate of W.H. Auden, reproduced by permission of Curtis Brown, NY and Random House, an imprint and division of Penguin Random House LLC, all rights reserved. Excerpts from 'The Landscape Near an Aerodrome' by Stephen Spender from *Collected Poems 1928–1953*; and a letter from Stephen Spender to Christopher Isherwood in September 1934 from *Spender, Sir Stephen Harold (1909–1995)*, copyright © The Estate of Stephen Spender, reproduced with permission of Curtis Brown Ltd, London, on behalf of The Beneficiaries of The Estate of Stephen Spender. Excerpts from 'Autumn Journal'; 'Bagpipe Music'; 'The Sunlight on the Garden'; and 'Prayer before Birth' by Louis MacNeice from *The Collected Poems of Louis MacNeice*, Faber & Faber, 1966, pp. 84, 97, 105–6, 193, reproduced by permission of David Higham Associates Ltd. Excerpts from 'Soliloquy in an Air Raid' and 'The Giraffes' by Roy Fuller from *Collected Poems, 1936–1961*, Andre Deutsch, 1962, pp. 44, 65, reprinted by permission of Welbeck Publishing. An excerpt from 'Song of the Dying Gunner A.A.1' by Charles Causley from *Collected Poems*, Macmillan, 1992, p. 6, reproduced by permission of David Higham Associates Ltd. An excerpt from 'Naming of Parts' by Henry Reed from *Collected Poems*, edited and introduced by Jon Stallworthy,

Oxford University Press, 1991, p. 49, reproduced with permission of the Licensor through PLSclear and The Royal Literary Fund. Excerpts from 'Sunday: New Guinea'; 'V-Letter'; and 'Elegy for a Soldier' by Karl Shapiro from *The Wild Card. Selected Poems Early and Late*, University of Illinois Press, 1998, pp. 62, 72, 73, reproduced by permission of Harold Ober Associates. Excerpts from 'First Snow in Alsace' and 'Mined Country' by Richard Wilbur from *Poems, 1943–1956*, Faber & Faber, 1957, pp. 18, 22, reproduced by permission of the publisher. Excerpts from 'Mail Call'; 'Absent With Official Leave'; and 'The Death of the Ball Turret Gunner' by Randall Jarrell from *The Complete Poems*, Faber & Faber Ltd, 1971, pp. 144, 170, 171, reproduced by permission of the publisher and Farrar, Straus & Giroux, LLC, all rights reserved. An excerpt from 'For Johnny' by John Pudney from *Dispersal Point and Other Air Poems*, Bodley Head, 1942, p. 24, reproduced by permission of David Higham Associates Ltd. Excerpts from 'When a Beau Goes In' by Gavin Ewart, *The Collected Ewart 1933–1980*, Hutchinson, 1980, p. 78, reproduced by kind permission of the Estate of the author. Excerpts from 'Picture from the Blitz' by Lois Clark, from *Chaos of the Night: Women's Poetry and Verse of the Second World War*, ed. Catherine Reilly, Virago, 1984, p. 27, reproduced by permission of Brown Book Group Ltd. Extracts and an excerpt from 'To Speak of the Woe that is in Marriage' from *Robert Lowell, Life Studies* by Robert Lowell, Faber & Faber, 1959 pp. 31, 81, 96, reproduced by permission of the publisher and Farrar, Straus & Giroux, LLC, all rights reserved. Excerpts from 'Skunk Hour' by Robert Lowell from *Selected Poems*, Faber & Faber, 1965, p. 54, reproduced by permission of Farrar, Straus & Giroux, LLC, all rights reserved. Excerpts from 'Dream Song #143'; 'Dream Song #145'; and 'Dream Song #366' by John Berryman from *His Toy, His Dream, His Rest: 308 Dream Songs*, Faber & Faber, 1969, pp. 70, 72, 298; and an excerpt from 'Dream Song #14' by John Berryman from *Dream Songs*, Faber & Faber, 2014, p. 16, reproduced by permission of the publisher and Farrar, Straus & Giroux, LLC, all rights reserved. An excerpt from 'After Auschwitz' by Anne Sexton from *The Complete Poems*, Houghton Mifflin, 1981, copyright ©

1981 by Linda Gray Sexton and Loring Conant, Jr, reproduced by permission of SLL/Sterling Lord Literistic, Inc.. Excerpts from 'Child on Top of a Greenhouse' by Theodore Roethke, copyright © 1946 by Editorial Publications, Inc; © 1966, renewed 1994 by Beatrice Lushington; and 'Elegy for Jane' by Theodore Roethke, copyright © 1950 by Theodore Roethke; © 1966, renewed 1994 by Beatrice Lushington from Collected Poems by Theodore Roethke, Faber & Faber Ltd, 1968, pp. 43, 102, reproduced by permission of the publisher and Doubleday, an imprint of the Knopf Doubleday Publishing Group, a division of Penguin Random House LLC, all rights reserved. Excerpts from 'Annus Mirablis'; 'This be the Verse'; 'Vers de Société'; 'Trees'; 'Myxomatosis'; 'An April Sunday brings the snow'; 'An Arundel Tomb'; 'Talking in Bed'; 'Afternoons'; 'Wants'; 'Aubade'; 'Here'; 'High Windows'; and 'Cut Grass' by Philip Larkin from Collected Poems, edited with an introduction by Anthony Thwaite, Faber & Faber Ltd, 1988, pp. 21, 42, 100, 110–11, 121, 129, 137, 165, 166, 167, 180, 181, 183, 208, reproduced by permission of the publisher and Farrar, Straus & Giroux, LLC, all rights reserved. An excerpt from 'The North Ship' by Philip Larkin from The North Ship by Philip Larkin, Faber & Faber Ltd, 1966, p. 8, reproduced by permission of the publisher. Excerpts from 'Further Requirements' by Philip Larkin from Further Requirements: Interviews, Broadcasts, Statements and Reviews, 1952–1985, Faber & Faber Ltd, 2001, p. 57, reproduced by permission of the publisher and The Society of Authors as the Literary Representative of the Estate of Philip Larkin. Excerpts from 'The Short Life of Kazuo Yamamoto' and 'The Terrible Shears' by D.J. Enright from Collected Poems, Oxford University Press, 1981, pp. 15–16, 107, reproduced by permission of Watson Little Ltd. An excerpt from 'One Flesh' by Elizabeth Jennings from New Collected Poems, Carcanet, 2002, reproduced by permission of David Higham Associates Ltd. Excerpts from 'Middlesex' and 'Baker St Station Buffet' by John Betjeman from Collected Poems, John Murray, copyright © 1955, 1958, 1962, 1964, 1968, 1970, 1979, 1981, 1982, 2001 by John Betjeman, reproduced by permission of John Murray, an imprint of Hodder and Stoughton Ltd. Excerpts from 'Not Waving But

Drowning' and 'Our Bog is Dood' by Stevie Smith from *Collected Poems and Drawings/Collected Poems of Stevie Smith*, Faber & Faber Ltd, 2015, copyright © 1957, 1972 by Stevie Smith, reproduced by permission of the publisher and New Directions Publishing Corp. Excerpts from 'Daddy'; 'Nick and the Candlestick'; 'Stings'; 'Lady Lazarus'; and 'Edge' by Sylvia Plath from *Ariel*, Faber & Faber Ltd, 1965, pp. 19, 40, 54, 55, 66–7, 85, copyright © 1965 by the Estate of Sylvia Plath, reproduced by permission of the publisher and HarperCollins Publishers. Excerpts from 'Fire-Eater'; 'Hawk Roosting'; 'Pike'; and 'Thrushes' by Ted Hughes from *Lupercal*, Faber & Faber Ltd, 2001, pp. 26, 33, 52, 56, reproduced by permission of the publisher. An extract from *Poetry in the Making: An Anthology of Poems and Programmes from 'Listening and Writing'* by Ted Hughes, Faber & Faber Ltd, 1967, p. 120, reproduced by permission of the publisher and Farrar, Straus & Giroux, LLC, all rights reserved. An excerpt 'The Envoy of Mr Cogito' by Zbigniew Herbert from *Mr Cogito*, translated by John Carpenter and Bogdana Carpenter, The Ecco Press, 1993, p. 61, reproduced by permission of The Wylie Agency (UK) Limited and HarperCollins Publishers. Excerpts from 'The Ministry of Fear'; 'Punishment'; and 'The Strand at Lough Beg' by Seamus Heaney from *100 Poems*, Faber & Faber Ltd, 2018, pp. 42, 47, 58; and 'Station Island' by Seamus Heaney from *Station Island*, Faber & Faber Ltd, 1984, p. 63, reproduced by permission of the publisher and Farrar, Straus & Giroux, LLC, all rights reserved. Excerpts from 'Omeros' and 'St Lucia Care Home' by Derek Walcott from *Omeros*, Faber & Faber, 1990, pp. 17, 46, 68, 200, 271, reproduced by permission of the publisher and Farrar, Straus & Giroux, LLC, all rights reserved. Excerpts from 'When I Think About Myself' and 'To a Man' from *Just Give Me a Cool Drink of Water 'fore I Diiie: Poems* by Maya Angelou, copyright © 1971 by Maya Angelou; 'Song for the Old Ones'; 'Now Long Ago'; and 'Artful Prose' from *Oh Pray My Wings Are Gonna Fit Me Well* by Maya Angelou, copyright © 1975 by Maya Angelou, © 1996 by Maya Angelou and Penguin Random House LLC; and 'To Beat the Child Was Bad Enough' from *And Still I Rise: A Book of Poems* by

Maya Angelou; audio rights from *And Still I Rise: A Selection of Poems Read by the Author* by Maya Angelou, copyright © 1978 by Maya Angelou, reproduced by permission of Little, Brown Book Group Ltd, Random House, and Penguin Random House Audio Publishing Group, imprints and divisions of Penguin Random House LLC, all rights reserved. An excerpt from 'On the Pulse of Morning' from *On the Pulse of Morning* by Maya Angelou, copyright © 1993 by Maya Angelou, reproduced by permission of Random House, an imprint and division of Penguin Random House LLC, all rights reserved. The poem 'The Summer Day' by Mary Oliver from *House of Light*, Beacon Press, copyright © 1990 by Mary Oliver, reproduced by permission of the Charlotte Sheedy Literary Agency, Inc. An excerpt from 'The Meaning of Existence' by Les Murray from *New Collected Poems*, Carcanet, 2003, p. 551, reproduced by permission of Carcanet Press Limited, Margaret Connolly and Associates and Farrar, Straus & Giroux, LLC, all rights reserved.

In some instances we have been unable to trace the owners of copyright material, and we would appreciate any information that would enable us to do so.

Index